THE CATHOLIC UNIVERSITY

AND THE SEARCH FOR TRUTH

THE CATHOLIC UNIVERSITY
AND THE SEARCH FOR TRUTH

CYRIL ORJI

ANSELM
ACADEMIC

Created by the publishing team of Anselm Academic.

Printed in the United States of America

7046

ISBN 978-1-59982-277-8

To my beautiful mother who gave me my first Catholic education: Mrs. Veronica Orji.

AUTHOR ACKNOWLEDGMENTS

Catholic intellectual tradition (CIT) is a collaborative endeavor and this book would not have been possible without the "collaboration" of many colleagues and friends. Special thanks to Paul Benson, Dean of the College of Arts and Sciences, University of Dayton (UD), for all the support and research (seed) grants that made this project possible. I also wish to thank Fr. Jack McGrath, the former UD Professor of Faith and Culture, who invited me to take part in campus-wide discussions on CIT. That invitation was the real seed that birthed this book. Special thanks also to the former chair of the Religious Studies Department, Dr. Sandra Yocum, who supported the idea of this book and supported me in every step of the way.

I cannot forget Fred Lawrence and Kerry Cronin who allowed me to use the Lonergan Center at Boston College (BC). It was at BC that I met Phil McShane, whom I consider a "mobile Lonergan archive." Phil directed this work and pointed me in the right direction. I also benefited from the kindness of Mark Shield, Daniel H. Monsour, and Robert Croken, who made available to me original and typescript materials at the Lonergan Research Institute (LRI), Toronto, Canada. Daren Diaz, OP, Br. Philippe LeBlanc, OP, and Michel Côté, OP, of the Dominican Community in Toronto offered me valuable help during my research at LRI. To you all I say thanks.

Thanks also to the following: Mark Morelli of the Lonergan Center at Loyola Marymount University in Los Angeles, who offered helpful critique and gave me the opportunity to "test" some of the ideas in this book at the Los Angeles Lonergan Conference; Denis Doyle of UD, who provided meaningful feedback at every step of the way; Marva Gray of UD, who provided much-needed logistical support; Timothy C. Hosterman, a friend of McShane's, who helped with original manuscript and documents. Finally, I wish to thank my publishers at Anselm Academic, particularly Paul D. Peterson and Jerry Ruff. You guys are the consummate professionals.

I also wish to thank many others who contributed in one way or the other to the manuscript. While the efforts and help of these genuine collaborators did engineer and steer this work in the right course, I do, however, take responsibility for any errors and shortcomings.

Publisher Acknowledgments

Thank you to the following individuals who reviewed this work in progress:

Richard J. Janet
Rockhurst University, Kansas City, Missouri

Margaret McGuinness
La Salle University, Philadelphia

CONTENTS

1

Catholic Intellectual Tradition (CIT) and the Catholic University

A serious debate has been taking place in recent years on the campuses of many Catholic colleges and universities on the nature of a Catholic university and the related question of Catholic intellectual tradition (CIT). "At issue is whether [Catholic institutions of higher learning] are likely to succumb, or have already succumbed, to the attenuating forces of secularization that evaporated the religious distinctiveness of mainline Protestant educational institutions a century ago."[1] There is also the related problem concerning tension between academic freedom and the Church's teaching office (magisterium), heightened most recently by the promulgation of Pope John Paul II's *Ex Corde Ecclesiae* (*From the Heart of the Church*, 1990), an Apostolic constitution that explains the nature of a Catholic university. The United States bishops issued general norms for implementing *Ex Corde Ecclesiae* in the United States in 1999 and began applying them

---

1. D. Paul Sullins, "The Difference Catholic Makes: Catholic Faculty and Catholic Identity," *Journal for the Scientific Study of Religion* 43 (2004): 83–101, at 83.

in 2001. There are those who claim that academic freedom means that professors and researchers, because they search for truth, cannot be brought under the jurisdiction or control of the magisterium. They argue that to be made to submit to the magisterium amounts to compromising the truth. There are also those who argue that a college or university operating within the Catholic tradition ought to recognize the place and role of the pope and the magisterium as legitimate interpreters of this ecclesial and intellectual tradition.

Our approach in this text is that CIT can be understood in a way that does not conflate this learning tradition with the magisterium or any ecclesiastical hierarchy, and also that Catholic institutions of higher learning can remain faithful to the pursuit of truth while still maintaining loyalty to the institutional Church. To suggest otherwise is to maintain an opposition between Catholicism and the ideal of learning. A Catholic college or university's privileged task is "to unite existentially by intellectual effort two orders of reality that too frequently tend to be placed in opposition as though they were antithetical: the search for truth, and the certainty of already knowing the fount of truth," (*Ex Corde Ecclesiae*, 1). Such opposition is inherently alien to the spirit of open inquiry that Catholicism engenders.

Chapter 1 looks at Catholic universities and the question of CIT. The chapter considers what it means to be Catholic in the contemporary world, i.e., how Catholic institutions of learning might contribute to fostering Catholic values. The nature of the question necessitates a clarification of the meaning of three key concepts: *Catholic*, *intellectual*, and *tradition*. The chapter concludes by considering why it is important for Catholic colleges and universities to preserve and develop their Catholic identity.

Chapter 2 revisits the issue of CIT in light of Cardinal John Newman's idea that the Catholic university needs theology and theology needs the Catholic university. The chapter considers how the difference between liberal and conservative theologians in a Catholic college or university helps that institution to understand and clarify its mission and identity. In order to better understand the role of CIT within Catholicism in general and Catholic universities in particular, the chapter briefly traces how CIT has been understood over time.

Chapter 3 examines the problem of secularization and the changing face of American Catholicism, i.e., the shift from the immigrant Catholicism of German, Irish, Polish, and Italian ethnic churches of the World War I and World War II eras to a post-Vatican II Church that is increasingly Latino. The chapter raises questions concerning the impact of this changing landscape on Catholic education.

Chapter 4 examines contemporary challenges facing Catholic colleges and universities, the debate surrounding CIT in the context of the rise of a new dominant subculture. It considers whether the post-Vatican II Church has assimilated attitudes and values of contemporary society and by so doing failed to be countercultural. In light of the many American universities that were founded by religious denominations, but have since lost all connection to those denominations, the question arises whether the continuing Catholic identity of Catholic colleges and universities is at risk.

"In Part 2 of this work, chps. 5–8 will narrow the focus to the work and thought of Bernard Lonergan (1904–1984), one of the foremost twentieth-century contributors to CIT. Lonergan devoted considerable attention to the issue of Catholic education, and his work can be instructive to Catholic colleges and universities today."

CHAPTER 1

Is There a Catholic Intellectual Tradition?

A number of approaches to the meaning of *Catholic Intellectual Tradition* (*CIT*) will be explored in the course of this book. In this chapter we shall introduce the topic by clarifying some key terms that are important to understanding what we mean by CIT. These terms are *Catholic, intellectual,* and *tradition.* The clarification will also offer us the opportunity for a brief survey of the history of Catholicism's involvement in education. Some years ago Rosemary Haughton wrote a book titled, *The Catholic Thing.*[1] There are ample items we can put under the umbrella of the "Catholic thing," education being one of them. *Catholicism,* as we shall see, is not a parochial or provincial term. It is all-encompassing and all-embracing and involves a belief system, prayer, mysticism, monasticism, scholasticism, education, saints, martyrs, confessors, and a whole set of other ideas and practices. Every element in this list can be properly called "the Catholic thing." What we call CIT is another "Catholic thing."

CIT is a relatively new concept. It is virtually a new field of investigation and research and its parameters are still being negotiated. Not everyone, not even all Catholics, accepts the designation CIT. There are still many who are confused as to what CIT means. Even among those sympathetic to the concept, not all accept the term. In 2009 I presented a paper at the annual meeting of the Catholic Theological Society of America (CTSA) in Halifax, Nova

---

1. Rosemary Haughton, *The Catholic Thing* (Springfield, ILL: Templegate, 1997).

Scotia, on the matter of CIT. In the question-and-answer period following, two participants engaged in a heated debate, one assuming CIT as a given, the other, livid, demanding to know, if CIT exists, *what* "it" is and *where* "it" can be located.

What and *where* continue to be divisive questions regarding CIT. There are also those who want to know how CIT can be independent of the Catholic Church's magisterial authority: How is CIT different from the revealed truth or "deposit of faith" that is safeguarded by the Church's magisterium? How is it different from Catholic dogma? How is it different from or related to Catholic social teaching? How is it different from the scholasticism of the Middle Ages? In what way is it related to the Thomism that Pope Leo XIII declared the official philosophy of the Catholic Church? If CIT is different from these, can it be broad enough to include different philosophies, and not just the one philosophy officially sanctioned by the magisterium?

Opposition to the designation CIT cuts across liberal (progressive) and conservative (traditional) lines. Both groups have serious questions regarding what is meant by the term. The liberal objection to CIT is that it can seem too catechetical and can become an indirect way of imposing Catholic teaching on non-Catholics on Catholic campuses. The conservatives or traditionalists who object to CIT think it can become too permissive and syncretistic, and thus can threaten to undercut traditions that are very dear to Catholics and, by so doing, undermine what is intrinsic to Catholicism.

The debate is far from settled and both sides have valid points. Even those who accept the existence of CIT concede that it may only be useful as an explanatory concept. Among these is Wolfgang Grassl who teaches theology at St. Norbert's College (Green Bay, Wisconsin). Grassl suggests that for CIT to be assumed in an unambiguous way it needs to undergo rational reconstruction.[2] Attempting to be sensitive to the arguments of both sides, we begin our foray into the nature of CIT by raising a series of questions: What do we mean by Catholic intellectual tradition? How might we speak of a Catholic intellectual tradition? Is there such thing as a Catholic intellectual tradition?

---

2. Wolfgang Grassl, "Is There Really a Catholic Intellectual Tradition?" (paper presented at the American Academy of Religion annual meeting, Montreal, November 7–10, 2009).

THE ISSUE AND CONTEXT

Every religious sponsored institution of learning has its own intellectual tradition—its own style of thought and philosophy, a prism through which it views the world. The style of thought of an institution shapes its members' views about God, the cosmos, and humanity. For example, Liberty Christian Academy, a Virginia-based college sponsored by Thomas Road Baptist Church, prides itself as a faith community that adheres to the core values of that church, namely commitment to Scripture, culture of prayer, lifestyle of worship, connection to community, heart of serving, and passion for excellence. They also speak of their intellectual tradition as being "based on the premise that man's ultimate purpose is to glorify God (1 Corinthians 6:19, 20; 10:31)."[3] On their website they proudly speak of themselves as a college that exists "to help each student reach his full potential by guiding him in developing spiritually, morally, personally, socially, and academically." Their faculty and staff "recognize that only when a student accepts Christ as Savior and yields to His Lordship can he realize his own unique potential (Romans 10:10–13)."[4] The point here is simple: every religiously sponsored institution has an identity. The identity of religiously sponsored institutions of learning is guided by the intellectual tradition and educational philosophy of the religion the institution professes.

The identity an institution assumes can shape that institution in much the same way that traditions shape those who embrace those traditions. In other words, self-styled identity can become a tradition. The term *tradition* means different things to different people. In the United States, *tradition* has a positive ring around the Thanksgiving and Christmas holidays. Hardly anyone questions the practice of giving and receiving gifts at Christmas, or the choice of turkey for dinner on Thanksgiving Day: it is a *tradition*. Analogously, tradition also guides and shapes the educational system of any religiously sponsored institution of learning. Apart from (covert or overt) proselytizing, religious groups sponsor institutions because they see education as worthwhile and fundamental to social

---

3. LCA Mission Statement, *http://www.lcabulldogs.com/media/9910/2011-2012% 20LCA%20Core%20Values.pdf.*

4. Ibid.

advancement. They constantly evaluate their teaching mission to determine the extent to which they have been faithful to the *tradition* that guides and sustains them. If they fail to do this, they risk losing their identity.

CIT is derived from a long history—or tradition—of Catholic involvement in the education of the whole person. Conceptually we can speak of this tradition in one of two broad and related ways as (1) the Catholic Church's intellectual identity or (2) an explanatory concept.

CIT as Roman Catholicism's Intellectual Identity

The Catholic Church's mission in the world has many dimensions, including spiritual, social, and intellectual elements. The Church establishes schools to further the intellectual aspect of this mission. Like any faith tradition that has its own schools, the Church has its own vision of education. The educational vision exhibits some similarities with and differences from all other visions of education, secular and religious. It is this intellectual Catholic "minding" that we speak of as the Catholic intellectual tradition (CIT). A great deal of this intellectual activity is cultivated in centers of learning like monasteries and Catholic institutions of learning. While CIT is not limited to the work of Catholic institutions of higher education, those institutions stand in unique relationship to CIT.

As a way of harnessing and collating ideas or treasures to be studied and handed on to posterity, these intellectual activities assume the form of tradition. There are many understandings of tradition associated with the Catholic Church. For example, it used to be that Catholics were associated with the tradition of not eating meat on Fridays. Catholics before Vatican II were also associated with the tradition of observing a liturgical fast before Eucharist and of going to communion at least once a year. Today Catholics are still associated with the tradition of going to confession for forgiveness of sins, and a tradition of devotion to Mary. Catholicism is also known for its emphases on living tradition—ways of doing things over the centuries, which include the primacy of the pope and the role of the magisterium in church leadership and governance.

Catholic tradition is multifaceted. It encompasses a way of devotion, spirituality, and intellectual patterns, characteristics, and rationales that have persisted over time and across cultures—patterns that shape the conversation we call CIT.

CIT as an Explanatory Concept

The Catholic intellectual conversation has continued for two millennia. It results from serious reflections on the part of Christians on the life and death of Jesus of Nazareth, whom Christians believe is the promised Messiah and Savior of the world. Catholics of all historical periods have always taken seriously the reflections of previous generations' belief in the person and activity of Jesus of Nazareth and have always found ways to apply these reflections to their lives. When schools and universities were established in the West, such schools became the centers of these reflections. The Catholic identity of Catholic colleges and universities where these reflections were cultivated and disseminated were for a long time taken for granted. Then, in the 1970s, Catholic colleges began to move toward secularization, particularly in the United States. As it became clear that these schools were fast losing their Catholic identity, agitation on the part of those who wanted to preserve Catholic intellectual heritage necessitated attempts to define CIT, at least as an explanatory concept. Catholic colleges and universities cannot claim to be Catholic if CIT is not part of their core understanding. It was in the context of trying to recover and maintain the identity of Catholic colleges that the term *CIT* was coined. It was introduced by persons concerned that the erosion of Catholic identity was doing harm to Catholic colleges and universities. Such persons generally invoked CIT as a mental and historical construct on which to build identity claims. This is the sense in which we say *CIT* is a term used, on the one hand, to reclaim, and on the other, to consolidate what Catholic educators and experts see as central and unique to the kind of education that Catholicism engenders.

At present the phrase *Catholic intellectual tradition* exists only in English. It is not found in Italian, German, Polish, French, or Spanish. Its equivalent in these languages, according to Grassl, is probably "Catholic thought." It is also not found in any papal encyclical or pronouncements. No papal statement on Catholic philosophy of education or guidelines issued by the Roman curia on Catholic education has used the phrase, in Latin or in English. But the fact that the phrase has yet to occur in a papal document does not render the term invalid. The expression may be American in origin, but the reality is as universal as Catholicism itself. When used as an explanatory concept, *CIT* addresses the question of what is "Catholic" about Catholic colleges and universities, ensuring that they are not just Catholic in name, but Catholic in fact.

Catholic institutions are guided by the Catholic tradition: two millennia of carefully worked-out treasures that include spirituality, monasticism, prayer, and reflection. While respectful of the spiritual element of the tradition, CIT's main emphasis is on the intellectual component. As an explanatory concept, CIT suggests that not only is the Catholic intellectual life central to Catholic identity but also that this tradition cannot be thought of as deposits of the past alone. It is a deposit of the present—a treasure that needs to be nourished, renewed, and handed on to future generations.

CIT: CATHOLIC AND ECUMENICAL

While the debate regarding what is meant by the designation CIT is far from over, few involved in the debate doubt the reality of the Catholic intellectual heritage. One commonly accepted aspect of that reality is that *catholic* can also be understood in the universal and ecumenical sense of the word. Whereas to be Catholic, in the sense of professing Roman Catholic faith, can sometimes be an object of suspicion and ridicule—in so far as Catholicism (rightly or wrongly) is perceived as dogmatic, intolerant, and closed-minded—in the realm of academics, the tradition of Catholic education is commonly lauded as thorough, comprehensive, tolerant, and nondogmatic, even by critics of Catholicism. It is not uncommon for parents who disagree with Catholicism on faith grounds to send their children to Catholic school to receive a Catholic education. This occurs because the *Catholic* intellectual tradition is *catholic*.

The catholicity (universality) of CIT mitigates against the reservations of both liberals and traditionalists regarding the use of the phrase. The *what* and *why* of CIT is ecumenically inclusive. Catholic campuses are for everyone, not just Catholics. In Catholic institutions one will find students, faculty, staff, and even administrators who are not Catholic and, in some instances, not affiliated with any religion. They all contribute to enhance the Catholic identity of these colleges and universities. The enterprise of Catholic education deals with questions common to all humanity: God, human origins, providence, human destiny, morality, death, judgment, an afterlife. As ecumenical, CIT is true to the spirit of Vatican II, particularly the vision that guided the Council's declarations on relations with non-Christian religions: "What is the meaning, the aim of our life? What is moral good? What is sin? Whence comes suffering, and what purpose does it serve? Which is the road to true happiness? What are death, judgment, and retribution after death? What, finally, is that ultimate inexpressible mystery that encompasses our existence: whence do we come, and where are we going?" (*Nostra Aetate* [*Declaration on the Relation of the Church to Non-Christian Religions*], 1). CIT embraces *Nostra Aetate*'s conviction that human life has meaning, and meaning can be found in the context of dialogue with other major religious traditions. As a body of thought and literature stretching over two millennia, CIT advances human understanding and human curiosity. This wealth of knowledge can be studied and illuminated by anyone, irrespective of his or her religious convictions.

The truth of God and human life can be fully grasped only in dialogue with other religions and cultures. The basic convictions of CIT are shared by Catholics and many non-Catholics alike. In fact, one of the driving visions of CIT is that Catholics can and do understand their own tradition better when they engage others in dialogue. The Catholic identity of Catholic colleges and universities "is more than just a matter of religious sponsorship or the personal faith of some members of the intellectual community, important as these are. It is a home for thoroughgoing intellectual and personal engagement with the ideas and traditions of Catholic culture and thought."[5] CIT sees diversity as strength not as weakness. Catholics and non-Catholics alike work in Catholic colleges and universities because they are all "committed in some way or another to help[ing them] succeed in this mission. No organization

---

5. See William J. Cahoy, "The Catholic Intellectual Tradition: What Is It? Why Should I Care?" *http://www1.csbsju.edu/catholicidentity/values/billcahoy.htm.*

can long survive, much less succeed, if its members either don't care about its mission or are opposed to it."[6] Everyone involved in Catholic colleges and universities—faculty, staff, and students, Catholics and non-Catholics—are that institution's identity. Institutional identities are carried by people, not by structures or documents.[7] The Catholic identity of Catholic institutions was, for a long time, embodied by monks, priests, and women religious who worked in those institutions. But as the number of priests and religious diminish and laypeople increasingly assume active roles in Catholic colleges and universities, these laypeople, together with the students of these institutions, become the flag-bearers of Catholic identity. "We can't take our Catholic identity for granted as something taken care of by the monasteries, by the fact that we have religious buildings, religious symbols, religious words in prominent places or a Department and School of Theology. These are very important expressions and sustainers of our identity. But by themselves they can be empty."[8] Catholic identity is meaningful only when carried on by people.

CATHOLIC, INTELLECTUAL, AND TRADITION

The Roman Catholic Church is a living Christian community that values all aspects of its tradition. This tradition is kept alive and maintained in a community with ecclesiastical leadership and political structures; the Church thus understands itself as united and yet divided, holy and yet sinful, human and yet divine. Keeping the tradition alive in a Church with many contradictions is not without its tensions. Some of the concerns of those who question the concept of CIT center around the issue of authority and the extent to which the participation of the lay faithful are encouraged: Who speaks for the community and why? By what criteria are these spokespersons chosen? To what degree are the things they say binding? Do they

---

6. Ibid.

7. Ibid.

8. Ibid.

always say the right things? What expectations do they have of other members and even nonmembers of this community?

Since one of the goals of this text is to demonstrate how the *why* and *what* of Catholic intellectual tradition exists, we shall also show in later chapters that this tradition is not constituted by one single person or authority. Yet it cannot exist apart from persons who are self-consciously Catholic, nor can it be maintained outside of the Church. In order to delineate how everyone contributes to this common fund we call Catholic intellectual tradition, it is necessary to clarify three important but problematic terms: *Catholic, intellectual,* and *tradition.*

Catholic and Catholicism

Catholicism is not something that can be reduced to oneliner bumper sticker expressions. Catholicism is multifaceted. It is a living reality and a community of persons that are rich in diversity and history. It is a Christian tradition and a unique way of life of a particular faith community that is specified by distinctive theologies, doctrines, ethics, spirituality, and ways of worship, ways of learning, and ways of acting. It is also a distinct network of peoples scattered all over the globe, but united with a common purpose. It has, among other things, a list of saints and martyrs, eremitical and cenobitical ascetic traditions, recognized mystics and visionaries, and doctors and intellectual giants. The early Church esteemed the eremitical and cenobitical forms of monasticism as the two best forms of Christian discipleship (far more than lay discipleship). Most of the Church's canonized saints and martyrs, mystics and visionaries, doctors and intellectual giants, at the beginning of the Church's history, were either hermits or monastics living in religious community. In other words, CIT in its beginnings developed in the monasteries and had an ascetic flavor (mysticism). It was not until much later (about the seventeenth century) when the study of theology was taken up by more nonclerics that the contributions of lay Christians became an integral part of CIT. That CIT had a somewhat ascetic or monastic origin is understandable since theology was done in the monasteries and only monks and clerics studied it.

THE EARLY MONASTICS

Eremitical Monasticism	Cenobitical Monasticism
St. Anthony of Egypt (c. 251–356 CE) is considered the founder of the eremitical tradition of monasticism. The words *monk* (from the Greek *monachos*, "alone") and *eremitic* (hermit) both point to a life in solitude or seclusion. After his conversion to Christianity, Anthony withdrew to the deserts of Egypt to live a life of solitude (eremitic monasticism) in prayer and fasting. According to Anthony's own story, there were already hundreds of others living alone in the desert when he withdrew there. But Anthony is referred to as the "father of monasticism" because of the inspiration of his life and his embodiment of Christian virtues. Later hermits who followed Anthony's example lived the life of a hermit to unite the mind and heart with Christ and free themselves from all earthly desires and worries.	Pachomius (c. 292–346 CE), a contemporary of Anthony, is considered the founder of cenobitical monasticism (monasticism in community). Before Pachomius some monks who withdrew from the world to the desert gathered weekly for common prayers and service. But they were not formally organized in a community. Pachomius gathered together monks of like mind to live in an organized community away from society. The goal of these *cenobites* (from the Greek *koinobios*, meaning "life in common") was the same as those of the eremites, except that they lived in formal communities. The early Church accepted the two forms of monasticism as ideal Christian living and exemplary ways of discipleship (following Christ).

The word *catholic* derives from the Greek *kat' holou*, meaning whole or entire. It denotes the opposite of incompleteness, faction, sect, or schism. Although the word *catholic* is related to *Catholicism*, it is not synonymous with it. They are two different words that can be used with different nuances. *Catholic*, for example, can be used as an adjective to designate things that have universal application, or as a noun. In its Christian usage, the origin of the term is traceable to St. Ignatius of Antioch (c. 50–117 CE), one of the early church fathers. Ignatius used the term in his exhortation letter to the Christian community in Smyrna: "Where the bishop is to be seen, there let all his people be; just as wherever Jesus Christ is present, we have the Catholic Church."[9] Like Ignatius, St. Augustine of Hippo (354–430 CE) also found the term helpful in his dealings with a notorious schismatic group that threatened the unity of the Church, the Donatists. Denouncing this sectarian group, Augustine spoke of the faith of the Church as *catholic* (universal) and orthodox, as against the Donatists, whom he condemned as separatists, sectarian, and unorthodox. Following Ignatius and Augustine, St. Cyril of Jerusalem (c. 315–386 CE), another important church father, also spoke of the Church as *catholic* because it extends through the entire world and brings under its umbrella all classes of people, rulers and subjects, learned and ignorant. Thus we see in the early Church and among the Fathers a common acceptance that the Church was *catholic* because it was inclusive. The first Council of Nicaea (325 CE) affirmed and accepted catholicity as an essential mark of the Church. The Council of Constantinople (381 CE) accepted the affirmations of Nicaea and developed a creed that spoke of the Church as *one*, *holy*, *catholic*, and *apostolic*.

The word *catholic*, in its pure and unadulterated sense (as used in the Nicene-Constantinopolitan Creed), was a rallying point and a source of unity for the early Church until about the eleventh century; the word took a new meaning and became divisive following the Great Schism of the East and West. The West, with Rome as its capital, held on to the title Catholic Church while the East, with Byzantium as its capital, severed all relations with Rome and called itself the Orthodox Church. The word was dealt another blow with the sixteenth-century Reformation when those who severed relations with Rome were called Protestants. The Church of Rome and those in communion with Rome, claiming continuity with the original Church, held on to the adjective *Catholic*. The schism and the Reformation severely impaired both the understanding and application

---

9. Ignatius of Antioch, *To the Smyrneans*, 8.2 (c.110 CE).

of the word, distorting its universal claims, and making it seem parochial. This parochial understanding persisted for a long time and was a source of disunity among Christians up to the twentieth century. The Second Vatican Council, in the spirit of the ecumenical movement of the time, rehabilitated the notion of *catholicity* to include, as it should, all the churches outside of the Roman Catholic communion. The Council's Decree on Ecumenism spoke of these churches as possessing varying "degrees" of catholicity.

Although the Second Vatican Council took an ecumenical step to broaden the notion of *catholicity*, other matters pertaining to catholicity and Catholicism were left unresolved. There was, for example, the question regarding whether Catholics who are in communion with Rome should be considered Roman Catholics or simply Catholics. According to the American theologian, Richard McBrien, there were some inside and outside the Catholic Church who thought it was ecumenically insensitive to drop the adjective "Roman" because so many Anglican, Orthodox, Protestant, and Oriental Christians also regard themselves as Catholic.[10] Others thought that *Roman* tends to confuse rather than define the reality of Catholicism. There was also the question of Eastern-rite Catholics who are in union with Rome but who, for obvious reasons, object to being labelled "Roman Catholic." Furthermore, apart from the Latin or Roman tradition, there are seven other non-Latin, non-Roman ecclesial traditions that are Catholic: Armenian, Byzantine, Coptic, Ethiopian, East Syrian (Chaldean), West Syrian, and Maronite. While every one of these is a Catholic church in communion with the Bishop of Rome, none of them is a *Roman* Catholic Church. The point is that Catholicism is neither narrowly Roman nor narrowly Western, but universal in the fullest sense of the word.

In light of the complex and varying understandings of the word *Catholic*, a word concerning how it is used in this book is in order. First, unless otherwise specified, references to the Catholic Church in this book are to that ecclesial communion of Churches headed by the bishop of Rome that is properly called the Roman Catholic Church. Second, allusions in this book to visions that drive the intellectual traditions of a Catholic university belong to a broader notion of Catholicity. The Catholic imagination or ethos,

---

10. Richard P. McBrien, *Catholicism* (New York: HarperCollins, 1994), 5.

although subtle, is profound. There is, "in purely historical and cultural terms, an immense, to some, an overwhelming objectivity about 'the Catholic thing.'"[11]

Intellectual

What do we mean by *intellectual?* Does *intellectual* refer to integral *humanitas* (integral humanism) or to the Renaissance idea of *Lebenskunst* (mastery of the art of living)? Or when we say *intellectual* are we referring to the late eighteenth-century German idea of modern education known as *Bildung* (liberation of the mind from "tradition" and superstition)? When we speak of *intellectual* we are swirling in the realm of academic vocation.

What might be classified or categorized as *intellectual* has a long and complicated history that predates the Catholic Church. But the Catholic Church has always been involved in the task of fostering and promoting education. Some consider the idea of a Catholic intellectual an oxymoron or at best a contradiction. Owing partly to a narrow conception of Catholicism and partly to the Enlightenment critique of religion (freedom from religion and autonomy of reason), they suggest that Catholics are not capable of thinking independently and therefore not capable of being legitimate intellectuals. They point out that the Church has a history of muzzling progressive ideas and astute thinkers. The Church certainly has had some anti-intellectual moments that feed this perception. Its dealings with Galileo and subsequent suppressions of scientific findings that seemed at odds with the Church's teachings rank high on the list.

It should be remembered, however, that education in part has its origin in religion in general and in the Church in particular. The origin of education goes back to the Greeks, who sought wisdom in all things and in all places. The ideals of education—"the Greek discovery of the mind"—has not always been separable from religion. The Greek quest for wisdom was all-inclusive in that it included temporal and spiritual dimensions of life. The Athenians accused Socrates of not believing in spiritual things (spiritual wisdom). Socrates replied that his belief in spiritual things (wisdom that comes

---

11. Anthony Kelly, "Researching Catholicity at ACU," *http://dlibrary.acu.edu.au/staffhome/ankelly/catholicityacu.htm.*

from the gods) was the reason for his search for human practical wisdom. He espoused an ideal unknown to non-Greeks by pressing the Athenians to pursue wisdom common to the Greeks and Barbarians when obeying the religiously binding laws of Athens. The theoretical and practical ideal that Socrates espoused is today considered one of the universal purposes of education.

Education, as we know it today in its formal Western style, began in Christian monasteries. Very early on Christian monks devoted themselves to asceticism and learning. They studied Greek, Hebrew, Aramaic, Syriac, and other ancient languages, and copied manuscripts. Origen of Alexandria (c. 185–254 CE), for example, who headed the catechetical school in that city, devoted his life to the study of the Bible, producing in the process the *Hexapla*, which presented the entire text of the Old Testament in Hebrew and various Greek versions, arranged in six columns. As monasteries began to flourish in the fifth century the monks made for themselves centers of learning comparable to Plato's academy. Later they made these centers (*cathedral schools*, as they were called) available to laypeople. In the cathedral schools, the method of *lectio divina* (Catholic practice of reflective reading of Scripture) was promoted. The prologue to the rule of St. Benedict (480–548) gives an insight both to the study of *lectio divina* and the ideal of learning that was promoted: "We are going to establish a school of the service of God, in which we hope we will establish nothing harsh, nothing burdensome."[12] Benedict saw the need to connect intellect with religion. The cathedral schools became centers of formal education and flourished for a long time. With the help of Charles the Great (d. 814), the monks built libraries and more schools, ushering in the "Carolingian Renaissance," named after Charles as a tribute to his patronage and devotion to education.

In the twelfth and thirteenth centuries, new educational centers that would be known as *universities* were opened thanks to the patronage of the Church. They were created to preserve the interest of those who wanted to pursue advanced studies, and were essentially educational cooperatives or guilds meant to protect teachers and students. The first center or the first university was established in

---

12. See J. Derek Holmes and Bernard W. Bickers, *A Short History of the Catholic Church*, Millennium edition (New York: Continuum, 2002), 51.

Bologna. Soon after, other universities were established in Paris and Oxford. Gradually, through both papal and royal patronage, the universities took on a life of their own and exercised their independence by creating structures suitable for their purposes. A masters degree (MA), which was then only in theology, took an average of five or six years, and doctoral degrees took an average of six to eight years.

With papal and royal patronage, there was for a long time a homogenous conception of education, even when Muslim and Jewish centers of learning were opened in Baghdad and Spain. Not distinguishing between universal and particular aims of education, together these centers of learning laid the foundation of what would become Western style education. Together with the influence of the Church, their homogenous conception of education in culturally diverse lands held Europe together until the political and religious crises of the fifteenth century culminated in the Reformation of the sixteenth century. Its aftermath was division and rancor in Europe: sectarian wars and wars of religion. The cultural revolution of the Enlightenment gradually also made Europe lose its Christian character. But the two educational goals that prevailed from the beginning—the Greek theoretical knowledge and the Hebrew practical wisdom—remained unchallenged until the Enlightenment.

The humanists, in particular Friedrich Alexander von Humboldt (1767–1835), Johann Wolfgang von Goethe (1749–1832), and Friedrich Schiller (1759–1805), advocated a more grand educational project. German classicists used an architectural metaphor, *Bildung*, to interpret education. They asserted that education consists essentially in what one makes of oneself. Earlier in the Renaissance, new discoveries had been made in the field of arts, music, poetry, and architecture. The printing press had been invented. These discoveries made possible the free flow of ideas that diminished the people's dependence on the Church. For some, the printing press constitutes the most important invention in the history of Western civilization. With the likes of Leonardo Da Vinci (1452–1519), Michelangelo Buonarroti (1475–1564), and William Shakespeare (1564–1616), and the ideals of uninhibited freedom they promoted, the Renaissance person became *homo universal*, an ideal person. But the uninhibited freedom they promoted, together with the ongoing technological development that culminated in the Industrial

Revolution, later forced Western culture to rethink the goals of education. Even so, as late as the twentieth century Max Weber (1881–1961) would continue to speak of education in terms and ideas that were religious in origin and implication. In the famous Munich University lecture (1918) on *Wissenschaft als Beruf*, Weber attacked what he thought was an elevated notion of the academic vocation that compartmentalized learning.[13] Using his understanding of Protestant ethics, Weber formulated a grandiose academic vocation that contradicted even his earlier view that we not only live in a world without God but that we must see to it that we live in a world without God. The new academic vision showed, for Weber, how a person can overcome life difficulties or surmount all odds by appropriating religious language for secular ends.

Modern educationists have today accepted most of the ideals Weber espoused in *Wissenschaft als Beruf*. Weber's vision of education still drives the educational philosophies of most of industrialized Europe and the United States, where the work of university faculty is conceived in terms of three main objectives: the making of knowledge (*Wissenschaft*), transmitting of knowledge and skills, and the cultivation of character (*Bildung*). Although these three objectives are by no means contradictory, some professors think of them as competing. Those who want to recover the Christian origins of education, particularly Catholic educationists who question the epistemological basis of the Weberian objectives, see the Catholic university as a place where these three objectives can be harmoniously integrated with the study of God (theology).

Tradition and Traditions

The post-Vatican II Catholic Church is in many ways different from the pre-Vatican II Church. In the era before Vatican II, the line of separation between Catholics and non-Catholics was clear because there was a distinctive Catholic social and religious etiquette; for example, Catholics did not eat meat on Fridays. Most significantly,

---

13. See Mark R. Schwehn, *Exiles From Eden: Religious and Academic Vocation in America*, (Oxford: Oxford University Press, 2005), 12. See also Max Weber, *The Protestant Ethic and the Spirit of Capitalism*, translated by Talcott Parsons (New York: Charles Scribner, 1958).

Catholics pledged allegiance to the pope and emphasized tradition. These two have long been the marks of identification for the Catholic Church. Unlike those ecclesial communions that stress the authority of the Bible as the final and supreme adjudicator of truth, the Catholic Church adds a caveat: the Bible itself is a product of many multilayered traditions. Before the canon of the Bible was set, the Christian faith was transmitted orally—through preaching, worship, catechesis, and witnesses of the martyrs. These elements (catechesis, worship, prayer, witnesses of the martyrs) were all parts of Christian tradition, and all carry weight in Catholic thinking.

The Catholic idea that tradition is intrinsically related to authority makes the concept complex. Some theologians have for this reason tried to distinguish between *tradition* and *traditions*. According to their distinction *tradition* (sometimes capitalized) refers to the authoritative body of teaching in the Church, like the magisterium, while *traditions* refer to the processes by which this body of teaching is communicated. The latter "can be analyzed as a cultural reality, with its own internal rules and structures, analogous to those of a language. Just as it is not possible to communicate the Gospel unless one follows the basic rules of language, so it is not possible to hand on the content of Tradition (or traditions) unless the basic rules of tradition processes are observed."[14] In the long history of the Catholic Church, there are, at times, tensions between tradition and traditions. "In the early Church, the criterion of authoritative doctrine was the unbroken connection with the 'teaching of the Apostles.' One could call this the historical criterion of authority."[15] The fifth-century Gallic writer St. Vincent of Lerins developed a formula that was widely accepted as a criterion of authenticity of doctrine in the early Church. In his *Commonitorium pro catholicae fidei, antiquitate et universitate* (434 CE), Vincent asserted that Catholic doctrine consists of that which is believed everywhere, at all times, by everyone. But as people began to study the history of the Church, it became

---

14. Brian Johnstone, CSsR, "What Is Tradition? From the Pre-Modern to Post-Modern" *Australian EJournal of Theology* 5 (August 2005) [no page numbers]. See also Yves Congar, *La Tradition et les Traditions: Il Essay Theologique* (Paris: Fayard, 1963), and Eamon Duffy, *Faith of Our Fathers: Reflections on Catholic Tradition* (London; New York: Continuum, 2004).

15. Ibid.

evident to them that some of the "doctrines and practices upheld by the Church in the present did not seem to have a basis, or at least an explicit foundation in the 'doctrine of the apostles' as it was presented in the early Church. This raised the question of the development of doctrine."[16]

To help clarify the issues, Brian Johnstone distinguishes between three models of tradition. This first is what he calls the participative model: tradition both participates in and draws its authority from the transcendent. This model views tradition as "timeless" ideas that are nonetheless manifest in history. To the extent that tradition participates in divine truth, it is authoritative. The second is what he calls the extrinsic authority model: tradition is an entity external to the Church community and imposed on the Church by an authority. "This model is correlated with the view that Tradition carries law-like propositions enunciating 'truths' to be believed or practices to be followed. Tradition was assumed to be something which went on within the Church, the Tradition once settled, was then to be communicated to others, as it was through worldwide missionary activity."[17] The third and final model is the communicate-critical model, which Johnstone derives from the documents of Vatican II. This model critically examines what conduces to holiness, i.e., what can lead the Church community to its final end, which is salvation. The role of tradition in this regard would be to encourage dialogue toward the fulfillment of this eschatological end of the Church community. It considers to what extent "this dialogue should be considered as communicating what is already in itself fixed, or whether the dialogue might contribute to the process of Tradition itself. In short what, if anything, can be accepted into the Tradition 'from outside'?"[18] Johnstone's analysis is helpful: while it accepts the role of authority and the place of the magisterium with regard to tradition, it does away with a juridical-authoritarian notion of tradition.

---

16. Ibid.
17. Ibid.
18. Ibid.

DOES IT MATTER?

Is it important that Catholic colleges and universities preserve and develop their Catholic identity? There are a number of reasons they should:

1. We can draw an analogy between the "why" of Catholic colleges and the "why" of education in the United States. Analogously speaking, we can say Catholics should care about the Catholic identity of Catholic colleges the same way Americans should care about education in general. Education in this country was founded to foster democracy and enhance the republican vision of the United States. Part of this republican vision is to lead the world in science and technology. Americans care about education for these reasons and more. Similarly, Catholic colleges and universities were established in the United States to give immigrant Catholics who were typically pushed to the margins of American socioeconomic life access to higher education and good job opportunities, in addition to preserving the Catholic identity of these institutions in a predominantly Protestant culture. Catholics should care about Catholic education for these reasons and, in particular, for the preservation of the Catholic intellectual tradition.

   The irony here should not be missed. Providing educational opportunities and access to American socioeconomic life to Catholics and preserving Roman Catholic culture and identity, the three reasons for which Catholic schools were established in the United States, ipso facto become the basis of tension in the mission of these Catholic colleges and universities. "The more successful they were in helping Catholics fit into the mainstream of American life (as they have been) the less distinctive they are likely to be and less successful they are likely to be in preserving Catholic culture and identity. On the other hand, success in preserving Catholic culture and identity makes it more likely that Catholics remain a separatist subculture and less a part of the mainstream culture."[19] The need to navigate this tension

---

19. Cahoy, "The Catholic Intellectual Tradition."

provides a compelling reason as to why Catholics should care about Catholic colleges and universities.

2. Catholic colleges and universities are also places for the preservation of Catholic intellectual tradition and are responsible for the ways and manner this rich tradition is developed and transmitted to future generations. Catholic identity can no longer be taken for granted as was done in the years before secularization had begun to break down the Catholic subculture. It is the responsibility of Catholics to build and foster this tradition because only they can preserve it. No one else will do it for them.

3. Catholics should care about the Catholicity of their colleges and universities because when an institution gives itself a name that identifies it as Catholic, intentionality is involved. This becomes the yardstick for measuring the success or failure of the institution's mission. When an institution identifies itself as Catholic, this is indicative of the way the university wants its mission and activity to be understood by its faculty, staff, and students, and this self-understanding has direct bearing on how the institution relates to and carries out its academic mission in the wider society.

4. Catholic colleges and universities not only mediate between faith and culture, they also have important roles to play in modern society. There is a rich body of Catholic teaching on social matters (Catholic social teaching) that Catholic schools bring to bear. Some of these teachings can be countercultural and can help society grow in matters of truth, human dignity, and the ultimate goal of human life. For example, in the early church when Christians were confused about whether or not it was legitimate to take part in war or to serve in the armed forces, some Christian thinkers, particularly Augustine, formulated a just war theory to help respond to this question. This theory has been refined and developed over the centuries and is today called the Catholic Just War teaching. In a war-obsessed culture such as ours, "preserving, understanding, and applying the idea of a just war is both true to the Catholic intellectual tradition" and our world.[20]

---

20. See ibid.

5. In mediating between faith and culture, Catholic colleges and universities integrate faith and reason and include in the curriculum of studies, not only theology but also philosophy and the social and behavioral sciences. In contrast to those faith traditions that focus only on revelation (Scripture), the Catholic tradition strongly emphasizes the need to consider the revealed word critically in light of the findings of modern science. Emphasis on philosophy or reason is by no means a rejection of faith, but faith seeking understanding—a way of educating the mind to help it clearly articulate the implications of faith. Among the values Catholicism shares with other religious traditions is the *Deus est fascinans* or yearning for transcendent reality that informs the way human life is lived as a community of persons. The human longing for communion with the divine is connected to the way people relate to others with whom they share a common humanity and destiny. Thus, by integrating faith and reason, a Catholic college or university helps in the education of the whole person in the true sense of the term.

CONCLUSION

What has been designated the *Catholic intellectual tradition* is a loaded term. CIT cannot be understood apart from Catholicism. *Catholic* and *Catholicism* are related but not synonymous terms. Because they derive from the same Greek root the two terms cannot be separated, but can be distinguished and nuanced. From their Greek derivation both words imply universality, completeness, and wholeness. Catholicity, in this inclusive sense, is understood as Christ's gift to the Catholic Church. The gift of the Church's catholicity, in turn, is central to the understanding of the Catholic intellectual tradition—a rich tradition that is inclusive, universal, all-encompassing, and all-embracing. CIT is a human search for the fullness of God's gift in Christ in a non-parochial, nonsectarian, and nondogmatic way. It is carried out everywhere and by everyone (Catholics and non-Catholics alike) who believes in truth and value, particularly in Catholic colleges and universities, in a spirit of open inquiry and academic freedom that Catholicism ought to engender.

For Further Reading

Cernera, Anthony J., and Oliver J. Morgan, eds. *Examining the Catholic Intellectual Tradition*. Fairfield, CT: Sacred Heart University Press, 2000.

Dulles, Avery. *The Catholicity of the Church*. Oxford: Clarendon, 1985.

Gallin, Alice, OSU. "American Catholic Higher Education: An Experience of Inculturation." In *Trying Times: Essays on Catholic Higher Education in the Twentieth Century*, edited by William M. Shea and Daniel Van Slyke, 99–119. Atlanta: Scholars Press, 1999.

Gallin, Alice, OSU, ed. *American Catholic Higher Education: Essential Documents, 1967–1990*. Notre Dame, IN: University of Notre Dame Press, 1992.

Landy, Thomas M. "Introduction: Yeast and the Measures of Flours." In *As Leaven in the World: Catholic Perspectives on Faith, Vocation, and the Intellectual Life*, edited by Thomas M. Landy, xi–xxii. Franklin, WI: Sheed and Ward, 2001.

McBrien, Richard. *Catholicism*. New York: Harper Collins, 1989.

Mize, Sandra Yocum. "On the Back Roads: Searching for American Catholic Intellectual Traditions." In *American Catholic Traditions: Resources for Renewal*, edited by Sandra Yocum Mize and William Portier, 3–23. The Annual Publication of the College Theology Society 42. Maryknoll, NY: Orbis Books, 1996.

Schwehn, Mark R. *Exiles from Eden: Religion and Academic Vocation in America*. Oxford University Press, 2005.

CHAPTER 2

Theology and
the Catholic University

The first universities were Christian in origin, and theology played a large role in defining this Christian identity. Then the liberalism of the eighteenth and nineteenth century that swept across Europe began to diminish the place of theology in a university curriculum. When Europe lost its Christian identity and the universities became secularized, the academic study of theology became one of the distinguishing characteristics of a Catholic university.

There is no Catholic university without theology. The Catholic university needs theology and Catholic theology needs the Catholic university. Theology is an ordered inquiry that investigates and locates the truth of God and human life. As a place for the study of the *universitas*—the totality of ideas, theories, and practices—the study of theology is integral to a Catholic university curriculum. Moreover, theology plays a key role in the transmission of values at the heart of the Catholic faith: human dignity, call to family, community, participation, human rights and responsibilities, preferential option for the poor, dignity of labor and right to just compensation, solidarity, and stewardship of God's creation.[1]

---

1. According to the United States Conference of Catholic Bishops (USCCB) pastoral, *Sharing Catholic Social Teaching: Challenges and Directions.* Washington, DC: USCCB, 1998, far too many Catholics are unfamiliar with basic Catholic social teaching and far too many do not understand that the social teaching of the Church is integral to the Catholic faith.

The place of theology in a university curriculum gained importance in the nineteenth century thanks to the efforts of John Henry Newman, who thought the study of the ancient wisdom of the church fathers might offer answers to the challenges posed by the wave of liberalism and secularism that was sweeping throughout Europe. Newman saw the university as a place for the study of universal knowledge. In his work, *The Idea of a University* (1852), Newman called for a liberal education that integrates Christian faith with the study of arts and sciences.[2] For him, a Catholic university curriculum without theology is defective because theology helps mediate discussion with the other disciplines. Referring specifically to Catholic theology, Newman noted that theology, Church, and university disciplines mutually influence one another and that a university teaching without theology is, to say the least, unphilosophical.[3]

The university has a unique function as the mind of the world. "The function of the mind is to identify, distinguish, and help the person-organism to relate itself to the different items in its experience. The more mature the mind, the better it can interpret the nature and value of the various possibilities for response, and thus further the purposes and satisfaction of the person-organism."[4] Newman went so far as to assert that no Catholic university can perform this function adequately and lay claim to universal knowledge unless it has a department of theology. The human mind speculates and systematizes, and if theology is absent from the university, other sciences that are foreign to theology will usurp its place, according to Newman. The Canadian Jesuit theologian, Bernard Lonergan, concurred with Newman that to omit theology in a university curriculum is to omit a significant component of knowledge, and by so doing destroy the curriculum itself. He asserted, like Newman, that the university is a place where all the branches of knowledge are professed and cultivated and "philosophic temper"

---

2. See John Henry Newman, *The Idea of a University* (Garden City, NJ: Doubleday, 1959).

3. Virginia M. Shaddy, "Newman on Theology in the University: Perspectives of a Convert," in *Catholic Theology in the University: Source of Wholeness*, ed. Virginia M. Shaddy (Milwaukee: Marquette University, 1998), 43.

4. Nels Ferre, *Christian Faith and Higher Education* (New York: Harper and Brothers, 1954), 235.

(i.e., the awareness that God is the beginning and end of human life) is instilled in students.[5]

More recently, John Paul II's Apostolic Constitution *Ex Corde Ecclesiae* (August 15, 1990) explicated the central role that theology plays in the synthesis of knowledge and how it helps mediate the dialogue between faith and reason. Theology "serves all other disciplines in their search for meaning, not only by helping them to investigate how their discoveries will affect individuals and society but also by bringing a perspective and an orientation not contained within their own methodologies."[6] While it enriches other disciplines, theology in turn is enriched by its interaction with these disciplines. They offer theology a better understanding of the world, "making theological research more relevant to current needs."[7] Every Catholic university should "have a faculty, or at least a chair of theology" because of theology's specific importance among the academic disciplines.[8]

Before *Ex Corde Ecclesiae*, some Catholics were expressing the concern "that the prominent role once given to philosophy and theology has been greatly reduced; that theology itself is dissolving into religious studies; that the general curriculum is becoming indistinguishable from that of secular universities; that little effort is being made to communicate the Catholic intellectual, artistic, cultural heritage; that the attempt at least to initiate some kind of integration of faith and reason has no institutional embodiment."[9] While John Paul II seemed to have addressed these concerns in this important document, the view that theology should occupy a central role in the university curriculum is not universally held. There are those that argue that theology should not be included in a university curriculum because it is alien to the spirit and character of university education. They offer three basic reasons: first, that the theologian cannot approach questions with the

---

5. Newman's and Lonergan's assertions are included here to illustrate the ideal relationship that the Catholic intellectual tradition envisions between theology and the other disciplines represented in a Catholic university.

6. John Paul II, *Ex Corde Ecclesiae*, 19.

7. Ibid.

8. Ibid.

9. Joseph A. Komonchak, "The Redemptive Identity and Mission of a Catholic University," in *Catholic Theology in the University: Source of Wholeness*, ed. Virginia M. Shaddy (Milwaukee: Marquette University Press, 1998), 73.

kind of openness and objectivity required by university standards; second, that theology is incompatible with academic freedom; and third, that theology infringes on the autonomy that belongs to universities, at least as they function in the American tradition.[10] These objections are not without their merits. In a study of the Catholic Church's view of academic freedom under the leadership of John Paul II, Kenneth Baker argues that the pope's understanding of academic freedom is different from current practices in North American universities. He shows that for John Paul II, academic freedom is a limited freedom, just as all freedoms are limited because the human person is a limited creature. Academic freedom, for this pope, is limited by rights of individual persons, by the rights of the community, and by the just claims of truth and the common good.[11]

What John Paul II opposed was the prevailing secular pluralism that insists that academic freedom requires that all should be free to hold and express whatever conclusions they arrive at through the exercise of free inquiry and that the Catholic university is a self-governing institution free from the control of religious authorities. Many advocates of Catholic education are uneasy about the idea of unlimited or unabridged freedom and the idea that the university is self-governing, self-constituting, independent and free from religious authorities. They look at the examples of some prestigious United States universities founded by Protestant communions, like Harvard, Yale, Princeton, Columbia, and the University of Chicago, which have now practically abandoned their religious character and have no identifiable religious identity. The fear is that if the Catholic authorities do not exercise the power of oversight on the leadership of Catholic colleges and universities, they too could lose their religious identity and go the way many Protestant colleges have gone. The consequence of this might be dire for CIT.

In institutions where the legitimacy of Catholic theology is expounded a commitment to an unlimited freedom without any

---

10. Avery Dulles, SJ, "The Place of Theology in a Catholic University," in *Catholic Theology in the University*, ed. Virginia M. Shaddy, 59–60.

11. Kenneth Baker, SJ, "Pope John Paul II and the Catholic University," in *The Mind and the Heart of the Church: Papers Presented at a Conference Sponsored by the Wethersfield Institute New York City, September 20, 1991*, ed. Ralph McInerny (San Francisco: Ignatius Press, 1992), 15–26.

Church leadership exercising the power of oversight is not without problems. There is in particular the problem of so-called liberalism. Roger Haight, the American Jesuit theologian, following and expounding on the massive survey of American liberal theology deriving from the renowned American Episcopalian theologian, Gary Dorrien,[12] posed the question: Do so-called liberal Catholic theologians have more in common with liberal Protestant theologians than with the Roman Catholic Church? The import of this question lies not only in the fact that it probes whether or not liberal Catholic theologians are more Protestant than Catholic but also because it seeks to ascertain "whether the liberal Catholic theologians represent a leakage in Catholic substance or identity."[13]

There is, according to Haight, a revolution in American Catholic theology, which had its beginnings from 1965 to 1975, a period when American Catholic theology developed six distinct characteristics:

1. the turn to experience (a transcendental or historically concrete set of experiences) that several theologians adopted as a point of departure for their theological reflection
2. the ecumenical turn of American Catholic theology in the period following Vatican II, when many Catholics began to read Protestant theology positively and learned a great deal from it
3. Catholic theology's integration of an emphasis on social praxis into its specifically theological reflection, and the elevation of this emphasis on social action as a criterion for the adequacy of a theological construction[14]
4. the "professionalization" of United States Catholic universities following World War II (and of course Vatican II), resulting in Catholic universities modeling themselves after secular universities—an act that caused revolution in departments of theology across Catholic campuses

---

12. See Gary Dorrien, *The Making of American Liberal Theology: Crisis, Irony and Postmodernity 1950–2005* (Louisville: Westminster John Knox Press, 2006), 449–50.

13. Roger Haight, "Liberal and Catholic?" *American Journal of Theology and Philosophy* 29 (2008): 146.

14. This development can be attributed to the agency of Vatican II, particularly the Council's document on the *Pastoral Constitution on the Church in the Modern World* (*Gaudium et Spes*), and the developments of liberation theology in many parts of Latin America.

5. the democratization of theology, by which is meant both theology's explosion into multiple subdisciplines and specialties (so that no theologian could control the "whole" as in the past) and a shift from clerical to lay practitioners of the discipline

6. increasing pluralism, such that Catholic theology today reveals a multiplicity of separate and unintegrated constituency-based and problem-defined theologies

Due to what is popularly perceived as the conservative nature of the Catholic Church and the negative connotations *liberal* has assumed for many since the nineteenth century, few Catholic theologians willingly accept the label, preferring the more or less neutral term *progressive*. But use of an alternate label does not or cannot detract from the liberalism of some American Catholic theologians.[15] Haight argues that liberal American Catholic theologians are distinctively Catholic when they appeal to analogical or sacramental imagination, to the classical theological tradition, to Catholic theologians around the world, and to a socially active dimension of theology.[16] And yet in three basic ways liberal American Catholic theologians resemble their Protestant colleagues:

- With respect to its method, liberal theology interprets Scripture and the official authoritative teaching of the Church through the lens of experience and reason. "Liberal American Catholic theology has taken a turn to experience. Sometimes it is characterized as theology from below. It is explicitly historically conscious and contextual. This contrasts with the Catholic Church in so far as it is represented by the hierarchy and an official insistence on unmediated didactic teaching of the Magisterium or the teaching authority of the church."[17]

- The liberal American Catholic theologian, appealing to common experience, addresses a broader audience. "Liberal theologians do not usually bear easily recognizable denominational labels. Rather they address an audience that transcends their particular church, whether it be Christians at large or society."[18]

---

15. Haight, "Liberal and Catholic?" 150.

16. Ibid.

17. Ibid., 148.

18. Ibid., 149.

- With respect to pluralism of positions on contested matters, "along with the democratization of theology has come an eclectic diversification of constituency for whom theologians write and the problem areas they treat. This stands out over against a growing concern within the Catholic Church for unity and identity, for authoritarian control of the church by its hierarchical leaders, and a disciplining of theologians that seems to be moving the church toward intellectual sectarianism."[19]

In sum, the liberal-conservative divergence and confluence in theology underscores the vital role and place of theology in a Catholic university. There are within both the liberal and conservative continuums a range of values each wants transmitted, values that would be difficult to transmit without theology. In teaching theology, a Catholic university not only transmits but also clarifies its values. "It is not the role of theology somehow to make the university or its students 'religious' and hence in some naïve way to legitimate Catholic foundation, but to offer informed perspectives on questions of Catholic Christian faith, to promote dialogue, intellectual rigor, and understanding, and to continue to clarify the nature of the values which are claimed to characterize the University's identity."[20] Because theology specifies the rich tradition of Catholic intellectual heritage, we now turn again to a consideration of the matter of Catholic intellectual tradition.

THE QUESTION REVISITED: IS THERE A CATHOLIC INTELLECTUAL TRADITION?

We are now at a better position to address the question posed in the previous chapter, even if only tentatively: Is there a Catholic intellectual tradition? The matter of CIT, as we have indicated earlier,

---

19. Ibid.; thus Haight thinks the solution might lie in an ecumenical environment where "a certain sense of community and interchange among liberal theologians of the many traditions may generate a good deal of common learning" (154).

20. Robyn Horner, "Issues for Teaching and Learning Theology in a Publicly-Funded Catholic University" *Australian EJournal of Theology* (February 2004), Issue 2 [no page numbers].

is difficult and highly contested. We suggested that such designation is valid but must be carefully nuanced. Because a definition can be problematic, it is perhaps best not to attempt one here, but to accept the existence of CIT as a given and then offer some general observations that will allow the reader to follow the arguments as we develop them in the next few chapters. These preliminary remarks will engage the work of John Haughey, who has offered one of the best clarifications in recent times on CIT.[21]

What CIT Is Not

The question—what is Catholic intellectual tradition?—suggests in the first place that there is something called the Catholic intellectual tradition. What then is "it"? Unfortunately, "it" is elusive. So we begin with what CIT is not.

- Catholic intellectual tradition is not the same thing as the Church's teaching authority or magisterium. "One of the main reasons for the poverty of educational theory in our Catholic colleges and universities" may be connected to the lack of clarity about the relationship between the Catholic intellectual tradition and the magisterium.[22] Confusion regarding the meaning of Catholic intellectual tradition will continue to exist and the problems will continue to plague our institutions until this distinction is properly understood. Understanding this distinction helps to eliminate any fear about ecclesiastical authority encroaching or usurping academics' freedom.[23]

- Catholic intellectual tradition is not synonymous with that sacred tradition from which the magisterium draws to teach authoritatively on matters of faith and morals. Catholic intellectual tradition is concerned only with the intellectual components of Catholicism. The magisterium is concerned with the authoritative doctrinal teachings of Catholicism.

---

21. See John C. Haughey, SJ, *Where Is Knowing Going? The Horizons of the Knowing Subject* (Washington, DC: Georgetown University Press, 2009).

22. Ibid., 61.

23. Ibid.

- Catholic intellectual tradition is not synonymous with papal teachings or pronouncements issued by dicasteries of the Roman curia. It is not the same as pronouncements issued by national or regional episcopal conferences or synods of bishops. While CIT may be guided by these, it is not synonymous with them.

How CIT Might Be Conceived

- Catholic intellectual tradition is, first and foremost, a learning tradition. No discipline is alien to it and no area of interest is irrelevant.[24] "There is a dialectical relationship between the Magisterium with its authority and the Catholic intellectual tradition, whose authority is located in the quality of the scholarship of each person seeking to connect the dots between his or her understandings and the doctrinal understandings of the Magisterium. The relationship between the Magisterium and the intellectual tradition has been largely beneficial to both, though they are not always on the same page."[25]

  Thus a distinction between the compound components of the Catholic entity, i.e., Catholic intellectual tradition and sacred tradition, according to Haughey, stands to benefit three main constituencies: the wider Catholic Church, the schools under the sponsorship of the Church, and the faculty, staff, and administrators of these schools. The Catholic intellectual tradition "helps the schools to be a school not a Church," while at the same time connecting the school's offerings to a tradition that has a continuous history, longer than any other educational tradition operating in the world today.[26] Another value to this differentiation is that it helps ease tension between Catholic institutions and Church authorities.[27] It also helps the Church prelates and authorities to relate to schools under their sponsorship pastorally, and not juridically. "A local bishop might then be a source of comfort to a campus, a sort of older brother in the faith, rather than the 'bad cop'

---

24. Ibid., 64.
25. Ibid., 62.
26. Ibid., 64.
27. Ibid., 67.

with the task of ensuring that orthodoxy is preserved. Respect for the religious authority of many bishops in the eyes of students, faculty, and administrators could be raised if both parties saw things this way."[28] More poignantly, Haughey observes rightly that there is "a unity-in-difference between the Sacred Tradition and the Catholic intellectual tradition; though distinguished, they cannot be separated. And while they exist in a reciprocal and interdependent relationship, the Sacred Tradition does not have the same function or mission as the intellectual tradition."[29]

- Catholic intellectual tradition has a very wide boundary, combining the realm of faith and realm of understanding.[30] Far from stressing one polar extreme at the expense of the other (faith at the expense of reason or reason at the expense of faith), in Catholic intellectual tradition faith and reason blend harmoniously. "There are, in other words, both a protology and eschatology in the tradition in which Catholic schools are rooted; such schools share in the Church's memory and destiny. For those who commit themselves to the Church's Sacred Tradition, it supplies a rule of faith."[31] A university is an enterprise in understanding; a Catholic university is "an enterprise in understanding that is linked to a faith tradition that has a history both of flights from understanding and deeper probes into understanding. Like all other universities, the Catholic university seeks knowledge, but it does so together with an intellectual tradition that is particularly open to the world in the light of faith."[32]

- Catholic intellectual tradition is not easy to locate because it is not in one place or in one mind.[33] It does not have a list of members. Rather, Catholic intellectual tradition is pluriform in that it both informs and at the same time is informed by different and vast bodies of knowledge.[34] It is a tradition that "consists in

---

28. Ibid., 64–65.
29. Ibid., 85.
30. Ibid., 66.
31. Ibid.
32. Ibid., 69.
33. Ibid., 75.
34. Ibid., 77.

the totality of all those instances in which a higher viewpoint has been sought and achieved, either by those who identify themselves with the Sacred Tradition or by those who don't, but whose higher viewpoint has been appropriated by the Church."[35]

- While one can and should speak of Catholic intellectual tradition, one should not do so in a boastful or triumphalistic way. The Church has had many anti-intellectual moments when the truth was ignored or those committed to the truth were persecuted for their devotion. "It took four hundred years before Galileo was given his due. And, of course, some of the greatest figures of the Catholic intellectual tradition shared the biases of their day (think, for example, of Aquinas's views on women)."[36] An important point to remember in talking about Catholic intellectual tradition is the fact that those who made major contributions to the tradition in the past "were naturally limited by their cultural and historical contexts, as all are. One thinks of Leo XIII, with his contribution to Catholic social thought and development of social questions on the one hand, and, on the other, his slamming of the door on Catholic scriptural scholarship. It took fifty more years before Pius XII could pry this door back open."[37]

The Difference "Catholic" Makes to CIT

So, what difference does the adjective *Catholic* make to this intellectual tradition? Is the adjective a fitting one for this intellectual tradition? Or would it be better to abandon the term and search for a more inclusive descriptor, in light of the suggestion that calling this tradition *Catholic* could wrongly suggest the exclusion of those who are not Catholics?[38]

The adjective *Catholic* is the right one for this tradition for reasons of etymology, ecumenism, and doctrine.[39] Etymologically,

---

35. Ibid., 75.
36. Ibid., 77.
37. Ibid.
38. Ibid., 71.
39. Ibid., 70.

catholicity, in contrast to what is incomplete, partial, sectarian, factional, exclusionary, tribal, and selective, connotes openness and that which is whole.[40] Ecumenically, *Catholic* is the right adjective because it suggests that people from other traditions "including some whose transcendental realm of meaning might not be Catholic, contribute to this tradition."[41] Doctrinally, *Catholic* fits because of the Church's doctrine of the nature of Christ as union of two natures—human and divine—a doctrine to which most Christian churches subscribe.[42] "That Jesus' humanity is at one and the same time other than God, and also united with his divine nature, is the key to understanding Christianity, and in turn Catholicism, and in turn Catholic schools. This is why Catholicism cannot accept a faith without reasoning or reasoning without faith. There is a direct link between the unique union of the two natures in Christ's person, and the Christian faith's insistence on reason."[43] Thus the adjective *Catholic* fits this intellectual tradition best, "not necessarily because of its connection to the Church, but because it connotes the whole connection with human intentionality and with all that was and is to be known."[44] In the final analysis, there is such a thing as the Catholic intellectual tradition, of which all Catholic schools must be aware. "A Catholic school that has no sense of this compound tradition does a disservice to students, leaving them ill equipped to deal with the confusions, ephemera, and biases of our contemporary culture."[45]

THE UNFOLDING OF THE TRADITION

The boundaries of the Catholic intellectual tradition are elastic and ever developing. The convergence of faith and understanding means that CIT will continue to grow and expand. As that which is always developing, CIT is a product of Christianity's interaction with the

---

40. Ibid., 40.
41. Ibid., 71.
42. Ibid.
43. Ibid., 72.
44. Ibid.
45. Ibid., 66.

cultures of which it has been a part. It is a learning tradition in that it borrows, adapts, and modifies things that it borrows from culture. In Catholic theology it is not uncommon to speak of two phases of theology: the mediating phase, known in Latin as *theologia in oratione obliqua* (theology encounters the past) and the mediated phase or *theologia in oratione recta* (theology looks forward to the future). In the mediated phase, one also understands that learning about the rich traditions and history of the past means that one must preserve and pass it on to future generations. But it is not sufficient just to assimilate and pass it on; one must also take a stand. In other words, one has to add one's own contribution. Only the person who is enlightened by the past can adequately confront the problems of his or her day. These two phases of theology offer a good way of envisioning CIT. To talk about CIT is to acknowledge a past with a rich history and tradition. History is concerned with change, i.e., change that also includes continuity.

Tracing the history of CIT is difficult because CIT has no list of members. Even if one were to attempt such a history, where does one begin and where does one end? Where does one draw the line? What are the legitimate criteria for determining who exemplified the tradition and what is in line with the tradition? Nevertheless, we can look at the different eras of the Church's life, beginning with Jesus, and extrapolate some important events or some persons who correctly connected "the dots between the Catholic intellectual life and doctrinal tradition, on the one hand, and the world on the other."[46]

The Origins of CIT

One thing we can say with certainty is that the history of the Catholic intellectual tradition begins with Jesus Christ and the first generation of early Christians and that the Catholic intellectual tradition is rooted in the Christian proclamation and confession of Jesus as the Christ, the anointed one of God. The seeds of the tradition were sown in the words and deeds of Jesus. The articulation of the tradition began with the first preaching of the Apostles, the *kerygma*—the proclamation of the death and Resurrection of Jesus. In other

---

46. Ibid., 105.

words, Catholic intellectual tradition began when the first disciples intellectually acknowledged the action of God in human history. This articulation was propelled by the Hellenist problem, the problem between the Jewish Christians and the Gentile Christians in the early Christian community (Acts chs. 6 to 8) that led to the election of the first seven deacons. It continued in the question of the Judaizers—whether Gentiles should be admitted to the Church without first going through Jewish circumcision rites (Acts 15). The wise decision of the Council that met in Jerusalem to accept Gentiles without requiring them to be circumcised opened the Catholic intellectual tradition in its primitive origins to Greek ways of thinking. Opening the door to Gentile Christians not only availed the Church of Greek concepts and ideas but also enlarged the Church's horizon. When the bishops gathered at Nicea to clarify the nature of the relationship between the persons of the Godhead (Trinity) in 325 CE, for example, they used Greek terms like *homoousios* (substance) to clarify the nature of the relationship between the persons of the Godhead. The use of Greek ideas helped the Church to specify a principal Christian affirmation, like the Trinity—one God and three persons. One wonders how the Church would have explained this and other Christian mysteries (such as the Incarnation and the union of the two natures in Christ) had the Church not opened the door to Greek Christians and Greek ideas (Hellenism).

The teachings of the apostles would form the cradle and centerpiece of any future intellectual discussion. Continuity with apostolic teachings would also become a necessary condition for determining compliance or faithfulness to the Catholic intellectual tradition. We have already mentioned Vincent of Lerin's formula of orthodoxy, that a dogma or teaching of the Church must be in accord with what was held everywhere, by all, and at all times. Many of the Fathers were Neoplatonists (a brand of philosophy deriving from Plotinus, an admirer of Plato who refined Plato's original ideas) and harmonized Neoplatonic teachings with Christian doctrine. They, as it were, used Neoplatonism to lay the philosophical foundation of Catholic intellectual thought.

Augustine was the most well read and the most influential of the Latin Fathers. His contribution to Catholic philosophy and theology in general was enormous. In his major writings can be found his program for Christian education, particularly the *Cassiciacum Dialogues* from which many leading thinkers in Catholic thought have derived valuable Christian pedagogies.[47] Apart from the *Confession*, the *Cassiciacum Dialogues* are classics in terms of what they add to the Catholic imagination. In *On the Trinity*, Augustine identifies some mental analogues for learning and points out what he terms the *amor studentium* (the sort of love that guides the learning process), suggesting that the more a thing is known without its being fully known, the more intelligence desires to know what is left to be known of that thing.[48] Augustine thus made the act of organizing intelligence the focal point of the learning process. In *On Order*, a work he wrote around December 386, about four months before his baptism, Augustine outlined a program of liberal education centered on the beatific vision as the object of learning.[49] He outlined the epistemological foundation of this program in the *Soliloquies*. In *The Teacher*, a dialogue with his son Adeodatus, he asserted that the object of inquiry is knowing all that needs to be known. Directing his instructions to both students and teachers alike, Augustine writes that one can truly claim to learn only when one has subjected one's interior convictions to a rigorous test.

Augustine's *Catechizing the Uninstructed* has yet to receive the attention it deserves in the larger scheme of the Catholic educational project. Written around 403 CE, *Catechizing the Uninstructed* was central to the formation of the clergy and monastic education in the centuries following Augustine's death. Augustine wrote this work in response to a question put to him by a deacon from Carthage named Deogratias, whom Augustine fondly referred to as a "brother." Deogratias requested from Augustine a sketch or a manual for instructing or catechizing beginners (*rudibus*) in the faith.[50] "The term *rudes* in the expression referred specifically to people who were

---

47. See K. Paffenroth and K. L. Hughes, eds., *Augustine and Liberal Education* (Burlington, VT: Ashgate, 2000).

48. See Raymond Canning, "Teaching and Learning: An Augustinian Perspective," *Australian EJournal of Theology* (August 2004), Issue 3 [no page numbers].

49. Ibid.

50. Ibid.

approaching the Church for the first time with the wish to become Christians. All classes were encompassed under the rubrics of the uneducated (16,24), the moderately well-educated (9,13), and the very well-educated (8,12)."[51] The designation *rudes* was applied even to the well-educated. They were expected to receive formal instruction in the faith from the hands of an authorized teacher. "The *rudes*, whatever their background, still had to take the step by which they would become catechumens (*catechumeni* or *audientes*, in Augustine's terminology), and further step that would make them petitioners for baptism (*competentes*, as Augustine calls these)."[52] Central to Augustine's pedagogy, as his instructions to Deogratias show, is 1 Timothy 1:5: "The aim of such instruction is love that comes from a pure heart, a good conscience, and sincere faith." For Augustine, learning leads to hope, and hope leads to love.[53]

The development of the Catholic intellectual tradition in the Middle Ages, in early universities and the cathedral or monastic schools, has been described in the previous chapter in our definition of the term *intellectual*. With regard to the importance of the cathedral school and universities in the Middle Ages for the development of CIT, we should only add that these universities produced intellectual giants like Albert the Great, Francis of Assisi, Thomas Aquinas, and Bonaventure. They continued the project of Augustine and the Fathers of harmonizing faith and reason. There was also Anselm of Canterbury (1033–1109) who made an important distinction between understanding and belief, showing how reason has every right to inquire into revealed truth in the quest to improve a person's knowledge and understanding about what is believed. The scholastics continued this harmonization of faith and reason

---

51. Ibid.

52. Ibid.

53. Ibid. Canning observes that for a contemporary Catholic university "it is not theologically unthinkable that this narrative of God's incarnational, self-emptying and humble love, and the responsive reciprocal love for God and neighbor that it kindles, might consciously shape a Catholic university's sense of identity and mission, the way curriculum is conceptualized and research priorities are determined and the types of review and quality assurance processes that are adequate, as well as acting as integral principles in the university's formulation of teaching and learning plans, policies and strategies."

and systematically arranged theological questions using arguments from reason. They also developed the *Quaestio* that became a standard method of argumentation in the universities. Their methods of inquiry, together with the founding of the universities, rank among the greatest contributions of the Catholic intellectual tradition. Pope Leo XIII idealized them in his encyclical, *Aeterni Patris* (1879), as the "Doctors of the Middle Ages" who did work of great magnitude. They diligently gathered together for their use and the convenience of those who came after them the rich and fruitful crops of doctrine that were scattered in the works of the church fathers. Within this scholastic tradition was Peter Abelard (1079–1142), who was the first to introduce the word *theology* to the Latin West. His *Sic et Non*, or dialectical method, challenged the hegemony of the Fathers and the authority the Fathers had previously enjoyed in the field of theology. Abelard's contribution was immense. With *Sic et Non*, the traditional teaching of the Fathers no longer enjoyed the unconditionally binding authority they used to have in academic circles because Abelard exposed, not only how the Fathers differed on many issues but also how they contradicted one another on some issues.

The scholastic ideal found particular expression in the works of two great giants: the angelic St. Thomas Aquinas and the seraphic St. Bonaventure, two men who saw ancient wisdom in the teaching of the Fathers. The Catholic Church regards Aquinas as the most influential philosopher of the Middle Ages and the most outstanding Christian thinker in Western civilization. His *Summa Theologiae* and *Summa Contra Gentiles* are unparalleled in Catholic history and thought. The authority of Aquinas in Catholic circles can be gleaned from the tribute Leo XIII paid him: "In the midst of the Council of Trent, the assembled Fathers so willing it, the *Summa* of Thomas Aquinas lay open on the altar, with the Holy Scriptures and the decrees of the Supreme Pontiffs, that from it might be sought counsel and reasons and answers."[54]

---

54. See encyclical letter *Aeterni Patris* of 1979 by Pope Leo XIII "On the Restoration of Christian Philosophy According to the Mind of St. Thomas Aquinas, the Angelic Doctor," in *St. Thomas Aquinas Summa Theologica*, trans. the Fathers of the English Dominican Province (Allen, TX: Christian Classics, 1981), xvi.

The Modern University and CIT

With the Renaissance and Enlightenment's critique of religion, the authority of the scholastics and their position in the Church became an object of suspicion as many began to distance the universities from the Church. While not discounting their contemporaries' critiques of religion, many Catholic thinkers still contributed to the growth of the modern university. The origin of the modern university is usually traced to the University of Berlin in 1810 and many Catholic thinkers helped make this happen. We already saw how the German idea of education as *Bildung* sought to liberate the mind from religion and tradition, which were viewed as "superstition," something to be done away with.

The synthesis of faith and reason, however, a hallmark of Catholic education was not lost on those Catholic thinkers who challenged the liberal idea of education that suppressed faith. Among these was the nineteenth-century Church historian, Cardinal John Henry Newman, who saw liberalism and its corollary, relativism, as a fundamental nineteenth-century problem that had to be confronted. His conversion to Catholicism was the culmination of a protracted intellectual and spiritual inquiry that led Newman to the conviction that the Catholic Church, not the Church of England, was the bona fide preserver of Christian truth. Newman, like many of his colleagues in the Oxford Movement, was convinced about the need to recover orthodox Christian truth and ancient wisdom in tradition and the study of the Fathers. In reaction against liberal individualism, Newman and his colleagues showed how human sense experience and ideas pale in comparison to the spiritual truths that are derived from revelation. In the face of the Enlightenment adulation of reason and the power of the human mind unaided by grace to attain truth, Newman maintained that reason alone was an insufficient guide for moral judgment. While not diminishing the power of reason to certain knowledge, Newman insisted that reason is still but only one faculty of human life and cannot be unduly made superior to revealed truths.

Newman was actively involved in Catholic education and served as the rector of the Catholic University of Ireland. As rector he gave many public lectures on university education, which were collected and published as *Discourse on a University Education* and *Lectures and Essays on University Subjects*. Together these two publications were

© Hulton-Deutsch Collection/CORBIS

John Henry Newman

refined and republished in 1873 as *The Idea of a University*, a work for which Newman became famous. In this work Newman provided a philosophical justification for a Catholic university.

Many in England at the time of Newman questioned whether theology was a legitimate academic discipline and denied that theology had any place in a university curriculum whatsoever. Theology, in their thinking, was alien to the spirit of modern science that a university upholds. Newman responded to these attacks by showing the significance of theology in a university curriculum. He also addressed the question of the ecumenical other—whether people of different faiths or no faith should be in a Catholic university. Newman was ecumenical before ecumenism became a catchword. He saw the university as a place for everyone, Catholics and non-Catholics alike. It

THE OXFORD MOVEMENT

Europe of the nineteenth century faced many political, social, and religious upheavals. The Enlightenment critique of religion had severely weakened the power the church exercised on society. The church was also undergoing a reform of its own. In 1833 the Church Temporalities Act was passed by Parliament to abolish three archbishoprics and eight bishoprics in Ireland. While many hailed the bill as a signal of society's freedom from the stranglehold of the church, not everyone was supportive. The most vocal opposition came from professors in the universities, most of whom were teaching at Oxford. One of these was John Keble who in 1833 preached a sermon in Oxford in the same year on "National Apostasy." At the time, John Henry Newman, then an Anglican, was returning from a visit to Sicily. Newman, along with two other Oxford professors, Hurrell Froude and William Palmer, joined Keble in condemning Parliament's action.

Newman and his three colleagues joined forces and began to preach sermons and produce tracts that condemned government interference in church matters. They were first known as the Oxford Tractarians because of the enormous number of tracts they produced. They argued that it was a sacrilege for the state to tell the church what to do. They were also against liberalism. The Tractarian Movement later became the Oxford Movement. Newman was the most famous of its members.

Newman saw the Oxford Movement as the beginning of the restoration of "ancient religion" to England after Roman and, subsequently, Anglican failures. It would ultimately lead him "to the conviction that history itself demonstrated that the Roman Catholic Church was the single, transcendent and yet visible entity that could embody, interpret, and judge all the facts of history." The Oxford movement would be, for Newman, not a digging of defenses of the old order, but a "revolution by tradition." In 1841 Newman published his famous Tract 90 that ended his involvement in Anglicanism. He equated Anglicanism with liberalism and became a Roman Catholic in October 1845. He was made a cardinal in 1879 by Pope Leo XIII.

is "a place where inquiry is pushed forward, and discoveries verified and perfected, and rashness rendered innocuous, and error exposed, by the collision of mind with mind, and knowledge with knowledge. It is the place where the professor becomes eloquent, and is a missionary and a preacher, displaying his science in its most complete and most winning form, pouring it forth with the zeal of enthusiasm, and lighting up his own love of it in the breasts of his hearers."[55]

Newman also argued that the primary business of a university is to foster liberal education. A university does not exist to inculcate virtues or prepare people for priestly vocation, but to train the mind. The other work for which Newman was well known is his *Grammar of Assent* (1870) in which he specifically addresses some nineteenth- and twentieth-century problems and defends Christianity against rationalism and skepticism. He was also concerned with method, a theme he began in *The Idea of a University*. Newman probed the nature of the human mind and raised some epistemological questions concerning what it means to know.

One of Newman's admirers was the Jesuit theologian Bernard Lonergan, one of the foremost twentieth-century theologians that have contributed to this rich Catholic tradition. His ideas and contributions will be explored more fully in later chapters, but a brief introduction to his thought is offered here. Lonergan was born on December 17, 1904, in Buckingham, Quebec, Canada. This was during the pontificate of Pius X, a time when liberalism and modernism seemed to many as if they were about to destroy the foundation of the Catholic Church. In general terms, the origins of modernism go back to the French Revolution (1789–1799) and the eighteenth-century humanists whose ideas led to it. The Church labeled "modernists" those whose infatuation with modern ideas or modern science carried over to their thinking about God and the Church's teachings about human life and afterlife. Modernists essentially advocated a radical transformation of the Church's understanding of the human person and of God.

The Church saw modernism as a threat to the Christian faith because of the way some modernists were applying scientific findings

---

55. John Henry Newman, *University Sketches*, ed. Michael Tierney (New York: Alba House, 1956), 15–16.

Bernard Lonergan

to revelation (Scripture) by using the historical method. These learned and progressive men were "characterized by a radical intellectual pride in the face of divine revelation," convinced that "the explanation of the religious form of life could be found in the human person."[56] Seminary training at the time seemed ill-equipped to handle the modernists' questions about human life, revelation, and the Church. The Church condemned modernism in the decree *Lamentabili Sane* [*The Syllabus of Errors Condemning the Errors of the Modernists*] (1907) and the encyclical *Pascendi Dominici Gregis* [*Encyclical of Pius X on the Doctrines of the Modernists*] (1907). Pius X also founded the Pontifical Biblical Institute in 1909 as a response to modernism

---

56. William Mathews, *Lonergan's Quest: A Study of Desire in the Authoring of Insight* (Toronto: University of Toronto, 2005), 23–24.

and entrusted its management to the Jesuits with the mandate to prepare a new kind of Catholic scholarship that could withstand the test of the time. "The response to modernism and the new promulgation of the Code of Canon law in 1917, which enshrined Thomism as the official theology and philosophy of the Catholic Church, were important events in defining the Catholic mentality and identity for much of the new century."[57]

It was in this climate that Lonergan joined the Society of Jesus (Jesuits) in 1922 in Guelph, Ontario. He had first encountered the Jesuits in 1918 as a student at Loyola College, Montreal, a Jesuit-run boarding school. His Jesuit superiors sent him to Heythrop, England, in 1926 to study philosophy and mathematics. From there he proceeded to Rome to study theology from 1933–1937. After his ordination to the priesthood he spent a few years studying theology at the Gregorianum before returning to Canada. Lonergan's two major works, *Insight: A Study of Human Understanding* and *Method in Theology*, continue to command great attention today. They stemmed in part from some disillusionment he felt while studying to become a Jesuit. At Heythrop, Lonergan witnessed firsthand the declining state of Catholic education. He saw the inferiority of Catholic schools when compared with secular schools such as the University of London, where he was doing overlapping studies. These "frustrations" led him to reflect seriously on what was wrong with Catholic education and how he might help to bring about a meaningful change.

Lonergan learned from Newman the maxim, "the human mind is the human mind"—that is, the human mind is vast and needing ongoing exploration; we cannot stop asking questions about how to improve ourselves as a community of persons. This slogan would direct Lonergan's life. He was committed to helping address the Catholic problem as he saw it. One of his early contributions to CIT was to fuse the ideas of Newman and Thomas Aquinas harmoniously. When he embraced Newman, although Newman was revered personally in the English Catholic community, his work was considered suspect by some neo-Thomists. "It was suspected, unjustly, of being the parent of Modernism, the heresy of Loisy and Tyrell condemned by Pius X. It was suspected, more justly, of being non-Thomist at a

---

57. Ibid., 24.

time when neo-Thomism was riding high. In the English College at Rome, it was said, the argument *secundum sanctum Thomam* [based on St. Thomas] carried greater weight than the argument *secundum veritatem* [based on truth]."[58] But it was Lonergan's genius to show that the ideas of Newman were not opposed to those of Aquinas. "Aquinas was a man of theory, system in particular, while Newman was a man of interiority, investigation in particular. It was Lonergan's later achievement to combine their horizons into a higher viewpoint."[59]

Using his synthesis of Aquinas and Newman, Lonergan understood the modernist crisis to be, in the final analysis, a human crisis. He felt it was the cumulative product of centuries of ambiguous change. To undo it would require what he called a differentiation of consciousness and an acquisition of new realms of meaning, something the university would have to play a key role to achieve. He saw the university as a reproductive organ of cultural community whose constitutive endowment lies not in its buildings or equipment, civil status or revenues, but in the intellectual life of its professors. The central function of the university is the communication of intellectual development. Both Catholic and secular universities, he argued, exercise the same function, though they do it under different conditions. The secular university, like the Catholic university, is caught in the ambiguities of civil and cultural development-and-decline and may lag in consenting to aberrations. But the Catholic university has ammunition that the secular university does not have: the supernatural virtues of faith and love that come through the study of theology.

Although the Catholic university may not be involved in the same kind of ambiguity as the secular university, still it is involved in ambiguity of its own: integrating revealed and acquired knowledge. The integration of sciences that deal with concrete human questions is to be sought not in philosophy but in theology. How is this integration to be accomplished? Lonergan suggests three practical ways. First, integration presupposes purification,

> "for human change is ambiguously good; it is development-and-decline; the aberrations of man's practical and speculative

58. S. A. M. Adshead, *Philosophy of Religion in Nineteenth-Century England and Beyond* (London: Macmillan, 2000), 210.

59. Ibid.

intelligence neither invalidate nor admit integration with his real achievements."[60]

Second, the purifier (the person trying to effect change) must be pure in the sense of undergoing intellectual, religious, and moral conversion. For "the true intellectual has to be humble, serene, detached, without personal or corporate or national complacence, without appeals to contemporary, let alone archaist, bias or passion or fads."[61]

Third, the integration must be carried out, not in abstract philosophical terms, but in dialogue with the empirical sciences in a way that addresses the concrete existential realities of the human person.

CONCLUSION

The contemporary idea of a Catholic university derives largely from the reform efforts of John Henry Newman, a key contributor to CIT. When the Irish bishops approached Newman about becoming the rector of the Catholic University of Ireland and charged him with the task of reforming their university, they wanted Newman to use the University of Louvain as a model or guide. Louvain at the time was one of the few Catholic colleges and universities remaining in continental Europe. The University of Louvain had a structure amenable to the kind of research and scholarship the Irish bishops desired. It had professional schools, like a School of Medicine, a School of Law, a School of Engineering, and a School of Theology.[62] The choice of Louvain as a model was also informed by another factor: Louvain had a history and structure the Irish bishops thought was adequate for addressing the problem of modernity.[63] In Louvain the scholarship of religion and science were separated, a separation

60. Bernard Lonergan, "The Role of a Catholic University in the Modern World," in *Collected Works of Bernard Lonergan: Collection*, ed., Frederick E. Crowe and Robert M. Doran (Toronto: University of Toronto Press, 2005), 108–113, at 113.

61. Ibid.

62. David Fleischacker, "The Place of Modern Scientific Research in the University According to John Henry Newman," *Logos: A Journal of Catholic Thought and Culture* 15 (2002): 101–117, at 103.

63. Ibid., 113.

the Irish bishops thought was a good thing. Such a separation, in their thinking, would appease the liberals who did not think theology had a place in a university curriculum. In hindsight we can say the bishops were thinking locally, to meet the needs of their time. But Newman had a global perspective. He was thinking far beyond the needs of the time. He would use the model of the University of Louvain, as the bishops demanded, but would also go beyond it. He would conceive a Catholic university in which the scholarship of science and religion would be integrated. A Catholic university, for Newman, exists as a counter to fragmentation of knowledge and "narrow-mindedness"; it promotes the integrative unity of truth and awakens the mind to all ranges of truth.[64] The Catholic university, in essence, is the intellectual light of the world.[65]

The Catholic university is a mirror of CIT. It is also the center of activity of CIT. Just like the Catholic university that is ever evolving to meet the needs of contemporary society, the boundaries of CIT cannot be limited. It is ever evolving as the needs of contemporary society change. In the final analysis, there is no single acceptable definition of CIT because the boundaries of CIT are too wide to be limited. CIT has its basis in faith in God's self-communication with creatures. People of faith do not see creation as a finished project or the world as a closed system. Rather they see the creation as ever evolving and ongoing as God is always communicating God's self anew to creatures. Similarly, CIT is not a closed system or a finished project. It is not just a deposit of the past. Rather it is an ever-evolving ever-unfolding treasure with a long history. It is always open to development and refinement.

Ordinarily, a school of thought has an original founder or founders whose set of ideas predominate to give the school a definite shape or scope. Or in the case of a movement there is an original founder whose belief system or charismatic personality becomes a rallying point for that belief system that his or her cult of personality has helped to shape. For example, Aristotelianism is derived from Aristotle, Platonism from Plato, and Buddhism derives largely from the set of ideas of Siddhartha Gautama, also known as the Buddha. The same cannot be said of CIT. Apart from Jesus Christ, whose life,

---

64. Ibid., 109.

65. Ibid., 105.

death, and Resurrection give meaning to CIT, there is no single individual whose set of ideas generated CIT. We can only point to eminent persons whose ideas and cults of personalities became catalysts for their disciples and devotees who produced works that became classics in this tradition. For example, Thomas Aquinas's ideas and cult of personality produced disciples in the sixteenth century who developed a philosophy that would become the official Catholic philosophy, Thomism, a work that to this day remains classic in CIT. Some twentieth-century refinements of Thomism that still contribute to CIT include neo-Thomism or Transcendental Thomism. Some neo-Thomists who have contributed to the tradition are the Dominicans Yves Congar, Marie Dominique Chenu, and Edward Schillebeeckx. The Jesuits Karl Rahner and Bernard Lonergan would be two examples of transcendental Thomists who have contributed to the tradition.

It is clear, then, that no one owns CIT. CIT is not easy to locate because it is not something neatly packed in one place. It is not embodied by one person nor is it found in one mind. There is no exhaustive list of its members. CIT is about a "community of being" or community of persons of which each contributor is a legitimate partner in his or her own right. In this community of being, anyone who pursues truth and value in an unrestricted and disinterested manner is a legitimate partner who contributes to the tradition.[66] This community of being is not confined to Roman Catholics. There are also non-Catholics and persons of no faith tradition who contribute to the tradition. For CIT, as it were, consists "in the totality of all those instances in which a higher viewpoint has been sought and achieved, either by those who identify themselves with the Sacred Tradition or by those who don't, but whose higher viewpoint has been appropriated by the Church."[67]

Finally, CIT is like a palimpsest. In the days when books were carefully handwritten on vellum, a valuable and expensive material, scribes recycled old manuscripts that were no longer needed by carefully erasing the writings in them to make the vellum usable for fresh texts. These texts, called palimpsests, have in them faint traces of the original stratum of writing that can be discovered either by a

66. Haughey, *Where Is Knowing Going?* 74.

67. Ibid., 75.

discerning scholarly eye or through the techniques of modern technology. CIT is like a palimpsest in the sense that it not only has traces of earlier strata of writings of earlier contributors but it is also a vellum that can be reworked, refined, and modified in accordance with the "signs of the time." Scribes who copied manuscripts did this work mostly in monasteries, which were at the time centers of learning. The center of activity of this palimpsest is no longer the monastery but the Catholic university.

For Further Reading

Baker, Kenneth, SJ. "Pope John Paul II and the Catholic University." In *The Mind and the Heart of the Church: Papers Presented at a Conference Sponsored by the Wethersfield Institute New York City, September 20, 1991*, edited by Ralph McInerny, 15–26. San Francisco: Ignatius Press, 1992.

Crowe, Frederick. *Lonergan.* London: Geoffrey Chapman, 1992.

Livingston, James C. *Modern Christian Thought: The Enlightenment and the Nineteenth Century.* 2nd ed. Upper Saddle River, NJ: Prentice Hall, 1997.

Lonergan, Bernard. "The Role of a Catholic University in the Modern World." In *Collected Works of Bernard Lonergan*, edited by Frederick E. Crowe and Robert M. Doran, 108–13. Toronto: University of Toronto Press, 2005.

Madsen, George M. "The Soul of the American University." *First Things* 9 (January 1991): 34–47.

Novak, David. "The Catholic University and the Promise Inherent in Its Identity." In *Catholic Universities in Church and Society: A Dialogue on Ex Corde Ecclesiae*, edited by John P. Langan, SJ, 95–100. Washington, DC: Georgetown University Press, 1993.

Schuster, George. "Reflections on Newman's *Idea*." In *The Catholic University: A Modern Appraisal*, edited by Neil McCluskey, SJ, 104–15. Notre Dame, IN: University of Notre Dame Press, 1970.

Teevan, Donna. "Tradition and Innovation at Catholic Universities: Ideas from Bernard Lonergan." *Catholic Education* 7 (2004): 308–19.

CHAPTER 3

Changes in the
Catholic Population

A discussion of the Catholic intellectual tradition in the United States must attend primarily to the state of Catholic institutions of higher education. But before examining the challenges facing Catholic colleges and universities, it is important to recognize that many of those challenges are symptomatic of broad changes within the Catholic population as a whole. This chapter takes a step back from the discussion of CIT per se in order to examine changes in the constituency of the Church that have had important implications for Catholic universities. Changes within the universities are best understood within this broader context.

DECLINE IN RELIGIOSITY

European culture has seen a general and significant decline in religious practices and belief systems since World War II.[1] Granted that there is sufficient data and anecdotal evidence to demonstrate differences in contemporary trends in American and European religiosities, the decline in religious vitality that is spreading throughout Europe is gradually becoming a feature of American life.

A Princeton Religious Research Center study (1980) provides evidence for both differences in religious vitality between the United

---

1. See Theodore Caplow, "Contrasting Trends in European and American Religion," *Sociological Analysis* 46 (1985): 101–8, at 102.

States and the other industrialized countries of the world, as well as for a general decline in religious attitudes and practices among them all. In this comparative study, young adults ages 18–24 were randomly chosen from the United States, Australia, United Kingdom, Switzerland, Germany (Western Germany at the time), France, and Japan and asked the question, "How do you spend your weekends?" Twenty-five percent of the United States respondents claimed they spend their weekends doing religious activities, compared with only about 5–8 percent of their European counterparts.

The survey suggests that although organized religion in the United States exhibits more vitality than organized religion in Europe, it is still significantly lower than in Latin America, Africa, and Asia (LaFricAsia). About 41 percent of young adults in the United States think religion is important in their life, compared to 11 percent of young adults in European countries.[2] How does one account for the difference? Some have attributed it largely to disparities in the church-state relationship in the United States and in Europe. In many of the European countries, unlike in the United States, organized religion is an aspect of the state, even in cases where the religion is not fully established. But in the United States, "the churches, for all their formal patriotism, are not only independent of the state but quietly antithetical to it. The state is universal, the denomination is particular; the state is founded on compulsion, the denomination is founded on voluntarism; the state gradually curtails other forms of local autonomy; but autonomy, in most American denominations, extends down to individual churches."[3] As the relationship between the individual and the state becomes more uncertain and even antagonistic in the United States, "the refuge offered by the churches against the insatiable demands of the state seems to become more attractive."[4]

---

2. Ibid. See also Princeton Religion Research Center, *Religion in America* (Princeton, New Jersey: Princeton, 1981). This research, although dated, is still a reference point for surveys in religious attitudes and landscapes of some of the world's industrialized societies.

3. Theodore Caplow, Howard M. Bahr, Bruce A. Chadwick, et al., *All Faithful People: Change and Continuity in Middletown's Religion* (Minneapolis: University of Minnesota Press, 1983), 301.

4. Ibid.

Unlike in the United States, church and state in Europe are intertwined in such a way that all religious affiliations have political connotations.[5] This makes political opinions and religious beliefs in Europe closely related and mutually determinative.[6] The state exercises, with varying degrees of commitment, its power over the religious beliefs of its citizens, although this power is almost always taken for granted. But in the United States the state does not hold any power over the religious beliefs of its citizens. So it is fair to say that in spite of the seeming resemblances of the United States to its European counterparts, there still exist profound differences in orientation and attitude of its citizens. "No matter how powerful the American state has become, its multifarious activities are still justified as contributing to the happiness of private persons rather than to any collective purpose," because the state's power over the beliefs of its citizens are curtailed.[7] Nevertheless, the United States also is trending toward secularization. Compared to the global South (Africa, Asia, and Latin America) where the religious attitude is on the upswing, the religious attitude in Europe and America is on the decline. What makes the United States' scorecard a little better than that of Europe, at least as far as Catholicism is concerned, one can attribute to the Latino/Hispanic factor. This cultural impact on United States Catholicism merits attention.

A SPECIAL CASE: LATINO AMERICANS

In the last twenty-five years the United States has seen an influx of immigrants, many of whom are Latinos (sometimes lumped under the category "Hispanics"), particularly Mexicans. The Latino population in general (immigrants from other Spanish speaking countries of Latin America) has increased rapidly in the same time frame through immigration and high fertility rates. According to the Pew Forum on Religion and the Public Life's 2006 study, Latinos are transforming the United States' religious landscape,

---

5. Caplow, "Contrasting Trends," 101.

6. Ibid., 104.

7. Ibid., 107.

particularly that of the Catholic Church, not just by their growing numbers but also by their distinctive form of Christianity: they
attend Church services regularly, revel in (often charismatic) ceremonies, love to worship in the Spanish language, and are given to incul-
turated Christianity—that is, they relate the Christian faith to their
culture. The Pew study found that nearly a third of all United States
Catholics are Latinos. More than two-thirds (68 percent) of Latinos
are Roman Catholics, about 15 percent are Evangelicals, while the
rest are scattered among the other Protestant denominations. The
Pew study projects that the Latino share of Catholics will continue
to climb for decades. The study finds that the increasing growth
of Latinos in the United States is resulting in "Latino-oriented
churches across the country," and that regardless of their religious
expressions—whether they are Catholics, "born again Christians," or
Evangelicals—"religious expressions associated with the Pentecostal
and charismatic movements are a key attribute of worship for Hispanics in all the major religious traditions—far more so than among
non-[Hispanics]."[8] This distinctive characteristic of Latino Catholicism, together with the demographic reality, according to the study,
ensures that Latinos will bring about some significant changes in the
nation's religious institutions.

This Latino boost to the religiosity of the United States is not
limited to the Catholic Church, however. The Pew study found that
a majority of the Latinos "who are joining evangelical churches are
Catholic converts. The desire for a more direct, personal experience
of God emerges as by far the most potent motive for these conversions."[9] About one in every ten Evangelical Latinos is an ex-Catholic.
The Pew study projects that if the pattern of conversion of the last
25 years holds steady, "the share of Latinos who are Catholic would
decline from 68 percent in 2006 to 61 percent in 2030."[10] Although
Catholicism, if the projection holds, will continue to be the dominant
faith among Latinos because of Latino population growth through
immigration and high fertility, conversions to other denominations

---

8. See Pew Hispanic Center, "Changing Faiths: Latinos and the Transformation
of American Religion," 1, *http://pewforum.org/newassets/surveys/hispanic/hispanics-
religion-07-final-mar08.pdf.*

9. Ibid.

10. Ibid., 13.

will continue to erode the number of Latino Catholics. Moreover, even though Latinos, as a group, are highly religious, nearly one in ten (8 percent) of them do not identify with any religion.[11]

THE INCREASINGLY SECULAR WEST

The pattern of steady decline of Christianity in the West has led to a characterization of these industrial societies as post-Christian; thanks to irreversible secularization, we have outlived the reigning convictions of a once Christian society.[12]

Robert and Helen Lynd conducted a study of social change in Muncie, Indiana (to which they gave the pseudonym "Middletown," a name borrowed from a village not far from Muncie), between 1890 and 1924.[13] The Lynds interviewed residents of Muncie, examined newspaper articles, and closely monitored some other measurable trends that could show the religiosity of the inhabitants of Muncie over the specified period of study. They thought that by studying Muncie they could give an accurate portrait of an average American city of the 1920s. They found that religious affiliation was declining—a groundbreaking and revolutionary conclusion at the time.[14] The Lynds returned to Muncie ten years later, after the Great Depression "to see what changes had been wrought by the intervening decade of prosperity and depression."[15] The two Middletown studies by the Lynds found contradictory trends in religious behavior in Muncie: while religious zeal was diminishing, people of different faiths were intolerant and hostile toward each other. They also found indications that religious zeal or enthusiasm was declining in every average American city.

---

11. Ibid.

12. Lamin Sanneh, *Whose Religion Is Christianity? The Gospel Beyond the West* (Grand Rapids, MI: Eerdmans, 2003), 1.

13. Their study focused on social change in such areas as work, family life, education, recreational activities, community activities, and religion. See Caplow et al., eds., *All Faithful People*, vii.

14. See Robert S. Lynd and Helen Merell Lynd, *Middletown: A Study of Modern American Culture* (Harcourt Brace, 1959).

15. Caplow et al., eds., *All Faithful People*, vii. See Robert S. Lynd and Helen Merell Lynd *Middletown in Transition: A Study in Cultural Conflicts* (New York: Harcourt Brace Jovanovich, 1982).

Forty years after the Middletown I and II studies (1976–1978), Theodore Caplow, Howard Bahr, Bruce Chadwick, and several of their colleagues returned to Muncie for another follow-up study, Middletown III. Using the same method as the Lynds and asking almost identical questions, they found, with few exceptions, similar contradictory trends in religious attitudes (intolerance among people of faith toward other faith traditions and diminution of religious fervor) as had the Middletown I and II studies. All three Middletown studies found "that modernization, the principal engine of recent social change, had been slowing down in the United States during the past half-century and that this deceleration has allowed some features of American culture to remain virtually unchanged."[16] Nevertheless, the Middletown III study identified trends toward secularization, as had Middletown I and II.

An important new finding of the Middletown III study was that, while religious intolerance persisted, it was markedly declining.[17] This represented a departure from previous hostile attitudes among different religious groups that the previous Middletown studies found. "Not only do Protestants speak well of each other and benignly of Catholics, they abstain from condemnation of the heathen and favor teaching about Buddhism in the public schools. There is no longer any teaching against the pope at revival meetings. There are no more diatribes against the Jews in Easter sermons."[18]

While the newfound ecumenical spirit of the Middletown III study was a welcome development for the researchers, the trend toward secularization was still very evident. Employing sociological tools, the researchers identified fifteen items that point toward increasing secularization.[19]

---

16. Lynd and Lynd, *Middletown in Transition*, x.

17. Ibid.

18. Ibid., 287.

19. The fifteen items are (1) a decline in the number of churches per capita of population, (2) a decline in the proportion of the population attending church services, (3) a decline in the number of rites of passage held under religious auspices, (4) a decline in religious endogamy, (5) a decline in the proportion of the labor engaged in religious activity, (6) a decline in the proportion of income devoted to the support of religion, (7) a decline in the ratio of religious to nonreligious literature, (8) a decline in the attention given to religion in the mass media, (9) a drift toward less emotional forms of participation in religious services, (10) a dwindling of new sects and of new

A more recent study by the Pew Forum on religion and public life agrees with the Middletown study: the trend toward secularization is gaining ground. The study showed that 16.1 percent of the adult population is not affiliated with any religion. One in four Americans ages 18 to 29 are unaffiliated with any religious group. Forty-four percent of adults have switched religious affiliations from one denomination to another or to no religion at all. Among Catholics the picture of mass defection is grim: one third of those raised Catholic have left the Church, and 10 percent of all Americans are either former Catholics who have found a home in a different religion or now have no religion at all.[20]

CAUSES FOR THE DECLINE IN AFFILIATION WITH THE CHURCH

The statistics on declining membership in the Catholic Church in the United States are troubling. What is responsible for the changing landscape of Catholicism? Some respondents in the Pew survey alluded to a number of factors that are not easily dismissible, including the Church's authoritarian character, its failure to grant equal status to women, its contested teachings on sexuality, and the scandal of pedophile priests. Some, with a conservative bent, assert that these problems are the result of the Church's laxity in upholding its teachings and having inappropriately accommodated the values and attitudes of contemporary American society. All seem to agree that the Church has struggled to find new forms of evangelization and enculturation in the face of an increasing shortage of vocations to the priesthood and religious life and overall demise of Catholic subculture.[21]

---

movements in existing churches, (11) increased attention to secular issues in sermons and liturgy, (12) a declining level of political activity by organized religious groups, (13) diminished interest in the religious credentials of candidates and officeholders, (14) less legislation of religious organizations by government, and (15) the removal of religious symbols from the ceremonies and insignia of the state and of patriotic symbols from the ceremonies and insignia of the church.

20. See "The Missing," *Commonweal* 135 (March 14, 2008): 5.

21. Ibid.

Decline in Vocations

According to the Center for Applied Research in the Apostolate (CARA) at Georgetown University in Washington, DC, in 1965 there were about 36,000 diocesan priests and 22,700 religious priests in the dioceses and eparchies of the United States. The number of diocesan priests declined to about 27,600 diocesan priests and 13,000 religious priests in 2008. In the same period, the number of priestly ordinations also dropped from 994 in 1965 to 480 in 2008. The consequence of this is a proliferation of parishes without a resident priest; the number increased from 549 in 1965 to 3,141 in 2008. "The drastic decline in the numbers of priests and seminarians in the United States since 1965 certainly suggests that there is cause for great concern."[22] Compounding the problem is the fact that while the number of priests in the United States has continued to decline, the Catholic population in the United States is rising because of a large Latino immigrant Catholic population. For example, the Center for Applied Research in the Apostolate estimated the Catholic population in 1965 to be about 45.6 million. In 2008, this number had increased to 64.1 million.

The CARA report is consistent with the latest report in the Vatican's Statistical Yearbook. The Vatican report, released periodically by the Vatican Publishing House, includes information on the main aspects of Catholic Church activity in various countries of the world. The 2008 Statistical Yearbook shows a steady decline in the number of men studying for the priesthood in the United States. While the number of seminarians rose worldwide from 63,882 in 1978 to 113,044 in 2004, the number of United States seminarians (diocesan and religious) fell from 9,021 to 4,555 in the same period—a decline of about 50 percent.[23] According to Archbishop Daniel E. Pilarczyk, former archbishop of Cincinnati, there are at least two reasons for this decline. "One is the self-serving culture in which we live that does not seem to esteem a life of dedication and service like that of the priest. Another is the turmoil in the Church caused by elements

---

22. *http://www.dioceseofgrandrapids.org/our_diocese/Documents/FAITH%20GR/2010/0102/2010%20Jan-Feb%20Year%20for%20Priests.pdf.*

23. Doug Culp, "What's Happening with Priestly Vocations?" *http://www.ignatius.com/Images/Products/USVocations.pdf.*

both inside and outside it, not excluding differences of opinion about married priests and the ordination of women."[24] The decline in numbers of priests, according to Archbishop Pilarczyk, "seems to be a localized phenomenon in highly developed countries and may say more about those countries than about the priesthood."[25]

The number of vowed religious women in the United States has similarly declined. Vowed religious women were once primarily responsible for staffing Catholic schools in the United States. Women religious orders in the United States grew in the 1950s, but experienced dramatic decline in the 1960s and 70s. Between 1950 and 1955, for example, the number of women religious in the United States rose by more than 23 percent, but dropped by more than 30 percent between 1966 and 1986. The decrease, which has been steady since then, is not without implications for Catholic higher education. A figure released in 2007 by the Leadership Conference of Women Religious (LCWR) reported an even more dramatic drop in the number of women religious in the United States in the last five years. Along this line, the CARA in 2009 reported that the average age of women religious in formation in the United States has risen to forty years (compared to nineteen to twenty-two in the 1950s). CARA also reported that 91 percent of women religious in final vows today are about sixty years or older. The number of new members decreased significantly, and a number of women left religious orders following the reforms of the Second Vatican Council (see "Catholic Schools and Declining Religiosity" below). The defection of women religious and the decrease in the number of new members have resulted in significantly fewer women vowed religious in the United States than in the 1950s.[26] Where in the past religious congregations had a good number of members to staff Catholic schools in the United States, today they can rarely fulfill this mission because they lack the personnel.

24. Daniel E. Pilarczyk, "What Is a Vocation?," *http://www.cincinnativocations.org/searching-for-answers/what-is-a-vocation-by-archbishop-daniel-e-pilarczyk/*.

25. Ibid.

26. Helen Rose Ebaugh, "The Growth and Decline of Catholic Religious Orders of Women Worldwide: The Impact of Women's Opportunity Structures," *Journal for the Scientific Study of Religion* 32 (1993): 68–75, at 69.

Catholic Schools and Declining Religiosity

The focus of much of the current research on Catholic schools has been on the long-term effectiveness and outcome of the religious attitudes of young adults. Studies show that parents who are deeply committed to the Catholic faith are, unsurprisingly, more likely to send their children to Catholic schools. Children who attend Catholic high school for at least three years are less likely to leave the Church. Moreover, the content of religious education provided in Catholic schools is crucial to the formation of active Catholics.[27] Catholic schooling, in other words, enhances one's commitment to the Church later in life and reduces the rate of disaffection and conversion.[28] The evidence also suggests that "Catholic schools may encourage modestly higher levels of church attendance and religious salience among adolescents."[29] Consequently, as enrollment in Catholic schools continues to decline, a higher percentage of Catholic young people leave the Church. Declining numbers of priests, coupled with a decline in religious vocations of all kinds, has important implications for Catholic educational institutions, which are increasingly staffed by laypersons. The change in staffing patterns has an impact on the Catholic identity of these institutions; the effects of this phenomenon on Catholic universities will be explored in subsequent chapters.

The Decline of a Catholic Subculture

David O'Brien and William Portier have shed light on a related problem: the decline of a Catholic subculture in America. They help us understand that the Catholic faith, like any faith expression, has its own political and social dimensions. In the American context, the social and political dimensions of the Catholic faith were strong in the early years of the Catholic Church in this country. For a long time the Catholic Church in the United States was an immigrant Church from Western Europe. This immigrant American Catholicism had an ethnic support

---

27. Paul Perl and Mark M. Gray, "Catholic Schooling and Disaffiliation from Catholicism," *Journal for the Scientific Study of Religion* 46 (2007): 269–80.

28. A. M. Greeley, W. C. McCready, and K. McCourt, *Catholic Schooling in a Declining Church* (Kansas City, KS: Sheed and Ward, 1976).

29. Jeremy E. Uecker, "Alternative Schooling Strategies and the Religious Lives of American Adolescents," *Journal of Scientific Study of Religion* 47 (2008): 563–84, at 580.

system: there were Polish, Irish, German, and Italian Catholic churches, among others. These ethnic churches had their strengths and weaknesses. The ethnic subculture that supported these different expressions of Catholicism "suggests that Catholicism can never be entirely identified with one or another of its cultural, or more accurately for us, subcultural expressions. It is always local and embodied."[30]

Historians who have researched immigrant Catholicism also help us understand the paradox of ethnic particularity vis-à-vis an expanded understanding of human solidarity—that in immigrant Catholicism, "French, German, and Polish parishes were always American congregations and they were also living embodiments of Roman Catholicism, with its universal claims, among them."[31]

According to O'Brien, the middle class Americanized Catholicism that succeeded the immigrant Church increasingly lacked the supportive subculture that is central to the Catholic experience. The "collapse of the American Catholic subculture, the buffer between Catholics and American individualism and pluralism, is the single most important fact of recent U.S. Catholic history."[32] While O'Brien sees potential for renewal in the decline of the American Catholic subculture, others view that decline negatively, one of them being American professor of history, Philip Gleason. "Gleason and I both saw subcultural decline as the crucial question," O'Brien writes. "Gleason tended to regard it negatively, most evident in his treatment of higher education but evident as well in his comments on the U.S. church as a whole. I tended to be more optimistic. I thought new identity could be achieved through a vision of shared responsibility for American society and politics at a moment when the use of American power was of critical importance, while Gleason was skeptical about social ministry and hinted at the need for the reestablishment of clear doctrine and sharp boundaries as better suited to the reinvigoration of institutions and communities."[33]

---

30. David O'Brien, "The Renewal of American Catholicism: A Retrospective," *U.S. Catholic Historian* 23 (2005): 83–94, at 85.

31. Ibid.

32. See David O'Brien's 2005 Marianist award lecture at the University of Dayton; published as *The Missing Piece: The Renewal of Catholic Americanism* (Dayton, OH: University of Dayton, 2005), 16.

33. Ibid., 88; see footnote 15.

O'Brien argues that, since the 1960s, the Church has experienced a long learning process about the realities of personal freedom, religious pluralism, and ecclesial self-government. He cites three reasons for the collapse of the American Catholic subculture.

1. **Americanization and Its Consequences**

   The Americanized Catholicism that succeeded the immigrant church was increasingly without a supportive subculture such that "even if there had been no Second Vatican Council, there would have been enormous pressures for change in the American Church."[34]

2. **The Vatican II Effect**

   Although the Second Vatican Council solved some American immigrant Catholic problems and even affirmed the American principles of religious liberty and religious pluralism, it also opened up new questions about personal faith and moral conscience, as in the birth control controversy of the 1970s (which in large part is still ongoing) and the debate regarding the morality of the Vietnam war that occupied the post-Vatican II American Church.[35]

3. **The Sociopolitical Climate of the 1960s**

   The third and final factor relates to the turmoil of American society of the 1960s. The civil rights movements and the Vietnam War were taking place about the same time as the Second Vatican Council.

In all, according to O'Brien, "something important did change dramatically. The combination of conciliar calls to conscience and American conflicts over race, war, and abortion accelerated the collapse of the American Catholic subculture and with it the death of Catholic Americanism."[36] The dissolution of the subculture is the context for understanding the reception of the Second Vatican Council and the Council's view of Church-world relations in the United

---

34. O'Brien, "The Renewal of American Catholicism," 87.

35. Ibid.

36. Ibid., 88.

States.[37] There are dangers in positing a sharp division between pre-Vatican II American Catholicism and post-Vatican II American Catholicism. Elements of continuity and change are always involved in the activities of a faith community and the American Catholic experience is no exception. Nevertheless, "the simultaneous convergence of changes in the Church with the dramatic conflicts in society did create for many a real sense of discontinuity most evident in questions of Catholic identity and integrity."[38]

CONCLUSION

The United States has changed since the founding of the major Catholic institutions of higher education. In the pre-Vatican II era, most American Catholics identified with one or another of the Catholic immigrant subcultures: they had a strong sense of identity as Catholics, and conveyed this to their children as well, sending them to Catholic schools and instilling in them Catholic values. Vocations to the priesthood and to religious orders were strong, providing a large pool from which the staffs of Catholic schools and Catholic universities could draw for their instructors. These institutions, in turn, played a vital role in reinforcing Catholic identity. With increasing secularization and the breakdown of Catholic subcultures, all this has changed.

The dissolution of American Catholic subcultures presents a new challenge for CIT. In light of this dissolution, what, if anything, does it mean to be truly Catholic in the contemporary world? What role might Catholic institutions of higher learning play in fostering authentic Catholic values? Are these institutions still places where the pursuit of truth is correlated with religious faith? Is it not after all the responsibility of Catholic colleges and universities, in an ecumenically conscious world, to articulate the Catholic tradition together with the values it shares with other religious traditions and cultures, present it to the youth, and represent it in the larger world

---

37. See William Portier, "Here Come the Evangelical Catholics," *Communio* 31 (Spring 2004): 35–66.

38. O'Brien, "The Renewal of American Catholicism," 88.

of academia in an intellectually meaningful way?[39] If so, why does a general air of uncertainty hang over Catholic institutions, rendering their identity ambiguous?[40] To these questions we turn next.

Further Reading

Brann, Eva. *Paradoxes of Education in a Republic.* Chicago: University of Chicago, 1979.

Brown, Peter. *The Rise of Western Christendom: Triumph and Diversity, A.D. 200–2000.* 2nd ed. Malden, MA: Blackwell, 2003.

Dolan, Jay P. *The American Catholic Experience: A History from Colonial Times to the Present.* Notre Dame, IN: Notre Dame University, 1992.

Gaillardetz, Richard. *Teaching with Authority: A Theology of the Magisterium.* Collegeville, MN: Liturgical, 1992.

Haughey, John. *Revisiting the Idea of Vocation.* Washington, DC: Catholic University, 2004.

Pius XII. *Humani Generis: Encyclical of Pope Pius XII Concerning Some False Opinions Threatening to Undermine the Foundation of Catholic Doctrine.* August 12, 1950.

Reuben, Julie. *The Making of the Modern University.* Chicago: University of Chicago, 1996.

Rist, John. *What Is Truth? From the Academy to the Vatican.* Toronto: University of Toronto, 2008.

Smith, Huston. *The Soul of Christianity: Restoring the Great Tradition.* San Francisco: Harper, 2005.

Wilcox, John R., and Irene King, eds., *Enhancing Religious Identity: Best Practices from Catholic Campuses.* Washington, DC: Georgetown University, 2000.

Woods, Thomas E. *How the Catholic Church Built Western Civilization.* Washington, DC: Regnery Publishing, 2005.

---

39. Philip Gleason, "What Made Catholic Identity a Problem?" in *Faith and the Intellectual Life: Marianist Award Lectures,* ed. James L. Heft, SM (Notre Dame, IN: University of Notre Dame Press, 1996), 90.

40. Haughey, *Where Is Knowing Going?* ix.

CHAPTER 4

Contemporary Challenges to Catholic Universities

Earlier we posed the question whether *Catholic* and *intellectual* are contradictory terms. In this chapter, we go a step further and ask whether the phrase *Catholic university* is an oxymoron.

The word *catholic*, as we noted, was used in a nonecclesiastical and nontechnical way before historical forces engendered its usage to designate a particular ecclesial communion of churches in communion with and headed by the Bishop of Rome (i.e., the pope). The Catholic Church, therefore, has a history that is rich and diversified. As a full-fledged historical entity, it has its own liturgy, its own tradition, its way of understanding the sacred text, its martyrs, saints, confessors, mystics, and doctors. The historical entity we call the Catholic Church has, in other words, its own incarnate meaning, which is at once artistic, symbolic, and linguistic.[1]

As a historical entity, the Catholic Church has its own intellectual heritage, some of which it may not be proud of, like the persecution of dissenters. Before the Reformation and the birth of Protestantism, Luther, together with some of his Catholic opponents, condemned Nicholaus Copernicus (1473–1543). The Catholic Church also attacked Giordarno Bruno (1548–1600) and Galileo Galilei (1564–1642) for their scientific investigations; the former was burned at the stake, while the latter died under house arrest.

---

1. See Bernard Lonergan, *Method in Theology* (Toronto: University of Toronto Press, 1996), 73.

Given such anti-intellectual moments of the Catholic Church, might the idea of a Catholic university or even a Christian university be a contradiction in terms, as George Bernard Shaw (1856–1950) asserted?[2] We have mentioned, in previous chapters, the rise of the modern university, with its ideal of unlimited academic freedom, and the resulting widespread skepticism that it is possible for an institution to be committed to a set of religious tenets and, at the same time, remain open to the free exchange of ideas and the findings of science. We must grant that today "the idea of a Catholic university seems so anomalous to contemporary consciousness, even some of its greatest supporters feel embarrassed when articulating the idea of a Catholic character to a skeptical audience."[3] Today there is no consensus on the notion of a Catholic university; it remains a matter of intellectual debate. In some instances the Catholic identity of Catholic universities is taken for granted and barely understood.[4] How can one account for the loss of Christian identity in these educational institutions that claim to follow the overtly religious educational ideals of the sixteenth and seventeenth centuries? To what extent has a "culture of disbelief" been a contributing factor in the erosion of Christian ideals in Catholic colleges and universities? In other words, how true is it that educated persons cannot be religious, or at least cannot take their religion very seriously?[5]

CULTURE OF DISBELIEF

In his highly acclaimed work, *The Culture of Disbelief: How American Law and Politics Trivialize Religious Devotion*, Stephen Carter writes eloquently about the assault on religion in American political life and describes how secularized forms of moral reasoning dominate American public life. "In the public sphere, religion is too often trivialized, treated as an unimportant facet of human personality, one

---

2. Mark W. Roche, *The Intellectual Appeal of Catholicism and the Idea of a Catholic University*, foreword by Theodore M. Hesburgh, CSC (Notre Dame, IN: University of Notre Dame Press, 2003), 1.

3. Ibid., 2.

4. Ibid., viii.

5. Ibid., 1.

easily discarded, and one with which public-spirited citizens would not bother."[6] Carter surmises that we have been led astray by the effort to banish religion for politics' sake. "In our sensible zeal to keep religion from dominating our politics," he writes, "we have created a political and legal culture that presses the religiously faithful to be other than themselves, to act publicly, and sometimes privately as well, as though their faith does not matter to them."[7] Carter makes the point that we pose a threat to our religious freedom and democracy when we try to keep religious voices out of the public square. "We do no credit to the ideal of religious freedom when we talk as though religious belief is something of which public-spirited adults should be ashamed."[8]

The culture of disbelief, which Carter argues is pervasive in American public life, is also a feature of Catholic higher education. A number of factors are conjointly responsible for the growth of a culture of disbelief within Catholic universities:

1. **Secularization Movement of the 1970s**

   According to Monika Hellwig, in the 1970s and 1980s United States Catholic colleges and universities began to move toward secularization at the expense of their Catholic identities. But the erosion of identity was not made out of conscious decision to abandon their particular religious identity, "but rather a combination of many new demands and the subtle influence of the secular expectations of the wider academy."[9]

2. **The Church's Anti-Intellectual Moments**

   Some critics blame the erosion of Catholic identity on the Church's darker, anti-intellectual moments, suggesting that the Church is its own worst enemy. According to this view, the Catholic Church "has occasionally undermined the concept of

---

6. See Stephen L. Carter, *The Culture of Disbelief: How American Law and Politics Trivialize Religious Devotion* (New York: Anchor Books, 1994), xv.

7. Ibid., 1.

8. Ibid., 10.

9. Monika Hellwig, "The Catholic Intellectual Tradition in the Catholic University," in *Examining the Catholic Intellectual Tradition*, ed. Anthony J. Cernera and Oliver J. Morgan (Fairfield, CT: Sacred Heart University Press, 2000), 2–3.

individual responsibility, acted irrationally in the face of advances of science, failed to rise to the challenges of the modern world, and fallen short of its own moral ideals."[10] Such critics cite the *Ex Corde Ecclesiae (From the Heart of the Church*, 1990), John Paul II's Apostolic Constitution that requires professors of theology to obtain a "mandate" from the ordinary of the place their Catholic college or university is located, as a recent example of the Catholic hierarchy's attempt to silence dissent and muzzle academic freedom. In a letter to alumni and students of Georgetown University on the delicate subject of academic freedom in a university that professes allegiance to the Catholic Church, the then rector of the college, Leo O'Donovan, SJ, stressed the need for a legitimate institutional autonomy in order to fulfill the mission of the college, which is to transmit ideas.[11] "The Catholic university does not flourish or serve the Church well, nor does it prepare its students for the conflicts and dilemmas of contemporary American life, by avoiding difficult discussions or by silencing thought."[12]

3. **Influence of Protestant Culture**

In the United States, the loss of the Catholic ideals of Catholic universities can also be attributed to the influence of a dominant Protestant culture that stresses individual autonomy and freedom of inquiry. The ideal of academic freedom and the recognition of the autonomy of the individual that was so much a part of the Protestant break from Catholicism are now the "heart and soul" of American Catholic universities.[13] American Catholic universities not only compete with secular and Protestant universities but also assimilate and integrate their best ideas and strategies. "An institution that measures itself against others is

---

10. Roche, *Intellectual Appeal*, 2.

11. Louis Dupre, "On the Task and Vocation of the Catholic College," in *Examining the Catholic Intellectual Tradition*, ed. Cernera and Morgan, 22–23.

12. Ibid., 23. Official Catholic interpretation of those in favor of *Ex Corde Ecclesiae* differs significantly from that of critics. According to Cardinal Pio Laghi's interpretation, for example, the document consists, first and foremost, in an institutional link with the Church, which means "neither teachers nor administrators should publicly embrace principles clearly in conflict with the doctrinal principles taught by the Church." See Dupre, "Task and Vocation," 22.

13. Roche, *Intellectual Appeal*, 3.

naturally encouraged to absorb and integrate the best ideas and strategies of the competition. A friendly rivalry forces an institution to bring to the fore the very best it has to offer, knowing that if it is deficient, others will supersede it."[14] Proponents of this view note that a significant difference in Catholic culture is observable in countries that are predominantly Catholic (e.g., Mediterranean countries) as compared with countries where Catholicism competes with other faith traditions (e.g., Germany and the United States). Active "engagement with others encourages a Catholic culture, or a Catholic university, to reach its greatest potential and to learn from other models."[15]

Be that as it may, in light of the contentious debates (discussed in earlier chapters) regarding the goal of education in general, it is apropos to raise the question: To what extent do the educational conditions imposed by contemporary North American society render it difficult for Catholic institutions of higher learning to maintain a Catholic identity in anything more than name? What might be the conditions for preserving this identity?[16] Is there, as Roche asked, a precise and clear view of a Catholic university that will appeal to students and faculty, parents and alumni, administrators and trustees, and donors and friends?[17] There is a longing, on the part of some in the university who profess faith in God, for meaning and purpose and a desire for integration and wholeness in their life—a desire and longing that leads to a consideration of the relationship between one's faith and one's teaching and scholarship.[18] This desire

---

14. Ibid., 4. Roche takes into account cautions by James Burtchaell, CSC, that the pull of mainstream culture is so powerful that a minority institution that integrates many of its features risks relinquishing its own distinguishing traits; that by integrating these secular and Protestant models Catholic universities risk the danger of becoming secular. See James Tunstead Burtchaell, CSC, *The Dying of the Light: The Disengagement of Colleges and Universities from their Christian Churches* (Grand Rapids, MI: Eerdmans, 1998).

15. Ibid.

16. Dupre, "Task and Vocation," 22.

17. Roche, *Intellectual Appeal*, viii.

18. Paula Powell Sapienza, "Catholic Intellectual Life: An Opportunity for the Church to Continue to Learn," in *As Leaven in the World: Catholic Perspectives on Faith, Vocation, and the Intellectual Life*, ed. Thomas M. Landy (Franklin, WI: Sheed and Ward, 2001), 17.

to connect faith and scholarship has made Catholic colleges, perhaps more than others, preserve "at least the ideal of a Christian liberal education, as formulated in the sixteenth and seventeenth centuries."[19] The task of educating the mind in a Catholic university is a serious business and often spoken of as a vocation and not a career.

A Catholic university espouses, among other things, the ideal of a Christian liberal education on which the first universities in Europe were founded. Being Catholic and being intellectual make demands that are vital,[20] not only for learning but also for day-to-day life in society. It is common to find at American Catholic universities a mix of Catholic and non-Catholic faculty. Two reasons quickly come to mind. First is the fact that Catholic universities make concerted efforts to recruit distinguished faculty members, Catholic or otherwise, who feel at home at a religious-sponsored college or university. A second reason is the related fact that as Protestant universities divest themselves of their Christian heritage, Catholic universities become one of the few places where religious and secular scholarship can truly flourish side by side.[21] This may explain why Catholic universities are becoming increasingly attractive to religious intellectuals of all kinds. The active presence of religious non-Christians helps Catholic universities realize, in the spirit of *Nostra Aetate* (the Vatican II decree on non-Christians that seeks the promotion of ecumenism), a richer sense of the community of humanity and the mystery of God.[22] Spirituality in general and Catholicism in particular enrich the liberal arts—they both seek to educate the whole person. "At a Catholic university prayer and liturgy are a central part of the student's experience. Spiritual questions arise in all disciplines. Perhaps only in a religious setting, where reflection on God, or metaphysically stated, the absolute, is prevalent do we address life's most fundamental questions, which are increasingly set aside at nonreligious institutions of higher learning."[23] Students at a Catholic

---

19. Dupre, "Task and Vocation," 22.

20. Dennis Doyle, "The Trinity and Catholic Intellectual Life," in *As Leaven in the World*, ed. Landy, 141.

21. Roche, *Intellectual Appeal*, 5.

22. Ibid.

23. Ibid., 6.

university engage in the study of theology "not as the disinterested science of religious phenomena but as faith seeking understanding. They study the history of the classics in order to learn not simply *about* the past but also *from* the past. Students employ the quantitative tools of the social sciences not simply as a formal exercise with mathematical models but in order to develop sophisticated responses to pressing and complex social issues."[24]

Monika Hellwig identifies six helpful marks or characteristics of a Catholic university: a continuity of faith and reason, a sacramental principle, tradition playing a guiding role, pursuit of integration of knowledge, affirmation of a communal dimension of life, and an antielitist bent.[25] We live in a world that is becoming disenchanted and ever more cynical; a Catholic university overcomes such cynicism by enriching the liberal arts with spirituality in ways that secular universities cannot. There is also the fact that theology is fully integrated, not separated from the curriculum or scholarship. Students in Catholic universities, through the study of theology, see faith, not as an add-on to learning, but as that which defines scholarship.[26] All these marks or characteristics that define Catholicism are not exclusively Catholic. Some of them can be found in non-Catholic and even secular colleges and universities. But while none of them is exclusive or unique to Catholicism, "they come together in the Catholic Tradition in a way that is distinctive, that characterizes Catholicism and its intellectual tradition."[27]

TOWARD AN IDENTITY CRISIS?
CHALLENGES FACING CATHOLIC UNIVERSITIES

The issue of identity of Catholic colleges and universities can be approached in three foci that are in themselves complementary: the

24. Ibid., 6–7.

25. See Hellwig, "The Catholic Intellectual Tradition in the Catholic University," 1–18.

26. Roche, *Intellectual Appeal*, 6–7.

27. William J. Cahoy, "The Catholic Intellectual Tradition: What Is It? Why Should I Care?" *http://www1.csbsju.edu/catholicidentity/values/billcahoy.htm*.

dogmatic teachings of the Church, the Church's traditions and emphases, and the institutional qualities of the Church.[28] The first two approaches pertain to the magisterial Church's self-understanding of its mission and identity: to proclaim the Gospel of Jesus Christ "whether the time is favorable or unfavorable; convince, rebuke, and encourage with the utmost patience in teaching" (2 Tim. 4:2). Paul's injunction that a time will come when people "will not put up with sound doctrine; but having itching ears, they will accumulate for themselves teachers to suit their own desires, and will turn away from listening to the truth and wander away to myths" (2 Tim. 4:3–4) is an admonition the Church takes to heart to avoid any threat both to the faith and its mission and identity. Because what the Church is has something to do with education,[29] it is worthwhile to pay attention to the Catholic hierarchical analysis of contemporary problems and challenges to Catholic education. This brings us to our third approach, i.e., the institutional qualities of the Church, which pertains to organs, structures, or Church-sponsored agencies, like the health and welfare sectors and educational institutes that help the Church fulfill its mission.

Parents who send their children to Catholic schools and the faculty, staff, and students of these schools assume, even if they do not articulate it, that the "Catholic Tradition offers something worth preserving, thinking about, and contributing to."[30] There is also a belief that Catholic colleges and universities emphasize personal values and community and that these values equip students with tools they need to effectively balance the often competing claims of faith and culture. In spite of the theoretical and practical helpfulness of Catholic schools, there are some negative elements in modern culture that seem to threaten Catholic identity, even to its foundations. These include: materialism, consumerism, individualism, and fragmentation of knowledge.[31] These pernicious "isms," together with some

---

28. James Heft, SM, "Catholic Identity and the Future of Catholic Schools," in *Catholic Schools for the Tweny-First Century: The Catholic Identity of Catholic Schools*, ed. National Catholic Educational Association (NCEA) (Washington, DC: NCEA, 1991), 5–20.

29. See Cahoy, "The Catholic Intellectual Tradition."

30. Ibid.

31. Heft, "Catholic Identity," 19.

"fundamental changes in the self-understanding of the Roman Catholic Church"[32] (like the many conflicting receptions of Vatican II and the outcomes of this reception, particularly in the United States and Europe) have further exacerbated the identity crisis of Catholic colleges and universities. In the United States, for example, the years following Vatican II, particularly 1965 to 1990, were tumultuous, and witnessed startling changes that even the schools were not prepared for.[33] The secularization that had threatened Protestant colleges in the century or two before has become a Catholic problem. When Protestant universities became secularized in the nineteenth century, Catholic universities vigorously resisted going that path. Catholic schools were largely successful in resisting such external threats because they were run by religious orders of nuns and priests. These religious orders had an age-long history of running schools and were steadfast in their educational mission that integrated learning, science, and scholarship with faith—a vision that made it much easier to resist and ward off secularization. In addition, the religious orders that ran Catholic schools had the support of the Vatican and could look to the Church's hierarchy for guidance and direction, while the hierarchy in turn was ready to intervene at critical moments and provide much-needed help.[34] These factors together served as a bulwark of resistance to anything that threatened the faith and its tradition.

In the 1960s, however, this resistance began to wilt due to some of the factors we have already identified. The United States experienced, in the 1990s, a shift to coeducation brought about by the civil rights movements of the 1960s. Coupled with the fact of decline in the number of vowed religious and clergymen in the United States, laymen and laywomen began to assume increasing responsibility in Catholic institutions, with large numbers assuming administrative responsibilities of schools that were hitherto run by clergy and religious. This is not to say that the laypeople who assumed new

---

32. Alice Gallin, OSU, "Introduction," in *American Catholic Higher Education: Essential Documents, 1967–1990*, ed. Alice Gallin, OSU (Notre Dame IN: University of Notre Dame Press, 1992), 1.

33. Ibid.

34. See Patrick Byrne, "The Good under Construction and the Research Vocation of a Catholic University," *Catholic Education: A Journal of Inquiry and Practice* 7 (2004): 320–38, at 321.

roles as administrators of these Catholic colleges and universities "have less to bring to their leadership responsibilities, as often they excel in other areas of competence, far more than their predecessors. However, in terms of their Catholic formation they have less depth and breadth."[35]

Changes in discipline and social mores followed. Some of the changes were momentous, and at times produced embarrassing differences from what had previously obtained on Catholic campuses. For example, in some campuses daily Eucharistic services soon became a thing of the past. Even the visible absence of priests and religious on campuses in their religious garb was itself a problem for institutions that for a long time were almost synonymous with priests and vowed religious.

These fast-moving and dramatic events caused those Catholic faithful who had not moved with the times to wonder what was "Catholic" in these institutions.[36] Historians like to point out that history does not repeat itself, but it is difficult not to see the parallels in the chain of events of the 1960s that affected the Catholic culture of Catholic colleges and universities and the chain of events that led to the secularization of Protestant colleges in the nineteenth century. The demise of Protestant universities in the United States, including Harvard, Princeton, Stanford, Michigan, and Chicago, came about when they began to adopt "models of research and the hiring of research faculty that were indifferent to the faith traditions of their founders. These decisions . . . meant that the faith traditions became increasingly irrelevant, first to the intellectual life, and eventually to student teaching, student formation, and indeed to every aspect of these institutions."[37] In the 1960s, Catholic colleges and universities adopted a similar model of research and hiring of faculty that at times seemed indifferent to their faith tradition and Catholic identity.

The soul searching that followed the events of the 1960s led to a rapid production of literature, some of it confusing, on the subject

---

35. Neil Ormerod, "Identity and Mission in Catholic Organizations," *Australasian Catholic Record* 87 (2010): 430–39, at 430.

36. Gallin, "Introduction," 1.

37. Byrne, "The Good under Construction," 321. See also G. M. Marsden, *The Soul of the American University: From Protestant Establishment to Established Nonbelief* (New York: Oxford University Press, 1994).

of the Catholic identity of Catholic institutions of learning in the contemporary world. This literature flourished along two divergent lines. There were works produced by the likes of Rev. James Tunstead Burtchaell, CSC,[38] who, like other so-called conservative Catholics, decried the secularization of Catholic colleges and the loss of their Catholic identities. In their view, Catholic universities and colleges, particularly in the 1960s and 70s, were guilty of a number of errors, including: relaxing ties to both the Church's hierarchy and the founding religious orders of these institutions, tolerating religious dissent among their faculty and staff, and muting references to the Roman Catholic Church in their mission statements in order to receive government funds or to make themselves more attractive to wider constituencies.[39] These authors argued that secularism— the absence of God in human or temporal matters—posed a great danger. This claim cannot be easily dismissed.

The other kind of literature was produced by the so-called liberals, who defended the secularization of Catholic colleges and their entry into the mainstream of higher education in the United States.[40] As the twentieth century wore on, some preeminent Catholic colleges and universities in the United States began to absorb the values and ideals of the secular society. Freedom of speech and religion, democratic organization, and individualism became increasingly visible on Catholic campuses.[41]

Freedom of speech particularly became a defining feature of Catholic campuses as more and more laypeople who were not formed in the culture of monastic life assumed faculty and administrative positions in these schools. Previously, the nuns and priests who had run these schools were trained in a monastic culture where the vow of obedience was emphasized. By the vow of obedience they committed

---

38. See J. T. Burtchaell, "The Decline and Fall of the Christian College (Part 1)," *First Things* 12 (1991): 16–29; "The Decline and Fall of the Christian College (Part 2)," *First Things* 13 (1991): 30–38.

39. Joseph A. Komonchak, "The Redemptive Identity and Mission of a Catholic University," in *Catholic Theology in the University: Source of Wholeness*, ed. Virginia M. Shaddy (Milwaukee: Marquette University Press, 1998), 73.

40. Alice Gallin, "American Catholic Higher Education: An Experience of Inculturation," in *Trying Times: Essays on Catholic Higher Education in the Twentieth Century*, ed. William M. Shea and Daniel Van Slyke (Atlanta: Scholars Press, 1999), 99.

41. Ibid., 101.

their will to their superior, meaning that they gave up their freedom of self-determination for the larger benefit of the community. They could not question or act contrary to the will of their superiors. This culture of strict adherence to the wishes of the superior evaporated as quickly as laymen and laywomen assumed positions in these schools. These laypeople felt free to question university policy. As leadership of Catholic schools shifted to democratically-minded American laypeople, decisions were no longer made by the hierarchy but by an elected body.

There were other shifts as well. Since the nuns and religious priests lived in community, they brought with them to Catholic campuses their respective visions of communal life. By the vow of chastity they committed themselves to a life of celibacy, which meant that they had minimal family responsibilities and could devote themselves to their communities. The vow of poverty meant that individual members of these religious orders and congregations could not own property or wealth. Competition for material goods was minimal, since the emphasis was on community, not on individual goods. They did not have to compete for tenure or promotion, since their apostolate depended on the need of the community. But as the presence of nuns and religious priests declined and the leadership of these schools came under laypeople, the emphasis on community soon gave way to individualism. Unlike vowed religious, laypeople have families to take care of and careers to pursue. These needs lead to some level of competition for the best available position and for tenure and promotion.

These changes did not take place all at once. They were gradual, but their impact was felt at every step of the way. Some of the changes (like the democratization of the decision-making process and competition on the part of faculty) turned out very well and became values to be cherished. But, for better or worse, the changes greatly altered the character of Catholic educational institutions. Because the changes were gradual, it seemed to many that the institutions had experienced radical changes before they realized what was going on. While many Catholic educators in the United States welcomed these new values, their counterparts in other countries were, in general, less sanguine.[42]

---

42. Ibid.

INTERNATIONAL DEVELOPMENTS

The absorption of these inherently American values came to dominate discussions between members of the International Federation of Catholic Universities (IFCU) from other countries and their American counterparts in the 1960s. There were repeated attempts on the part of the Americans to dialogue with colleagues in other countries and with the Sacred Congregation for Catholic Education on the question of what makes a university Catholic? In the course of these dialogues it became apparent that there were many divergent understandings of these basic American values and the relationship of these values to a Catholic university.[43] Major questions were left unresolved. For example: "Given the secular foundation of cultures (i.e., the basic physical, social, and political realities), how could secularization (understood as the absence of God from human discourse and the irrelevance of Christian ideals in the academy) be avoided? Did the American experience have anything to offer as a solution?"[44]

In the post–World War II years there were sentiments in favor of solidarity and international cooperation in almost every facet of social and political life. Pius XII also wanted at the time to bring together a seemingly fragmented Catholic world that was beset by spiritual and cultural crisis. At his request, leaders of Catholic universities around the world, in collaboration with the Sacred Congregation for Catholic Education, formed in 1949 the umbrella group the IFCU.[45] The central mission of the IFCU at the time of its formation was primarily to address the identity question, i.e., to articulate the role of a Catholic university in a modern and fast-changing world. It was thought that by fostering a shared common identity among its members the IFCU would promote the unity that Pius XII wanted to see among its members. At the time of its formation, there was great optimism that the IFCU would be successful in this regard; Pius XII went so far as to call upon the IFCU to serve as liaison to the United Nations.[46]

---

43. Ibid.

44. Ibid.

45. Gallin, "Introduction," 2.

46. Gallin, "American Catholic Higher Education," 101.

Although the Catholic Church has always valued education, which the Church sees as an arm of its teaching mission, before the formation of the IFCU there was no concerted effort on the part of the Catholic hierarchy to articulate a special role for Catholic universities and colleges in an ecclesial context. "The Code of Canon Law promulgated in 1917 passed over universities in silence, addressing only schools and seminaries."[47] In truth, there was little or no need for any articulation of Catholic schools in an ecclesial context when Catholic colleges were staffed and administered by religious. The need to articulate the role of Catholic universities in the world emerged only with the rising wave of secularism and as the leadership of Catholic schools moved from the religious to laypeople. Even by the time most universities in Europe were secularized and became state institutions, the Church "contented itself with securing the right to appoint the teachers of theology on faculties attached to state universities."[48] This was how "canonical mission," the permission to teach Roman Catholic theology, began.[49] But as the need arose for the Church to articulate the role of a Catholic university in a modern world, the IFCU provided the opportunity for this engagement. With the support and encouragement of Pope Paul VI, the IFCU became an independent organization in 1963 with Rev. Theodore Hesburgh, CSC, the president of the University of Notre Dame, as its president. "At its meeting in Tokyo in 1965, the IFCU decided to formulate a statement on the distinctive purposes of a Catholic university that would have as its context the Vatican II document, 'The Church in the Modern World.'"[50]

The IFCU's statements on the distinctiveness of the Catholic university in a contemporary context were gradually developed over time and were brought into sharp focus following regional meetings at Buga, Colombia; Manila, Philippines; Paris, France; and Land O'Lakes, Wisconsin. The statement at the Land O'Lakes regional meeting was particularly significant because it insisted on two fundamental principles as necessary ingredients for the survival

---

47. Gallin, "Introduction," 2.

48. Ibid.

49. Ibid.

50. Ibid.

of a Catholic university: institutional autonomy and academic freedom. Its reasoning was that the Catholic university "participates in the total university life of our time, has the same functions as all other true universities and, in general, offers the same services to society. The Catholic university adds to the basic idea of the modern university distinctive characteristics which round out and fulfill that idea."[51] The Land O'Lakes meeting created as many questions as it answered.

At the Third International Congress in 1989, the IFCU delegates sought "to clarify for one another the legal and educational systems within which they lived and which would need to be taken into account in any statement on the nature and mission of a Catholic university."[52] The delegates, some of whom had a more canonical approach to the question of Catholic identity, did not universally share the American value of free debate and participatory decision-making.[53] Their position stems from an understanding of a crucial text of canon law: "The Church has the right to erect and to supervise universities which contribute to a higher level of human culture, to a fuller advancement of the human person and also to the fulfillment of the Church's teaching office" (Canon 807). An additional canon law text insists that "even if it really be Catholic, no university may bear the title or name Catholic university without the consent of the competent ecclesiastical authority" (Canon 808).

ANALYSIS BY THE CHURCH'S HIERARCHY

In a 1989 address to members of the International Meeting on Catholic Higher Education, Pope John Paul II suggested that the two-poled entity university-Catholic must receive greater efficacy in any attempt to address the Catholic identity of Catholic colleges and universities. According to the pontiff, university-Catholic is "an entity whose two poles complete and enrich one another, in which both poles must be maintained and brought to ever greater

---

51. See Land O'Lakes Statement on "The Nature of a Contemporary Catholic University," in *American Catholic Higher Education*, 7.

52. Gallin, "American Catholic Higher Education," 101.

53. Ibid., 101–2.

perfection in order to fulfill a task which remains always new and exciting."[54] He described the problem of the Catholic identity of Catholic schools as convergent and critical, because not only does the Church look to the Catholic universities but society also looks to and needs these Catholic universities.[55] The pope traced the origin of the crisis of the university to the period around World War II when the world was faced with not only organizational but also spiritual and cultural crises. For him, the crisis of the university was not merely one of identity or purpose but also one of values.[56]

In Catholic understanding, education is a ministry, although the Church has yet to properly determine what goes under the rubric of educational ministry. The Catholic Church often lumps a virtually endless catalogue of programs under the rubric of education,[57] but it is clear that education is an expression of the mission entrusted to the Church by Jesus Christ, and it takes that mission seriously. Catholic education, particularly education of adult Catholics, "is situated not at the periphery of the Church's educational mission but at its center."[58] The Second Vatican Council mandated, in its *Declaration on Christian Education*, that national episcopal conferences regularly issue statements and guidelines on educational ministry in the context of the Church and their own society.[59] "Through education the Church seeks to prepare its members to proclaim the Good News and to translate this proclamation into action. Since the Christian vocation is a call to transform oneself and society with God's help, the educational efforts of the Church must encompass the twin purposes of personal sanctification and social reform in light of Christian values."[60]

In spite of its many great achievements, due largely to "the dedicated teachers who have expressed their Christian vocation through

---

54. John Paul II, "Address, John Paul II to International Meeting on Catholic Higher Education," in *American Catholic Higher Education*, 385.

55. Ibid., 386.

56. Ibid., 387.

57. USCCB, *To Teach as Jesus Did* (Washington, DC: USCCB, 1973), 1.

58. Ibid., 13.

59. Ibid., 1.

60. Ibid., 3.

the apostolate of Catholic education,"[61] the Catholic school system is "shrinking visibly" as the result of many complex sociological, demographic, and psychological factors.[62] Financial problems have contributed significantly to the present crisis. Education, at the public and nonpublic levels, according to the United States Conference of Catholic Bishops, has been burdened by spiraling costs. Even in instances where the legislative arm of the government has intervened, such interventions have been set back by courts that "have rejected laws favorable to nonpublic education, sometimes on grounds which many find extremely difficult to understand or accept."[63] Speaking generally and without citing specific examples, the USCCB pointed out that the main "obstacle to meaningful public aid to nonpublic elementary and secondary schools continues to be the United States Supreme Court's interpretation of the First and Fourteenth Amendments."[64] To some it seems "that the Court has raised an impenetrable barrier between government and church-sponsored schools; but to others, who are knowledgeable about its jurisprudence and procedures, it appears that the Court, having acknowledged that it is walking a tightrope between the First Amendment's free exercise and establishment clauses, may eventually see a way to give realistic support to parents' freedom to choose a nonpublic school."[65] Since the Court only decides cases that are brought before it, it is possible that some plan whereby public funds could be used to assist nonpublic schools may yet prove acceptable.

Of the many issues besetting Catholic education there is none more pressing than the challenge of providing adequate and efficient education for Catholic youth. "The history of American education is testimony to the deeply held conviction of American Catholics that Catholic elementary and secondary schools are the best expression of the educational ministry to youth."[66] According to the USCCB, rapid population expansion, ethnicity, and scientific and technical

61. Ibid., 32.
62. Ibid.
63. Ibid.
64. Ibid.
65. Ibid., 32–33.
66. Ibid., 23.

progress have led to new problems in need of urgent attention. There are "some strong pressures to secularize Catholic institutions."[67] There are also "contemporary trends and pressures to compartmentalize life and learning and to isolate the religious dimension of existence from other areas of human life."[68]

Might not a solution lie in the study or promotion of theology in Catholic schools?

SHOULD CATHOLIC UNIVERSITIES BE CATHOLIC?

In *Contending with Modernity*, Philip Gleason provides a detailed account of the shifts and changes that have taken place in United States Catholic colleges and universities since the twentieth century, enumerating not only the effects of the two World Wars on American Catholicism but also the effect of the turbulent social and political climate of the 1960s that practically left American Catholic educators with two options: either accommodate or contend with modernity.[69] To draw an analogy from government-funded public schools, critics of the American educational system in general sometimes compare the educational sector with the health care system. Just as critics claim that the latter is too often shaped not by concerns for the well-being of patients but by the profiteering appetite of the insurance industry, so too, some would argue, much of what goes on in American public schools is shaped by politicians who are more concerned with winning elections than the best interests of students.[70] In the public school system, various pressure or interest groups try to influence decisions about American education at primary, secondary, and tertiary levels.[71] Interest groups in American

---

67. Ibid., 19.

68. Ibid., 29.

69. See Philip Gleason, *Contending with Modernity* (New York: Oxford University Press, 1995).

70. Parker Palmer, "On the Edge: Have the Courage to Lead with Soul," *National Staff Development Council* 29 (2008): 12.

71. See Roy Adam, "Interest Groups in American Education," *Comparative Education* 11 (1978): 165–78.

education exhibit the "complexity and instability that characterizes the real power structure in the governance of education in the United States."[72] Any educational system, regardless of how well conceived, will be hampered when educational decisions are made by politicians and pressure groups rather than educators.[73]

While many would claim that special interest groups have hijacked public schools, there is no data to suggest that Catholic schools have suffered in this way. Nevertheless, the question of the "Catholic" nature of Catholic colleges and universities has recently become a pressing issue. We have already discussed one of factors involved, the fact that "the leadership of these institutions has moved from persons who have been formed within the culture of priestly or religious life, to a lay leadership, who, while professionally competent, does not have the same depth and breadth of Catholic formation as the previous generation of leaders."[74] Another factor is the question of how to understand the mission and identity of Catholic schools in an ever-changing world. Some assert, that, while Catholic schools today may not necessarily be driven by the interests of politicians, the air of uncertainty that continues to blur the mission of Catholic schools stems from similarly mundane interests, not the Catholic vision of their schools, and that the net result of this is a catechetical crisis and loss of the distinctive Catholic identity of these institutions.

The "Catholic" nature of Catholic institutions of learning is not just an American problem. A worldwide study conducted on the mission and identity of Catholic colleges and universities in Australia found a wide range of disagreements among faculty, not only on curricular matters and their connection to the mission and identity of the college but more importantly on the connection with their own religious faith and teaching.[75] Religion is entwined in its human

---

72. Ibid., 165.

73. Bernard Lonergan's interview with Canadian *Register* at Xavier University, Cincinnati, where he conducted a two-week seminar on the philosophy of education. Material is preserved at the Lonergan Research Institute (LRI), Toronto, Ontario.

74. Ormerod, "Identity and Mission in Catholic Organizations," 430.

75. See Judith A. Dwyer and Charles E. Zech, "American Catholic Higher Education: An ACCU Study on Mission and Identity, Faculty Development and Curricular Revision," *Current Issues in Catholic Higher Education: ACCU* 19 (1998): 3–32; at 17–18.

roots and too pervasive to be restricted to personal habit or pref-erence.[76] As human beings, scholars bring their personalities with them to their work, including their convictions—although hopefully not in such a way as to impair their objectivity.[77] But now it is felt that *religious* convictions can only get in the way of true scholar-ship. Indeed, today these two dimensions, religious faith and schol-arship, are presented as near polar opposites. They seem to occupy two separate and hermetically sealed compartments.[78] Western cul-tural tradition, beginning with the Greeks (as previously discussed), began with the search for truth. When the first universities were established in the Middle Ages by the Church, their goal was still the same: to witness to the truth. While faith and reason are dis-tinct, they are also mutual reference points for dialogue and recip-rocal enrichment.[79] Anselm of Canterbury, following Augustine, ingeniously brought together faith and scholarship in his ontologi-cal argument, which he termed *fides quarens intellectus* (faith seeking understanding). "In his encyclical letter, *Fides et Ratio*, Pope John Paul II recalls the long and great history of their mutual interaction, especially in the writings of Thomas Aquinas, who, at the very dawn of European universities, provided the finest expression and deepest synthesis of faith and reason."[80]

If scholarship is objective and faith subjective, and the two must be kept separate lest scholarship be distorted, then the era of robust Catholic institutions that harmonized faith with scholarship must be consigned to the annals of history. In the mid-twentieth century, i.e., before the collapse of the Catholic subculture, Catholic universities had no identity problem; the Catholicity of Catholic colleges was a given and Catholic institutions "made no bones about *professing* their

---

76. Lamin Sanneh, *Whose Religion Is Christianity? The Gospel Beyond the West* (Grand Rapids, MI: Eerdmans, 2003), 7.

77. James Heft, SM, "Preface," in *Faith and the Intellectual Life: Marianist Award Lectures*, ed., James L. Heft, SM (Notre Dame, IN: University of Notre Dame Press, 1996), x.

78. Ibid.

79. See Walter Cardinal Kasper, "The Role of the Church and a Catholic Univer-sity in the Contemporary World, *Sacred Heart University Review* 21, no. 1 (2001): 58. Available at: *http://digitalcommons.sacredheart.edu/shureview/vol21/iss1/5* .

80. Ibid.

Catholicity."[81] As Philip Gleason succinctly puts it, no one "regarded it as a problem anymore than they regarded it as a problem that a college was a college and not a filling station or a furniture factory."[82] The reason why Catholic colleges then "could be unself-consciously Catholic was that Catholics were still self-consciously 'different.' That is, American Catholics were so conscious of holding distinctive religious beliefs that it seemed perfectly obvious that they needed their own schools to perpetuate the outlook on life that flowed from those beliefs."[83]

If Catholic institutions of learning had intentionally remained self-consciously "different" and maintained a distinctive Catholic subculture perhaps the contemporary problem of identity of Catholic colleges would not have emerged.[84] But as it is, Catholic colleges and universities that are not self-consciously Catholic might be their own worst enemies. Is a crisis then looming in American Catholic higher education? Some would answer in the affirmative.[85] Wilson Miscamble, a professor of history at the University of Notre Dame, having carefully studied the identity problem facing Catholic universities today, thinks these institutions are now at the tipping point: "While their buildings are quite real, what goes on within them has increasingly lost its distinctive content and come to resemble what occurs in secular institutions of higher learning. Students emerge from Catholic schools rather unfamiliar with the riches of the Catholic intellectual tradition and with their imaginations untouched by a religious sensibility." [86] Melanie Morey and John Piderit point to the issue of faculty hiring as the heart of the problem. They argue that one way to get out of the present impasse is through a renewed commitment to hiring committed Catholic faculty members. Miscamble develops their argument:

---

81. Philip Gleason, "What Made Catholic Identity a Problem?" in *Faith and the Intellectual Life*, ed. Heft, 89.

82. Ibid.

83. Ibid.

84. Ibid.

85. See Melanie Morey and John Piderit, SJ, *Catholic Higher Education: A Culture in Crisis* (Oxford: Oxford University Press, 2006).

86. See Wilson D. Miscamble, "The 'Faculty' Problem: How Can Catholic Identity Be Preserved?" *America* (September 2007). Also available at *http://www.america magazine.org/content/article.cfm?article_id=10176*.

An examination of the present situation at the University of Notre Dame suggests that the tipping point is at hand—a parlous situation that assuredly is replicated in all the major Catholic universities. Dramatic action will be required to secure the school's Catholic identity. If even Notre Dame, with its abundant resources and its storied role in Catholic education, fails in this effort, one must wonder who can succeed. Some specific details illustrate the nature of the crisis as it exists at Notre Dame. Notre Dame's mission statement draws upon *Ex Corde Ecclesiae* and rightly declares that the "Catholic identity of the University depends upon . . . the continuing presence of a predominant number of Catholic intellectuals" on the faculty. Nonetheless, the last three decades have seen a dramatic decline in the number of Catholic faculty members. The figure as of 2006 was 53 percent, which is somewhat inflated by those who answered "Catholic" on the faculty questionnaire but for whom the practice of the faith appears nominal at best. The prospects for the immediate future clearly worry senior administrators. Notre Dame's provost, Thomas Burish, has explained: "When the prospective rate of Catholic retirements is plotted against the contemporary rate of Catholic hires as a constant, it is clear that soon Notre Dame will no longer have the predominant number of Catholic faculty members whom we require."

In Catholic universities, as in their secular peers, the academic department constitutes the key entity where hiring decisions are made. Today at Notre Dame, however, few departments conscientiously and enthusiastically support the mission statement's call for a predominant number of Catholic faculty; the theology department and the law school are notable and honorable exceptions.[87]

Miscamble interprets the faculty hiring problem as a sign of Notre Dame's secularization.[88] He suggests that to halt the trend "a major board decision calling for two-thirds of all future appointments to be committed Catholic scholars is essential. This would

---

87. Ibid.
88. Ibid.

require very different ways of hiring from the department-based procedures of today. The university would need to engage in what might be termed strategic hiring or hiring for mission."[89] Only by taking such drastic measures can schools that want to preserve their Catholic character be truly different from secular schools.[90] Miscamble is, in essence, calling on Catholic colleges and universities to self-consciously return to their mission by hiring for this mission. Here Miscamble's example of an accomplished professor at Notre Dame who branded herself an atheist comes to mind. This distinguished professor "wanted her atheism to have a major impact on her scholarly work."[91] Although she recognized the importance of religion to the academy, her intellectual suppositions were very much at odds with a Catholic worldview.[92]

A number of social factors constitute countercurrents that work against the Catholic identity of Catholic colleges and universities. Especially problematic are "the continuing social assimilation of the Catholic population, and the concomitant acceleration of the process by which Catholic colleges and universities adjusted themselves to prevailing standards in the larger world of American higher education."[93] Concern about Catholic identity and the mission of Catholic institutions and colleges predates *Ex Corde Ecclesia* (1990). Although the document became controversial in the United States and some other countries in the West, largely because of the issue of *mandatum*, the 1983 revised Code of Canon law required that a *mandatum* be granted by a local ordinary to theologians teaching in Catholic schools. The USCCB interpreted *mandatum* to mean "fundamentally an acknowledgment by Church authority that a Catholic professor of a theological discipline is a teacher within the full communion of the Catholic Church."[94] While theologians who have reacted negatively

89. Ibid.
90. Ibid.
91. Ibid.
92. Ibid.
93. Gleason, "What Made Catholic Identity a Problem?" 90–91.
94. Dennis Doyle, "Communion Ecclesiology, *Mandatum*, and Prudential Judgments," *Pro Ecclesia* 11 (2002): 20–23, at 20; quoting "*Ex Corde Ecclesiae*: The Application to the United States," *Origins* 30 (June 15, 2000): 68–85 and "Guidelines Concerning the Academic *Mandatum*," *Origins* 31 (June 28, 20001): 128–31.

to this interpretation see *mandatum* as a threat to academic freedom, those who favor the idea that the religious identity of a university needs to be carried by a "critical mass" of its committed faculty see the *mandatum* as addressing this need.[95]

> This document enforced new, stricter requirements for colleges and universities that call themselves Catholic, touching off a spate of discussion, policy review, and church politicking as America's 230 Catholic post-secondary institutions, along with the Catholic bishops, worked out how to apply the new norms in the United States. . . . [According to the document,] "in order not to endanger the Catholic identity of the University or Institute of Higher Studies, the number of non-Catholic teachers should not be allowed to constitute a majority within the institution, which is and must remain Catholic" (ECE II:4.4).[96]

Contrariwise, there are those who argue that the Catholic identity of a college constitutes a liability.[97] It is feared that stressing the Catholic identity of an institution leads to exclusion. In other words, "faculty who have played central roles enlivening their institution for decades can suddenly fear that emphasis on what's 'Catholic' will mean that they no longer belong there as first-class citizens."[98]

In the debate over the identity of Catholic schools, therefore, two broad camps emerge: those who argue that Catholicism makes a positive contribution to teaching and learning versus those intent on showing that it either makes no difference or actually mitigates against good academic policies. The Catholic hierarchy and those concerned with how to maintain Catholic education, at least in the United States, face two fears. The first fear is the experience of Yale, Brown, Kings College, and similar institutions: that Church-related colleges and universities, following a historical pattern in

95. See D. Paul Sullins, "The Difference Catholic Makes: Catholic Faculty and Catholic Identity" *Journal for the Scientific Study of Religion* 43 (2004): 83–101.

96. Ibid., 83.

97. Thomas M. Landy, "Introduction: Yeast and the Measures of Flour," in *As Leaven in the World*, ed. Landy, xiv.

98. Ibid.

American higher education, tend to drift from their denominational identities.

The second fear is that, as large secular institutions gain the upper hand, religious institutions will not survive unless they embrace their true identity.[99] John Haughey asserts that the early Protestant universities in the United States lost their distinctive religious identities because they failed to properly work out the connections between reason and faith in Christ. "It was precisely this weakness that eviscerated their institutional commitments to their religious origins in the face of the Enlightenment and the primacy of reason. Faith commitments were relegated to the private sphere of the individual believer's preferred beliefs."[100] Haughey argues, "The great strength of Protestant Christianity has been its emphasis on the responsibility of the individual believer to appropriate his or her own faith. While the strength of that kind of faith is to be admired, Catholicism need not go the same route Protestants did with their universities."[101]

CONCLUSION

If Catholic colleges and universities fail to embrace their identity, they may "go the way Yale, Princeton, and Brown have gone, which may not seem too dire. But they may also go the way scores and even hundreds of others have gone—they are gone and no longer remembered at all. This possibility catches the attention."[102] Embracing Catholic identity does not have to entail a narrow conception of Catholicism. Catholicism properly understood is a broad and inclusive term. Non-Catholic faculty and staff can and do contribute enormously to the Catholic mission of an institution. A true Catholic institution reaches out, not only to non-Catholic faculty and staff but also collaborates with non-Catholic institutions. There are many

---

99. Ibid.

100. Haughey, *Where Is Knowing Going?* xiii.

101. Ibid.

102. Joseph Tetlow, "Intellectual Conversion: Jesuit Spirituality and the American University," in *Spirit, Style, Story: Essays Honoring John W. Padberg, SJ*, ed. Thomas Lucas (Chicago: Loyola Press, 2002), 94.

examples of Catholic and Protestant colleges collaborating in the last decade to organize conferences on the future of religious identity of their colleges as well as the compatibility of faith and science on issues pertaining to faith and the intellectual life.[103] Commendable in this regard also is the effort of Collegium, a colloquy on faith and intellectual life, at the College of the Holy Cross, Worcester, Massachusetts. It numbers about sixty Catholic colleges and universities that collaborate to foster Catholic intellectual life and the mission of Catholic higher education. Collegium emphasizes the importance of Catholic intellectual tradition, although it has never been primarily for Catholics. It seeks out "the participation of faculty who are not familiar with the Catholic intellectual tradition or the particular mission of their institution, and who the institutions believe will play an important role shaping the future of the colleges."[104] Thus while it takes as its starting point Catholic higher education, Collegium is geared toward providing individual faculty members the opportunities to shape their own intellectual vocations and help them discern how they could best contribute to the mission of their institutions, taking into consideration the faculty member's particular faith, talents, and desires.[105]

Reflecting on the valuable work of the twentieth-century historical theologian, Friedrich von Hugel, who wrote at length on the mystical, institutional, and intellectual dimensions of the Church, James Heft rightly remarked that a Catholic university is at its best when it keeps a balance between its mystical (religious), institutional, and intellectual dimensions.[106] That balance is today threatened by lack of consensus on "the substantive content of the ensemble of religious beliefs, moral commitments, and academic assumptions that supposedly constitute Catholic identity, and a consequent inability to specify what that identity entails for the practical functioning of Catholic colleges and universities."[107] It is for reasons such as these that the educational goals of Catholic colleges and universities need

103. Landy, "Introduction," xv.

104. Ibid., xii.

105. Ibid.

106. James Heft, S.M., "The Open Circle: The Culture of the Catholic University: Creativity – Character – Culture," *Australian EJournal of Theology* 2 (February 2004) [no page numbers].

107. Gleason, *Contending with Modernity*, 320.

to be rethought and reevaluated if they are to reclaim what United States Secretary of Education William Bennett termed a "legacy."[108]

The social and political complexities of the twenty-first century have affected the educational landscape, thereby imposing on Catholic colleges and universities a mandatory self-scrutiny. Monika Hellwig focuses this process of self-scrutiny with the following questions: Are Catholic universities sacrificing depth of knowledge for the sake of breadth? Are they abandoning efforts toward the integration of knowledge? And in what ways are they in danger of losing their distinctive Catholic identity?[109] These are complicated questions for which there are no easy answers. The issue is not whether one can answer them, but whether one can answer them in a way that does not do disservice to the rich and active Catholic intellectual tradition, a tradition that is alive and growing.

The onslaught of secularism has made it very difficult for universities to be fully Catholic and at the same time committed to their institutional identity, and free.[110] Catholic universities mediate between the Church and society. The crisis of the university is the crisis of the world.[111] It is not clear to what extent the chaos that results from drifting intellectual and moral values and the dissolution of the human person will play out in contemporary Catholic education.[112] How might one characterize contemporary Catholic education in light of the debate between conservatives and liberals, progressives and advocates of tradition? The descriptors *ambiguity, tensions, change, turmoil, silencing, segregation, flux, fragmentation, burdens,* and *crises* are all fittingly applied to contemporary Catholic education.[113] If it is fair

---

108. See John Tracy Ellis, "Moral Values in Higher Education," in *Faith and the Intellectual Life,* ed. Heft, 7.

109. Hellwig, "The Catholic Intellectual Tradition in the Catholic University," 1.

110. Theodore Hesburgh CSC, "Preface," in *The Catholic University: A Modern Appraisal,* ed. Neil McCluskey, SJ (Notre Dame, IN: University of Notre Dame Press, 1970), vii.

111. See Nels Ferre, *Christian Faith and Higher Education* (New York: Harper and Brothers, 1954), 233.

112. Ferre, *Christian Faith and Higher Education,* 22; see also M. C. Jeffreys, *Glaucon: An Inquiry into the Aims of Education* (London: Pitman and Sons, 1950), 53.

113. Sandra Yocum Mize, "Introduction," in *Trying Times: Essays on Catholic Higher Education in the Twentieth Century,* ed. William M. Shea and Daniel Van Slyke (Atlanta: Scholars Press, 1999), ix.

to say that contemporary Catholic universities have been successful in living out their mission and identity in the face of mounting odds, it is in part because ambiguity has led to interaction, fragmentation has led to integration, tensions have brought possibilities, and burdens have come with blessings.[114] One can be alternately optimistic and pessimistic about the present state of the Catholic university.[115]

It is for this reason that we will turn next to Bernard Lonergan, who shows us how, through the study of the past, we can come to our own in the present and understand what we hold and teach.[116] The paradoxes of pairing burden and blessing, fragmentation and integration, and tension and possibilities are more meaningful in light of the changing demographics of United States Catholic schools in the past few decades. The closure of Roman Catholic high schools in some United States cities due to the ongoing consolidation of Catholic parishes has an impact on Catholic colleges. As the United States population continues to grow, more and more ethnic minorities are gradually absorbed and integrated into Catholic schools, posing challenges in multicultural education, especially in urban areas.[117] There is also the fact of ambiguities arising from the changed theological understanding of the Church itself and the roles universities ought to play in the process of inculturation.[118] We shall examine how these challenges can be better met later when we pair Lonergan's cognitional method with Howard Gardner's Multiple Intelligence (MI) theory. Lonergan was critical of aspects of the Church's program of studies—which he thought were framed for a time before electric lights and printing presses were discovered. Lonergan's criticism of scholasticism was not against scholastic theology as such, which he considered a monumental achievement. Rather, he was aware that the defects of scholasticism were the defects of its

---

114. Ibid.

115. Hesburgh, "Preface," vii.

116. Frederick E. Crowe, *Old Things and New: A Strategy for Education* (Atlanta: Scholars Press, 1985), 119.

117. See National Catholic Educational Association, *Catholic Schools for Children and Youth in Poverty: Conversations in Excellence 2003: A Component of SPICE: Selected Programs for Improving Catholic Education, a National Diffusion Network for Catholic Schools* (Washington, DC: NCEA, 2004), 8.

118. Gallin, "American Catholic Higher Education," 100.

time. He saw in scholasticism many conflicting currents, productive and counterproductive, good and bad, hopeful and fearful.[119] The present situation, like a Chinese ideograph, signified for Lonergan both crisis and opportunity.[120]

Further Reading

Boeve, Lieven. *Interrupting Traditions: An Essay on Christian Faith in a Postmodern Context.* Louvain, Belgium: Peeters, 2003.

Buckley, Michael. *The Catholic University as Promise and Project.* Washington, DC: Georgetown University, 1999.

Clooney, Francis X., ed. *Jesuit Postmodern: Scholarship, Vocation and Identity in the Twenty-First Century.* Lanham, MD: Rowman and Littlefield, 2006.

Haughey, John. "Catholic Higher Education: A Strategy for Its Identity." *Current Issues in Catholic Higher Education* 16, no. 2 (1996): 25–32.

Heft, James, ed. *Believing Scholars: Ten Catholic Intellectuals.* Bronx, NY: Fordham University, 2009.

Hellwig, Monika K. *Public Dimensions of a Believer's Life: Rediscovering the Cardinal Virtues.* Lanham, MD: Rowman and Littlefield, 2005.

John Paul II. *Ex Corde Ecclesiae. Origins* 20 (October 4, 1990): 265–76.

Marsden, George. *The Soul of the American University: From Protestant Establishment to Established Nonbelief.* New York: Oxford University, 1994.

Ong, Walter J. "Yeast: A Parable for Catholic Higher Education." *America* 162 (April 7, 1990): 347–63.

Prusak, Bernard. *The Church Unfinished: Ecclesiology through the Centuries.* New York: Paulist Press, 1989.

---

119. Hesburgh, "Preface," viii.
120. Ibid.

2

Bernard Lonergan's Thought as a Possible Way Forward

Part 1 of this work explored the concept of a Catholic intellectual tradition, the challenges that tradition faces, and the Catholic universities that play such an important role in the transmission and development of CIT. Part 2 narrows the focus to the work of Bernard Lonergan. Lonergan was not only one of the foremost twentieth-century contributors to CIT, he also devoted considerable attention to the issue of Catholic education. Lonergan raised many critical questions that can be of help to Catholic colleges and universities.

Lonergan addressed problems facing Catholic education like the ones we raised in Part 1 of this work. His concerned view that the rich Catholic heritage was somehow adrift is everywhere evident in his writings. He asked, should education, in general, assume the form of a "banking procedure in which the teacher hands over parcels of information that the pupil daily stores in the safety-deposit box of the mind, and draws out as occasion demands, especially the occasion of examinations? Or should education be a freely developing evolution of inner resources, where the pupil is put in a sandbox and left to grow in self-realization with the expectation that he or she will advance steadily from sandbox to, say, a laboratory for nuclear physics?[1] The desire to foster an intellectual tradition that promotes the latter is, for Lonergan, a driving force behind Catholic education. We have attempted to present something of the rich treasury of Lonergan's writings on this topic in a way that readers unfamiliar with his works will find accessible.

Chapter 5 concerns intellectual authenticity and its foundational importance to achieving any meaningful change in the culture of Catholic higher education. It is a journey into the mind of Lonergan—how Lonergan embarked on his project of reforming Catholic theology and Catholic education. The chapter discusses how one can attain intellectual authenticity by showing how Lonergan himself attained it in the context of his work of reform: from a classicist worldview that thought of human culture as one and only one (i.e., European Christian culture) to modern pluralist culture that recognizes that there are multiple human cultures; from an apprehension of men and women in terms of human nature to an understanding of men and women through human history; and from the Aristotelian-Thomistic method that deduced everything from what was called "first principles" to a modern empirical method that takes into consideration the findings of the modern sciences.

Chapter 6 examines issues pertaining to understanding and learning styles. It is a "comparison by contrast" in anticipation of an argument we shall advance in chapter 7 that Catholic intellectual tradition must be attentive to pluralism of cultures and multiple ways of understanding. Here we apply to education what Lonergan calls the transcendental precepts: be attentive, be intelligent, be reasonable, and be responsible. The chapter brings into the conversation Howard Gardner, whose groundbreaking work on Multiple Intelligence (MI) revolutionized school reform efforts in the United States in the 1980s. Correlating Gardner's work with Lonergan's cognitional method (CM), this chapter shows how Lonergan and Gardner, albeit independently in their multidimensional work, uncover how knowledge is acquired and pin down the acts of human understanding.

---

1. Frederick E. Crowe, SJ, *Old Things and New: A Strategy for Education* (Atlanta: Scholars Press, 1985), ix–x.

This comparison by contrast shows that while Lonergan's CM can aid MI considerably in the task of educational reform, MI can as well aid Lonergan's view of human capacity for thought as ground for self-transcendence.

Chapter 7 conceives of CIT as a kind of palimpsest. Like all palimpsests, CIT can also be reworked, refined, and modified according to the "signs of the time." The chapter considers how Lonergan, as one of many contributors of this tradition, has reworked, refined, and added to this palimpsest. To make his contribution easier to grasp and reader friendly, it is broken into eight "modules" that reflect characteristics of CIT or Catholic education.

Chapter 8 considers the overlap between two questions: *What* is Catholic intellectual tradition? and *Why* Catholic intellectual tradition? Drawing upon insights of behavioral sciences, the chapter presents a fresh, pragmatic strategy that could lead to greater understanding of Catholic identity and the Catholic intellectual tradition, resulting in fundamental reform in Catholic colleges and universities.

CHAPTER 5

The Search for Intellectual Authenticity

Evidence presented in Part I suggests then that United States Catholic colleges and universities have become a place of conflict between two very different cultural institutions: the Catholic Church, with its devotion to revealed truth backed by hierarchical authority, and the American higher educational system, with its commitment to free inquiry and democratic ideals. To be at once a contemporary American institution of higher education and a Catholic institution has become problematic. The problem is "symptomatic of a changing conception of education on the part of U.S. colleges and universities and a changing conception of education on the part of the Catholic Church."[1] This chapter will explore how theologian and Catholic educator Bernard Lonergan handled the apparent conflict between revealed truth vis-à-vis free inquiry and democratic ideals through his work on method, with a view to shedding more light on his contribution to the Catholic intellectual tradition.

Before his breakthrough work on method in 1965, Lonergan went through a period of transition brought about by new philosophical currents that threatened the system of education in which he was brought up.[2] He survived these challenges by unyielding fidelity to

---

1. Jacob Dumestre, "The Contribution of Bernard Lonergan toward the Recovery of a Catholic Philosophy of Education" (PhD diss., Vanderbilt University, 1990), 1–3.

2. See Bernard Lonergan, *Philosophical and Theological Papers 1958–1964*, ed. R. Croken, F. E. Crowe, and R. M. Doran, in *Collected Works of Bernard Lonergan* (Toronto: University of Toronto Press, 1988), xii.

© The Jesuit Fathers of Upper Canada

Bernard Lonergan

what he would later term *authenticity*. Authenticity would be central to his new conception of method and would also become an apt summary of his life quest.[3] His newly discovered method, aimed at discovering a person's deepest need and most prized achievement, is not infallible; it stands or falls on authenticity.[4] A Catholic education remains faithful to the tradition only to the extent that the education and the tradition are authentic. Moreover, the method Lonergan introduces into theology will help resolve ambiguities surrounding Catholic intellectual tradition.

---

3. Robert Doran, *Psychic Conversion and Theological Foundations II* (Milwaukee: Marquette University Press, 2006), 46.

4. Bernard Lonergan, *Method in Theology* (Toronto: University of Toronto Press, 1996), 254.

INTEGRATING OLD AND NEW

The problem of authenticity comes down to the question: who am I, really and truly? Am I something beyond my family name? Beyond our personal and social identities, we share with others a human identity that is comprehensive and foundational.[5] The authenticity-test question is not limited to the individual. It can also be extended to groups, societies, and communities with common goals and meanings, like the Christian or Catholic community. Lonergan's concern that the Catholic community was grappling with the problem of authenticity, which was responsible for the crisis of culture (not of faith) it was embroiled in, made him confront head-on the question, what, really and truly, does the Catholic Church stand for? An authentic Catholic theology has not only to become historical and existential but must also ask questions about the human person, not in the abstract, but in the concreteness of one's living and dying.[6] Lonergan devoted himself to attaining personal authenticity before wrestling with how authenticity might be achieved and sustained in the Catholic tradition.

If the attainment of authenticity was one of Lonergan's most valuable achievements, it came by way of his work on transposition— going beyond the riches of the past in order to meet the challenges of his time. He saw the transposition of Catholic philosophy, theology, and education as a requisite demand. Before one can transpose a thing one must know it; one cannot transpose what one does not know. Furthermore, transposition suggests an act of understanding of what is already out there. The new is analogous to the old, and the new can therefore preserve all that is valid in the old by achieving a higher synthesis.[7] Lonergan had a good understanding of what had

---

5. Joseph Flanagan, *Quest for Self-Knowledge: An Essay in Lonergan's Philosophy* (Toronto: University of Toronto Press, 1997), 3.

6. Bernard Lonergan, "Dimensions of Meaning," in *Collection: Papers by Bernard Lonergan, SJ*, ed. F. E. Crowe (New York: Herder and Herder, 1967), 266.

7. Matthew Lamb, "Lonergan's Transpositions of Augustine and Aquinas: Exploratory Suggestions," in *The Importance of Insight: Essays in Honor of Michael Vertin*, ed. John Liptay, Jr., and David Liptay (Toronto: University of Toronto Press, 2007), 4; referencing Bernard Lonergan, "The Scope of Renewal" and "Horizons and Transpositions," in *Philosophical and Theological Papers 1965–1980*, vol. 17 of *Collected Works of Bernard Lonergan*, ed. Robert Croken and Robert Doran (Toronto: University of Toronto Press, 2004), 282–98, 409–32.

to be transposed and assumed at its heart was the program of Leo XIII to revive Thomism.

Lonergan identified at least five broad categories of transposition:

1. transposition from the metaphysics of the soul to the self-appropriation of the subject
2. transposition from logic to method
3. transposition from a classicist worldview to that of modern empirical science
4. transposition from an apprehension of men and women in terms of human nature to an understanding of men and women through history
5. transposition from Aristotelian first principles to transcendental method[8]

These five bold realities, related and interconnected, will be elaborated in our chapter on modules. Here we simply point out that Lonergan's success in effecting his program of transformation was made possible by three separate but interrelated ideas that shaped his life and work: (1) the synthesis of tradition and modernity in thinking, (2) the promotion of the "not too numerous center" in the Church, and (3) the detachment of a long-range point of view in society.[9]

Tradition and Modernity

Lonergan was at once critical and respectful of the advances of modern science, just as he was both critical and respectful of the achievement of scholasticism. In Lonergan's view, one of scholasticism's great achievements was integration of faith and reason. But scholasticism also had limitations: whereas advocates thought it to be a perennial philosophy that was valid for all times and places, Lonergan saw this

---

8. Robert Doran, *Theological Foundations* (Milwaukee: Marquette University Press, 1995), 2:342. See also Bernard Lonergan, "The Future of Thomism," in *A Second Collection: Papers by Bernard J.F. Lonergan, SJ*, ed. William Ryan and Bernard Tyrell (Toronto: University of Toronto Press, 1974), 43–53.

9. Robert Doran, "Introduction—Lonergan: An Appreciation," in *The Desires of the Human Heart: An Introduction to the Theology of Bernard Lonergan*, ed. Vernon Gregson (Mahwah, NJ: Paulist Press, 1988), 2–3; referenced also in Dumestre, "Contribution," 107.

view as antithetical to the new methods and spirit of open inquiry that the times demanded. His writings "can be filtered through the hermeneutic grid of his respectful attention to, learning from, and critical reorientation of, both tradition and modernity."[10]

This spirit of inquiry motivated Lonergan to honor the charge of Leo XIII's *Aeterni Patris* (*Of the Eternal Father*). Leo's encyclical letter of 1879 should not be confused with the Apostolic letter *Aeterni Patris* (June 1868) of Pius IX. The latter was issued by the pope to summon the first Vatican Council. The *Aeterni Patris* of Leo XIII called for the revival of scholastic philosophy according to the mind of St. Thomas Aquinas, a program summed up in the Latin phrase *vetera novis augere et perficere* (to augment and complete the old with the new). It was this call that Lonergan responded to and, in effect, assumed. He wrote to his religious superior (provincial) in 1935: "My purpose has been the Leonine purpose, *vetera novis augere et perficere,* though with this modality that I believed the basic task still to be the determination of what the *vetera* (old) really were."[11] This commitment and determination led him to decipher what the old and new (*nova*) can become at a time when many were still unclear about these. The key, for him, was in grasping the truth of tradition, i.e., the process of meaning used by the Church's forebears "to address the concerns of their day, and an understanding of the many biases that determined their answers."[12] In grasping both the truth and possibilities of these traditions, Lonergan was able to draw from the past and at the same time look forward to modernity, as a way of augmenting and completing the old with the new.[13]

Lonergan's fundamental orientation was "to preserve, monitor, and reawaken in modern culture the differentiations of consciousness that are displayed in the writings of Plato and Aristotle, in the Christian gospel and the development of dogma in the Church, and in the classic Christian theologies of Augustine and Aquinas."[14] A

---

10. Ibid., 3.

11. Ibid., 4; citing Bernard Lonergan, *Verbum: Word and Idea in Aquinas*, ed. David Burrell (Notre Dame, IN: University of Notre Dame Press, 1967), 215.

12. Dumestre, "Contribution," 107.

13. Ibid., 108.

14. Doran, *Psychic Conversion and Theological Foundations II*, 65.

GRACE: A CASE IN POINT

In the late sixteenth century, a crisis arose concerning different understandings of grace, and more pointedly, how to interpret Thomas Aquinas on the subject of grace. Aquinas, whose writings had been adopted by the Church, had written extensively on grace in the *Summa Theologiae*. The Dominicans (members of Aquinas's religious order) and the Jesuits (who were founded at the time of the Reformation to defend the Catholic faith) each championed their own interpretation. The animosity between the two groups was bitter and led to name calling, each one charging the other with heresy.

This rancor was felt especially in Spain, which was at the time a Catholic nation with a great center of learning in Salamanca. The Dominican position on grace was represented by Domingo Banez (1528–1604), a Spanish Dominican theologian whose position is sometimes referred to as Banezianism, while the Jesuit position was represented by Luis de Molina (1535–1600), a Spanish Jesuit theologian whose position is sometimes referred to as Molinism. The Dominicans, claiming to be the accurate interpreter of Aquinas on the subject, accused the Jesuits of Pelagianism (the heresy of Pelagius that was condemned by the Church because it denied God's grace in human affairs) and the Jesuits in turn accused the Dominicans of Calvinism (the teaching of the reformer John Calvin that denied human free will and affirmed only predestination, which was condemned by the Council of Trent). The controversy escalated to such an extent that the Vatican had to appoint an *ad hoc* committee to intervene. First Pope Clement VIII tried to resolve the matter, without success. Finally his successor, Paul V, decreed on September 5, 1607, that neither side could accuse the other of heresy and asked both sides to consider the matter closed.

Lonergan, in his doctoral dissertation, *Gratia Operans: A Study of Speculative Development in the Writings of St. Thomas of Aquin*, showed that the rancor between the Dominicans and Jesuits stemmed from lack of historical consciousness on the part of commentators of Aquinas who tried to project forcefully onto Aquinas questions he never considered. The other problem Lonergan pointed out was that

Continued

GRACE: A CASE IN POINT   *Continued*

the two opposing camps of Dominicans and Jesuits presented their arguments in syllogisms. Syllogisms sometimes contain unnoticed fallacies; in this case, the fallacy was an exaggerated view of the objectivity of truth, and both sides were guilty of it. Lonergan also showed how the mind of Aquinas was not a finished project, but something that was ever developing. In so doing, he pointed out ways of making Aquinas relevant to our time—a kind of intellectual authenticity Lonergan effected in himself and advocated for CIT.

---

differentiation of consciousness, for example, seeks to understand why Plato, Aristotle, or Aquinas wrote what they wrote and the kind of problem they were addressing, cognizant that their minds were not finished projects and that they were also conditioned by the biases of their time. Lonergan's integration of the positive gains of modernity with the rich heritage of the past is a challenge to our age: problems in our understanding of reality and our world cannot be reconciled with the riches of the Catholic heritage unless inherited tradition is purified and radically transformed.[15]

The Not Too Numerous Center

Before the Second Vatican Council, Lonergan served in different capacities in various Vatican commissions, like the Secretariat of Non-Believers. He was one of the original members of the International Theological Commission that was appointed by Paul VI. His dedication to these projects led Robert Doran to surmise that Lonergan's "main ecclesial concern after the Second Vatican Council was with the depth, both religious and intellectual, to which the Church must penetrate if it is really to achieve 'Pope John's intention.'"[16]

Lonergan's writings on authenticity show the depth of his commitment to the *aggiornamento* program. While committed to

---

15. Ibid.
16. Doran, "Introduction," 4–5.

the pope's reform program, he was also mindful of forces within the Church that could scuttle the renewal.[17] "There is bound to be formed a solid right that is determined to live in a world that no longer exists. There is bound to be formed a scattered left, captivated by now this, now that new development, exploring now this and now that new possibility. But what will count is a perhaps not numerous center, big enough to be at home in both the old and the new, painstaking enough to work out one by one the transitions to be made, strong enough to refuse half-measures and insist on complete solutions even though it has to wait."[18] Concerned about two extreme groups, the "scattered left" and the "solid right," working against real renewal, Lonergan sought the ground of unity in the love of God, religious conversion. Human authenticity, he believed, begins with the acceptance of God's gift of love that constitutes religious conversion and leads to moral and intellectual conversion.[19]

The Long-Range View

The extraordinary balance that Lonergan's mind reached between fidelity to tradition and respect for modernity, and between fidelity to doctrine and the promotion of responsible pluralism, is a function that characterizes both Lonergan's own mode of thinking and the cognitive authenticity he would encourage or chart for CIT.[20] Lonergan was a long-range thinker and his pattern of thinking is befitting of a long-range project like CIT. His pattern is one of concern for the preeminent position of "the role of human intelligence in history and society, and on the relation of intelligence to social and cultural progress and decline, especially in view of the distinct dangers confronting human society today."[21] His long-range point of view was geared toward the cumulative development of the individual and the Church:

---

17. Ibid., 5.

18. Lonergan, "Dimensions of Meaning," 366–67.

19. Doran, "Introduction," 6.

20. Ibid., 7.

21. Ibid., 8.

In the *Verbum* articles, Lonergan wanted to vindicate and to retrieve the genius of St. Thomas both in the substance of his Trinitarian thought as well as in the method of his theological procedure. Lonergan wrote in response to the manualist tradition,[22] which lumped together dogmatic and speculative elements to meet its aim of establishing proofs of faith. In contrast to the manualist aim, Lonergan took as his goal the Thomist theological ideal of understanding the truths of faith.[23]

The manualist tradition was not geared toward helping a person understand Christian teaching. Its main concern was to prove the truth of the faith. But Lonergan's aim, like that of CIT, was understanding, not proofs. His emphasis on the speculative procedure used by Thomas in the *Summa Theologiae* as a way of attaining theological understanding would become a useful tool for CIT, in so far as CIT seeks to understand and appropriate the treasures of the past as means of meeting the needs of the present.

The Lonergan enterprise is ultimately oriented to the practical and programmatic for the future.[24] Lonergan, according to Crowe, is not a "now" theologian, but one whose task is to build for the future. His long-range concern "looks to a complete restructuring of theology as the answer to our most fundamental need; and his energies have been devoted consistently toward attaining that goal, however distant it still remains."[25] His dedication to Leo's program of renewal or transposition indicates the Catholic character of Lonergan's work and its importance for CIT: realizing that the higher fulfills and corrects but does not negate the lower, the newer does not negate

---

22. Manualist tradition refers to the roughly three-hundred-year period in which Catholic priests instructed the lay faithful in matters of morality and sin from a codified set of instructions called manuals. This tradition, which was ended by the reforms of the Second Vatican Council, tended to be rigorous and rigid. For more on the Manualist Tradition see Eric M. Genilo, *John Cuthbert Ford, SJ: Moral Theologian at the End of the Manualist Era* (Washington, DC: Georgetown University Press, 2007).

23. Craig Boly, *The Road to Lonergan's Method in Theology: The Ordering of Theological Ideas* (Lanham, MD: University Press of America, 1991), 48.

24. Frederick Crowe, *Method in Theology: An Organon for Our Time* (Milwaukee: Marquette University Press, 1980), 10.

25. Ibid.

but enriches the older. Authenticity, after all, demands that one remains open to new questions for understanding and not be fixated on one's viewpoint or past insights alone.[26] Transposition is not a once-and-for-all event, but as ongoing as the method based on one's authentic interior quality or character.[27] Thus Lonergan's theology of history and long-range point of view are essentially what is needed in a Catholic university—history and perspective that integrate the old with the new and make Christian witness, fellowship, and service practical.

THE VIRTUALLY UNCONDITIONED

When Lonergan speaks of authenticity he almost always applies it to the task of interpreting the "old" in light of the "new," making the old relevant to the contemporary context. Three terms are relevant to his formulation of authenticity: *self, commitment,* and *values.* A person (self) who collaborates with others (commitment) to work together for the common good (values) is related to other members of that community by reason of their shared values. The human person is a subject or knower who experiences, understands, and judges. He or she is a doer who deliberates, evaluates, chooses, and acts and because he or she is a free and responsible subject; such doing affects, changes, and modifies both the person and the world in which the person lives. Here we identify how Lonergan changed, modified, and integrated the "old" Catholic tradition with the "new" that gives us reasons for speaking about his contribution to CIT.

1. **The Nature of Transposition**

   Although the Christian tradition has transposed the great achievements of the past before Lonergan (Augustine transposed Platonic and Neoplatonic themes and Aquinas transposed Aristotelianism and Augustine's teaching, for example), Lonergan was the first to give attention to the very nature of transposition itself and the need to understand it—a phenomenon that will come to

---

26. Tad Dunne, *Lonergan and Spirituality: Towards a Spiritual Integration* (Chicago: Loyola University Press, 1985), 61.

27. Lamb, "Lonergan's Transposition of Augustine and Aquinas," 4.

characterize the Catholic intellectual tradition (CIT). He spoke of transposition and the effort to understand its nature as a moment of authenticity and appropriation of one's own rational consciousness.[28] Authenticity is achieved in self-transcendence (going beyond oneself). Human knowing is oriented toward action in that we desire to know because we desire to act and act intelligently. One's experiencing, understanding, and judging is directed not just to knowing reality but also to creating reality, not just to what is but also to what is to be done, thereby creating and developing a personality in the process. A person's spirit of attentive, intelligent, and critical inquiry becomes for that person a responsible decision and action.[29]

2. Catholic Theology's "Turn to the Subject"

Modern philosophers like Georg F. W. Hegel (1770–1831), Søren Kierkegaard (1813–1855), Martin Heidegger (1889–1976), and Martin Buber (1881–1965), reacting against previous neglect of the subject (i.e., the human person) in the quest for truth, emphasized the subject. Catholic theology had long resisted this modern "turn to the subject" for fear that it would inevitably lead to idealism, relativism, immanentism, and neglect of the cognitive opening upon the realm of absolute transcendence.[30] Although these suspicions have not completely disappeared from Catholic thought, thanks to the efforts of Lonergan (and Karl Rahner), Catholic theology has today embraced the "turn to the subject." Lonergan points out that in trying to emphasize the objectivity of truth, older Catholic theology did not pay attention to the human person as a knower (subject). He notes that if there is, among Catholics, a widespread alienation from the dogmas of the Church, it is "not unconnected with a previous one-sidedness that so insisted on the objectivity of truth as to leave subjects and their needs out of account."[31]

---

28. See Bernard Lonergan, *Verbum: Word and Idea in Aquinas*, vol. 2 of *Collected Works*, 227.

29. Walter Conn, "The Desire of Authenticity: Conscience and Moral Conversion," in *Human Heart*, ed. Gregson, 36.

30. Doran, *Theological Foundations*, 130.

31. Lonergan, "The Subject," in *A Second Collection*, ed. Ryan and Tyrell, 71.

Long neglect had left the subject "truncated," says Longergan, "not only without but within the Church, when we find that the conditions of the possibility of significant dialogue are not grasped, when the distinction between revealed religion and myth is blurred, when the possibility of objective knowledge of God's existence and of his goodness is denied."[32] He blamed this truncation on traditional metaphysics and the according of too much primacy to Aristotelian philosophy:

> In the later Middle Ages, Aristotle's work was redis-
> covered and enthusiastically adopted by medieval
> scholars. His followers called him *Ille Philosophus* (The
> Philosopher), or "the master of them that know," and
> many accepted every word of his writings—or at least
> every word that did not contradict the Bible—as eter-
> nal truth. Fused and reconciled with Christian doctrine
> into a philosophical system known as Scholasticism,
> Aristotelian philosophy became the official philosophy
> of the Roman Catholic Church. As a result, some sci-
> entific discoveries in the Middle Ages and Renaissance
> were criticized simply because they were not found in
> Aristotle. It is one of the ironies of the history of sci-
> ence that Aristotle's writings, which in many cases were
> based on first-hand observation, were used to impede
> observational science.[33]

3. **Learning to Be Oneself**

Although existentialism has since shed more light on the study of the subject in its self-determining freedom, it still has not solved the ancient problems of cognitional theory (what one is doing when one is knowing), epistemology (how one knows that one knows), and metaphysics (what one knows). Loner-gan developed a cognitional theory (as we shall see in the next chapter) that addresses issues pertaining to how we know what we know, showing how an authentic human subject cannot

---

32. Ibid., 86.

33. "Aristotle (384–322 B.C.E.)," *http://www.ucmp.berkeley.edu/history/aristotle.html.*

brush aside the questions of epistemology, cognitional theory, and metaphysics. When he speaks of the subject, Lonergan is in effect addressing the existential question of how one can be oneself. He acknowledges in particular the existentialism of Karl Jaspers, for whom the idea of the *subject* is a relative term that can be used in a variety of ways, and for whom also the idea of being oneself was paramount.[34] Lonergan observes that for Jaspers the meaning of *subject* varies with what the subject is subject of: Grammatically the subject denotes the function of a sentence; logically the subject denotes the function in the proposition; metaphysically the subject is the recipient: matter is the subject of form, potency of act; and psychologically there is the subject in the stream of consciousness. When Lonergan speaks of the subject he is concerned mainly with the latter, i.e., the subject of the stream of consciousness that is orientated on knowing, on trying to know, and on choosing and doing.[35] It is the flow of consciousness relevant to being a person.

4. The Slipperiness of Authenticity

Lonergan shows that human authenticity is a complex business and cannot be taken for granted. He speaks of a sense in which we all live in our own worlds, with fixed boundaries and fixed ranges of interest; the extent of our knowledge and the reach of our interests fix a horizon within which we are confined. "Such confinement may result from the historical tradition within which we are born, from the limitations of the social milieu in which we were brought up, from our individual psychological aptitudes, efforts, misadventures."[36] For Lonergan, ontologically everyone is capable of an intentional self-transcendence, "of going beyond what he feels, what he imagines, what he thinks, what seems to him, to something utterly different, to what is so" because of the objectivity of truth.[37]

---

34. Bernard Lonergan, Collected Works of Bernard Lonergan: *Phenomenology and Logic: The Boston College Lectures on Mathematical Logic and Existentialism*, ed. Philip J. McShane (Toronto: University of Toronto, 2001), 234.

35. Ibid., 234–35.

36. Lonergan, "The Subject," 69.

37. Ibid., 70.

Lonergan had some affiliation with the Louvain tradition, but on his own terms. The Louvain tradition was founded in 1889 at the University of Louvain at the request of Pope Leo XIII, who wanted to revive the study of Thomism. The members of the Louvain tradition engaged the post-Kantian philosophical current that was active at the time in dialogue. Post-Kantian philosophy was critical of knowledge and denied the objectivity of truth. In denying the objectivity of truth they denied some of the truths of the Christian faith. Members of the Thomist school of the Louvain tradition used the findings of modern science to refute the post-Kantian philosophical currents and assert the objectivity of truth. While refuting the post-Kantians, Lonergan was also mindful of people on the opposite end of the spectrum (people he sometimes referred to as naïve realists and fideists) who have an exaggerated view of the objectivity of truth. Such people tend to disregard the very conditions by which truth is attained. Guarding against the post-Kantians on the one hand and those who have an exaggerated view of the objectivity of truth on the other hand, Lonergan calls his own position "critical realism." A critical realist understands that the criterion by which one arrives at truth is virtually unconditioned. Unlike the formally unconditioned, which has no conditions whatsoever, the virtually unconditioned has conditions. That which is virtually unconditioned can be said to involve three elements: (1) a conditioned, (2) a link between the conditioned and its conditions, and (3) the fulfillment of the conditions. Something is virtually unconditioned when all conditions have been fulfilled.[38] Lonergan's point is that although truth is objective it does not exist independent of the knowing person. He cautions against those who get too fixated or too preoccupied with the objectivity of truth even to the extent of disregarding the very conditions (conception, gestational parturition, etc.) that make truth possible. The truth one seeks in CIT is not formally unconditioned, but virtually unconditioned in that the truth of CIT is attained only through a laborious process of conception, gestation, and parturition of an authentic subject.

---

38. Hillary Mooney, *The Liberation of Consciousness: Bernard Lonergan's Theological Foundations in Dialogue with the Theological Aesthetics of Hans Urs von Balthasar* (Frankfurt Am Main: Verlag Josef Knecht, 1992), 31.

HOW AUTHENTICITY FURTHERS CIT

The authenticity achieved in self-transcendence, far from remaining only in the order of knowing (cognitive level), in the final analysis has to become moral. In other words, authenticity results in a way of living. Because we can ask questions and answer them and live by the answers, we can effect in our living a moral self-transcendence.[39] "My 'knowing' is genuinely cognitional exactly in so far as it is authentic. Noetic objectivity is functionally identical with authentic 'noetic' subjectivity. My 'cognitional' performance is true precisely to the extent that my experiencing is attentive, my understanding is intelligent, my judging is reasonable, and my evaluating is responsible."[40] An intellectually authentic person is one who not only experiences, understands, and judges but also deliberates, evaluates, chooses, and acts. One makes oneself what he or she is going to be in a free and responsible action. "Such doing, at first sight, affects, modifies, changes the world of objects. But even more it affects the subject himself. For human doing is free and responsible. Within it is contained the reality of morals, of building up or destroying character, of achieving personality or failing in that task."[41] In practical terms, this means that a person who has taken steps to find out answers to questions of ultimate relevance will act in accordance with his or her beliefs. Not even the threat of death can deter such a person because he or she is morally self-transcendent. In Christianity, some of the early Christians who chose martyrdom rather than recant their faith are examples of intellectually authentic persons. Other religious and spiritual traditions might cite their own examples of intellectually authentic persons willing to undergo great hardship and even death in order to act according to their beliefs.

Lonergan was not only concerned with the authenticity of individuals but also with the authenticity of the tradition of which the individual is a part, understanding that if left unchecked, unauthenticity can spread and even become a tradition.[42] A good example

---

39. Lonergan, *Method in Theology*, 104.

40. Michael Vertin, "Gender, Science, and Cognitional Conversion," in *Lonergan and Feminism*, ed. Cynthia Crysdale (Toronto: University of Toronto Press, 1994), 56.

41. Lonergan, "The Subject," 79.

42. Lonergan, *Method in Theology*, 299.

would be the story of the monk who had a cat; because the cat always ran around and distracted the monks during prayer he instructed his disciples to always tie the cat before prayer. It became an accepted practice to tie the cat before prayer. Years later the monk died and the monks still tied the cat before prayer. And years later the cat died and the monastery bought a new cat to be tied before prayer. It became a tradition, and no one questioned how the practice began. This is an unauthentic tradition.

Let us take another concrete example from the teaching of St. Thomas Aquinas, which is integral to CIT. Aquinas accepted many of the teachings of Aristotle, "baptizing" in the process some truths that he saw in pagan philosophy. Aristotle's philosophical system led him to the conclusion that women were, in effect, made from defective genes. Aquinas accepted this Aristotelian notion of the inferiority of women. Now, one can be dedicated to Thomism without accepting Aquinas's teaching on the inferiority of women, as many Thomists have done. It takes authenticity to make the distinction— that Aquinas might be right on many other Aristotelian issues, but the Aristotelian view of women was based on crude science. So a person can be authentic within an undifferentiated or partially differentiated consciousness (as in the example of the monks that tied a cat before prayer), but unauthentic within the realms of meaning, just like a person can be authentically faithful to an unauthentic tradition.[43] When a tradition is inauthentic the original (Christian) message is then watered down and recast "into terms and meanings that fit into the assumptions and convictions of those that have dodged the issue of radical conversion."[44]

Let us take as an example the creation story in Genesis. It is part of the Christian tradition that God created the earth for humans to enjoy. But some Christians have wrongly interpreted the injunction "fill the earth and subdue it" (Gen.1:28) as a command to dominate. This kind of interpretation used to be very common and has contributed to environmental degradation.

So Lonergan in effect speaks of two types of authenticity: the authenticity of the tradition and authenticity of the individual who is part of the tradition. Whether of the individual or tradition, authenticity is dialectical in character. It is "not some pure quality, some serene freedom from all oversights, all misunderstanding, all mistakes, all sins. Rather it consists in a withdrawal from unauthenticity, and the withdrawal is never a permanent achievement. It is ever precarious, ever to be achieved afresh, ever in great part a matter of uncovering still more oversights, acknowledging still further failures to understand, correcting still more mistakes, repenting more and more deeply hidden sins."[45] We might say the same thing of CIT that it has a dialectical character in that it is ever more precarious. CIT stands or falls on authenticity. A person who contributes to CIT is one who, among other things, preserves and transcends the riches of the past by helping to uncover oversights, failures, and biases in the tradition and adds to and complements the tradition by helping to correct them.

TRANSPOSITION AS GUIDE TO ACADEMIC VOCATION IN A CATHOLIC UNIVERSITY

In light of Lonergan's work on transposition that interprets the old in light of the new, how might a given cultural value, such as the American value of right to autonomy and academic freedom, be blended with a well-articulated philosophy of education that accommodates the values of Catholicism?[46] There is, according to Frederick Lawrence, in the concrete and practical programs of *Insight* and *Method in Theology*, a framework for healing the fragmented and alienated modern university and a strategy for creative collaboration within the university.[47]

> In universities today education for specialized professionals (technocrats or bureaucrats) has all but supplanted genuinely liberal education; and education for careers has

---

45. Ibid., 252.

46. Dumestre, "Contribution," 3.

47. Frederick Lawrence, "Lonergan as a Political Theologian," in *Religion in Context: Recent Studies in Lonergan*, ed. Timothy Fallon and Philip Riley (Lanham, MD: University Press of America, 1988), 19.

practically displaced education for citizenship. Anyone who knows what goes on in universities today cannot but agree that they have become seminaries for what Max Weber called "specialists without spirit or vision and voluptuaries without heart." If there is a possibility for a revival of liberal and liberating education that is not simply anachronistically oblivious of the claims of authentic and needed specialization, I believe that it resides in the virtualities of Lonergan's method. For just as *Insight* and *Method* specify the conditions for theology as a principle for shaping and transforming culture, so, too, can they be used heuristically for determining the implementation of the core of liberal and liberating education for citizenship.[48]

The process of ascent in education will require, in addition to intellectual, moral, and religious conversion, "first, an individual and communal process of purification and enlightenment; and second, the fostering of the breakthrough experiences that are conditions for real purification and enlightenment."[49]

In Lonergan's program, the supposed conflict between revealed truth and the truth attained through "democratic ideals" and "free inquiry" cannot be sustained in one who is authentic, because human understanding is systematic. In an April 1959 lecture to the Society for Theological Studies at Nottingham University, Lonergan offered five precepts or rules that guide learning: (1) understand (2) understand systematically (3) reverse counterpositions (4) develop positions and (5) accept the responsibility of judgment.[50]

The precept "understand systematically" means that understanding is the ideal goal of learning. The "ideal goal of understanding is completeness. Common sense operates within a cultural horizon. It settles for a mode and measure of understanding that suffice to enable one to live intelligently. But human intelligence wants more; it heads for the complete explanation of all phenomena; it would

48. Ibid. See also Max Weber, *The Protestant Ethic and the Spirit of Capitalism*, trans. Talcott Parsons (New York: Charles Scribner and Sons, 1958), 182.

49. Ibid., 20.

50. The content of the lecture is published in *Philosophical and Theological Papers 1958–1964*, 29–53.

understand the universe. It distinguishes endlessly; but it does so only to relate intelligibly; and ideally the network of relations is to embrace everything."[51] Thus when Lonergan speaks of understanding as systematic he is speaking of the complete network of relations that makes intelligible every aspect of the concrete universe.[52]

Reality is complex. "A cultural tradition will contain very many things, and each of them may be authentic in some ways and unauthentic in others. Still, this complexity is not the main issue. That lies in the fact that merging horizons are a matter not only of the present moving into the past but also of the past becoming alive in the present and challenging the assumptions both of the individual scholar and of the tradition that has nurtured him."[53] There is a sense in which this relates to the Catholic educator. A Catholic educator operating within CIT at a Catholic college or university will say to students: come to know your own mind and your own heart; come to live your own life on the basis of an affirmation of the exigencies of your own intelligence, rationality, and existential openness and transcendence.[54] This is true because the cultural matrix with which a contemporary Christian educator mediates the significance and role of Christian religion can no longer be parochial; it must be global.[55] Knowledge is not fixed, but admits of development. The possibility of development is the possibility of revising earlier views, and the possibility of revising earlier views gives continued existence to the structure itself.[56] The empirical notions of culture and developments in the modern world have combined to raise new questions concerning the intelligibility of doctrines.[57]

Intelligibility of what has been affirmed as true by the Catholic tradition is, for Lonergan, the task of the functional specialty systematics. Drawing from the Augustinian-Thomist tradition, Lonergan

---

51. Ibid., 35.

52. Ibid.

53. Ibid., 60.

54. Doran, *Psychic Conversion and Theological Foundations II*, 55–56.

55. Doran, *Theological Foundations*, 4.

56. Lonergan, *Method in Theology*, 343.

57. Matthew Ogilvie, *Faith Seeking Understanding: The Functional Specialty, "Systematics," in Bernard Lonergan's Method in Theology* (Milwaukee: Marquette University Press, 2001), 9.

accepts the idea, employed by the First Vatican Council, that reason illumined by faith, when it inquires diligently, piously, and soberly, can with God's help attain a highly fruitful understanding of the mysteries of faith both from the analogy of what it naturally knows and from the interconnection of the mysteries with one another and with a person's last end. The end of human life, according to the Christian tradition, is beatitude (happiness or union with God). The promotion of such understanding of the mysteries of Christian faith is the principal function of systematics. Systematics, however, presupposes doctrines; its aim is "not to increase certitude but to promote understanding. It does not seek to establish the facts. It strives for some inkling of how it could possibly be that the facts are what they are. Its task is to take over facts, established in doctrines, and to attempt to work them into an assimilable whole."[58]

Lonergan's insistence on functional specialization, especially the distinction between systematics and doctrines, far from being a novelty, has solid basis in Catholic intellectual tradition, particularly during the Middle Ages. In every field of inquiry "there comes a time when a scattered set of discoveries coalesces into a rounded whole. Pythagoras established his theorem long before Euclid wrote his *Elements*. Galileo and Kepler established laws before Newtonian mechanics deduced Kepler's laws from a set of principles. Much important work was done in chemistry prior to the creation of the periodic table. But it is only from the moment when a Euclid, a Newton, a Mendeleev comes along with a system that a subject has a well-defined existence, that it can be treated as a unity, that it can possess a method of its own."[59] Functional specialization is, therefore, a return to the type of systematic theology found in Aquinas's *Summa Contra Gentiles* and *Summa Theologiae*. "Both are systematic expressions of a wide-ranging understanding of the truths concerning God and man."[60] They aim at understanding and present a single unified whole, not two separate parts that tend to overlook the primacy of conversion and overemphasize the significance of proof.[61]

---

58. Lonergan, *Method in Theology*, 343.

59. Lonergan, *Philosophical and Theological Papers 1958–1964*, 44.

60. Lonergan, *Method in Theology*, 340.

61. Ibid.

Lonergan cites the decrees of the Fourth Lateran Council and Vatican I to show that there is no theological or philosophical system that can fully master the mystery of God. According to the former, "between creator and creature no similarity can be noted without a greater dissimilarity being noted" (DS 806); whereas, according to the latter, "the divine mysteries so exceed created intellect that, even when given in revelation and received by faith, they remain covered over by the very veil of faith itself" (DS 3016).[62] This means for Lonergan that there is an exception to the scholastic adage: *nihil amatum nisi preacognitum* (nothing precedes love except knowledge) because it is not human knowledge that conditions us to God's gift of love, but rather God's gift of love precedes our knowledge of God—an orientation toward an unknown.[63]

> There is a still further consequence of the shift from a faculty psychology to intentionality analysis.[64] It is that the basic terms and relations of systematic theology will be not metaphysical, as in medieval theology, but psychological. As had been worked out in our chapters on method, on religion, and on foundations, general basic terms name conscious and intentional operations. General basic relations name elements in the dynamic structure linking operations and generating states. Special basic terms name God's gift of his love and Christian witness. Derived terms and relations name the objects known in operations and correlative to states. . . .
>
> Finally, the approach eliminates any authoritarian basis for method. One can find out for oneself and in oneself just what one's conscious and intentional operations are and how they are related to one another. One can discover for oneself and in oneself why it is that performing such and such operations in such and such manners constitutes human

---

62. Ibid., 341.

63. Ibid.

64. Lonergan at first followed Aquinas's faculty psychology (derived from Aristotle), which speaks of intellect and will, theoretical and practical reason, etc. He later effected a shift in his intellectual journey, and came to speak of levels of intentional consciousness: experiencing, understanding, judging, and deciding.

knowing. Once one has achieved that, one is no longer dependent on someone else in selecting one's method and in carrying it out. One is on one's own.[65]

Lonergan understands that when mysteries of God are expressed in dogmatic formulas such formulations are problematic. The scholastics of the Middle Ages made a distinction between order of discovery and order of teaching, Lonergan appeals to this distinction. "Not only does the order of teaching or exposition differ from the order of discovery but also the terms and relations of systematic thought express a development of understanding over and above the understanding had either from a simple inspection or from an erudite exegesis of the original doctrinal sources."[66] Lonergan again appeals to the decree of Vatican I to show that the understanding of dogmas "grows and advances down the ages" (DS 3020).[67] Doctrines therefore need systematics; no repetition of formulas can take the place of understanding.[68] "Doctrines are concerned to state clearly and distinctly the religious community's confession of the mysteries so hidden in God that man could not know them if they had not been revealed by God. Assent to such doctrines is the assent of faith, and that assent is regarded by religious people as firmer than any other."[69] Systematics helps bring the understanding of doctrine to the level of one's times.[70] "If one does not attain, on the level of one's age, an understanding of the religious realities in which one believes, one will be simply at the mercy of the psychologists, the sociologists, the philosophers, that will not hesitate to tell the believers what it really is in which they believe."[71]

Thus doctrines and systematic are two instances of truth and two instances of understanding. Both aim at understanding the truth, although they do so in different ways. "Doctrine aims at a clear and distinct affirmation of religious realities: its principal concern is

---

65. Lonergan, *Method in Theology*, 343–44.

66. Ibid., 346.

67. Ibid., 347.

68. Ibid., 351.

69. Ibid., 349.

70. Ibid., 350.

71. Ibid., 351.

the truth of such an affirmation; its concern to understand is limited to the clarity and distinctness of its affirmation. On the other hand, systematic aims at an understanding of the religious realities affirmed by doctrines. It wants its understanding to be true, for it is not a pursuit of misunderstanding. At the same time, it is fully aware that its understanding is bound to be imperfect, merely analogous, commonly no more than probable."[72] While dogmas may be permanent, the mysteries revealed, which the Church defines, can still in the course of time be better understood. "For Aquinas' thought on grace and freedom and his thought on cognitional theory and on the Trinity were genuine achievements of the human spirit. Such achievement has a permanence of its own. It can be improved upon. It can be inserted in larger and richer contexts."[73]

Since the natural objective of our intellectual desire to know is the concrete universe, theology can succeed as a systematic understanding only if it is assigned a determinate position in the totality of human knowledge, with determinate relations to all other branches,"[74] i.e., accorded a unique place in the natural and human sciences. "This further step was taken by Aquinas. Where Bonaventure had been content to think of this world and all it contains only as symbols that lead the mind ever up to God, Aquinas took over the physics, biology, psychology, and metaphysics of Aristotle to acknowledge not symbols but natural realities and corresponding departments of natural and human science."[75]

REVERSING COUNTER POSITIONS

Lonergan's idea of the authentic existential subject that is good or bad by his or her choices and actions was his way of calling for authenticity in Catholic theology and in the tradition as a whole. The attainment of truth and value is a personal as well as a communal achievement. Persons who engage in the study of theology or religion do so to understand the origins and sources of a religion

---

72. Ibid., 349.

73. Ibid., 352.

74. Lonergan, *Philosophical and Theological Papers 1958–1964*, 45.

75. Ibid., 45–46.

and communicate the meaning and significance of that religion to the culture in which they direct their concern.[76] "Theologians are, therefore, mediators between the riches of the past and the riches of the present. But that mediating must also be a discerning and an evaluating, for not everything in the past of a tradition is something to be treasured, sometimes far from it, nor is everything in the present culture something to be treasured, again sometimes far from it."[77] A Catholic educator or theologian with a classicist mind set,[78] for example, is wont to lapse into inauthenticity because classicism minimizes the achievements of Catholic tradition and stifles its creativity.[79]

Authenticity calls for intellectual conversion. In our five precepts or rules mentioned earlier, the third precept calls for reversal of counterpositions and the fourth for the development of positions. Both precepts pertain to the authenticity of the individual or the person's own personal development: "My first rule was: Understand. In virtue of that first rule I conclude that all genuine discoveries must be retained. My second rule was: Understand systematically. In virtue of that second rule I divide the formulations of discoveries into two classes: positions and counterpositions. Positions are formulations that can be retained unchanged within the new way. Counterpositions are formulations that have to be recast before they can be made coherent with the new way."[80]

Lonergan had no doubt that the old way of dogmatic theology was out of date. The old way was based on proof-texting—making propositional statements of faith and finding evidence from Scripture and Tradition (writings of the church fathers and ecumenical councils) to justify them. The empirical notion of culture renders obsolete the old classicist normative view in which there was *de jure* one culture for all peoples. Culture, as was then conceived, was understood in terms of mastery of Greek and Latin, classical literature and art,

---

76. Vernon Gregson, "Theological Method and Theological Collaboration I," in *Human Heart*, ed. Gregson, 74.

77. Ibid., 75.

78. Classicism is the idea that there is only one culture, which is permanent and universal, and that everyone must aspire to the ideals of this one culture.

79. Ogilvie, *Faith Seeking Understanding*, 23.

80. Lonergan, *Philosophical and Theological Papers 1958–1964*, 37.

and the so-called perennial philosophy. But by drawing from anthropology and critical history, Lonergan reconceived culture empirically as a set of meanings and values that inform the way of life of a community, a function of the development of human consciousness.[81] There is no longer one normative culture. It is an incredible conceit to suppose that one's culture is the one and only uniform and universal culture. Rather cultures are many and varied, each with its own notable ideals and deficiencies. "Cultures can decline rapidly, but they develop only slowly, for the development is a matter of coming to understand new meanings and coming to accept higher values. Moreover, any notable culture has a long history: it has borrowed from other cultures; it has adapted what it borrowed into its new context; it has effected the development of its own patrimony."[82] Cultural advance is rooted in differentiation and cultural regression in a reversion to unmediated or less mediated compactness.[83] In other words, one must learn to make distinctions based on where the best available evidence leads. Not to be open to inquiry is to revert to primitiveness. This is what it means to be a historical person, for all human actions occur within a context of culture. Cultures have histories, they develop and decline, providing the matrix within which a person develops and finds meanings and values. "The culture that flows from undifferentiated consciousness is either archaic and mythical or regressive, depending on whether or not the differentiation of various realms of meaning is part of the heritage that it could have appropriated."[84] Catholic philosophy and theology are matters, not just of revelation and faith but also of culture, for both have been fully and deeply involved in classical culture. "The breakdown of classical culture and, at last in our day, the manifest comprehensiveness and exclusiveness of modern culture confront Catholic philosophy and Catholic theology with the gravest problems, impose upon them mountainous tasks, invite them to Herculean labors."[85]

---

81. Bernard Lonergan, "Revolution in Catholic Theology," in *A Second Collection*, ed. Ryan and Tyrell, 232.

82. Ibid.

83. Doran, *Psychic Conversion and Theological Foundations II*, 33.

84. Ibid.

85. Lonergan, "Dimensions of Meaning," 266.

As the Catholic view of faith makes theological understanding a grasp of converging lines that focus upon uncomprehended mystery, so too it places human wisdom and judgment within a context of communicated divine wisdom and divine judgment. As the Catholic theologian accepts a divine revelation, so also he believes in its providential preservation. Nonetheless, this does not liberate him from also accepting the responsibility of making judgments of his own. We learn from Geoffrey of Fontaines that, in the 1290s, the theological students at the University of Paris believed they would be excommunicated if they read the writings of Thomas Aquinas. In 1323, forty-nine years after his death, Thomas Aquinas became St. Thomas Aquinas. Two years afterwards the Archbishop of Paris officially removed the ban against him. Clearly, if today Aquinas holds a preeminent position in Catholic theology, it is because he had the daring that is needed to understand, and the courage to make far-reaching judgments on the basis of his daring understanding. Moreover, if the decisions Aquinas made were momentous, the element of decisiveness is not removed when one turns from the man of genius to the ordinary honest worker. Everyone engaged in theology as something more than an exercise in repetitiveness has to make decisions and . . . would be deceiving himself if he thought that there existed some automatic technique onto which he could shift the burden.[86]

At times Lonergan spoke joyfully of the changes taking place in Catholic theology and talked about them in terms of revolution:[87] "More rapidly in the fields of patristic and medieval studies, more slowly in the field of Scripture, there gradually have been accepted and put into practice new techniques in investigating the course of history, new procedures in interpreting texts, new and more exacting requirements in the study of languages."[88] These innovations are necessary to eliminate the old style dogmatic theology and its normative conception of culture:

86. Lonergan, *Philosophical and Theological Papers 1958–1964*, 52–53.
87. Lonergan, "Revolution in Catholic Theology," 232.
88. Ibid., 231.

For the old style dogmatic theologian was expected: (1) to qualify his theses by appealing to papal and conciliar documents from any period in church history and (2) to prove his thesis by arguing from the Old Testament and the New, from the Greek, Latin, and Syriac Fathers, from the Byzantine and medieval Scholastics, and from all the subsequent generations of theologians.[89]

The problems that have occurred in Catholic theology are not solved simply by assenting to the propositions that are true and rejecting the propositions that are false. Rather, it is a matter of intellectual conversion, of appropriating one's own rational self-consciousness, of finding one's way behind the propositions, proofs, judgments, and thoughts of our forebears who contributed, in their own way, to the rich Catholic treasure we call CIT. Without self-appropriation and the critical appraisal it generates one may repeat all that Augustine says of *veritas* (truth) and all that Aquinas says of *esse* (being) without still raising oneself to their level.[90]

There is a difference, in other words, between the reality that is presented and the reality that one encounters, the thought that is presented and what one actually thinks for oneself. This explains why Lonergan conceives method of inquiry as a set of related and recurrent operations cumulatively advancing toward an ideal goal.[91] A theologian discerns, evaluates, and mediates the riches of the past and the riches of the present by following the eight functional specialties that are functionally interdependent: research, interpretation, history, dialectic, foundations, doctrines, systematics, and communications. "Functional specialties are intrinsically related to one another. They are successive parts of one and the same process. The earlier parts are incomplete without the later. The later presuppose the earlier and complement

---

89. Ibid., 231–32.

90. Lonergan, *Philosophical and Theological Papers 1958–1964*, 38. The editors of the *Collected Works* note how Lonergan regularly relates Augustine's *veritas* to Aquinas's *esse*. Augustine developed the notion of judgment as fundamental in knowing, the *veritas*, and Aquinas added a metaphysical equivalent, the *esse* in the composition of the finite being. For more see Bernard Lonergan, *Topics in Education*, ed. R. M. Doran and F. E. Crowe (Toronto: University of Toronto Press, 1993), 170ff. Lonergan, *Method in Theology*, 125.

91. Ibid., *Method in Theology*, 125.

them."[92] One does not necessarily engage in any full extent in all of the tasks, not only because the field of religion has become too extensive but also because theology is a collaborative endeavor.[93] The functional specialties, therefore, serve as a challenge to the members of the Catholic family, educators and theologians in particular, "to broaden their horizons to the whole related set of questions that alone can lead one from the riches of the past (research) to that kind of action which responsibly creates the future (communications)."[94]

BULVERISM: A THREAT TO CIT

A willful and deliberate refusal to realize oneself in transcendence imposes on a person a different kind of burden: inauthenticity and alienation, two major factors that can undermine CIT. In an insightful essay in honor of Lonergan, Hugo Meynell recounts the story of Ezekiel Bulver, a fictional savant of the nineteenth century, insufficiently known to social scientists.[95] In this story, the turning point in Bulver's life came when Bulver heard his father trying to prove the Pythagorean theorem to his mother that the square of the hypotenuse of a right triangle is equal in area to the sum of the squares of the other two sides. Bulver's mother won the argument by declaring, "You only say that because you're a man." According to Meynell, "The young Bulver realized that he need never again attend to the tiresome question of whether the arguments presented to him were sound or unsound; if he wanted to dismiss them, he had only to direct attention to the psychological history or socioeconomic circumstances of those who advanced them."[96] Meynell observes that Christians are guilty of Bulverism when they too readily attribute opposing arguments to sin.

Bulverism illustrates the tension inherent in every human person between knowing and doing, the desire to know, to understand,

---

92. Ibid., 126.

93. Gregson, "Theological Method and Theological Collaboration I," 75.

94. Ibid., 79.

95. Hugo Meynell, "Values in Social Science: Foundations and Applications," in *Religion in Context*, ed. Fallon and Riley, 23. The story of Bulver comes from C. S. Lewis, *Undeceptions*, ed. Walter Hooper (London: Bles, 1970), 223–28.

96. Ibid.

and to come to grips with contradictions in oneself and one's social milieu. The desire to know includes all that one knows as well as all that can be known. Until one arrives at a complete set of answers to a complete set of questions there will always be unresolved questions arising from the true or false judgments one has already attained.[97] Bulverism is a counterpoint to the authenticity that CIT requires. It is inauthenticity or alienation from oneself, which is destructive of both the person and community. Alienation is a person's disregard for the transcendental precepts: be attentive, be intelligent, be reasonable, and be responsible. It is a refusal to seek self-transcendence. This alienation from oneself often leads one to adopt misguided remedies, finding justification in divergent meanings or ideologies that corrupt the social good and turn progress into cumulative decline.[98] "As common meaning constitutes community, so divergent meaning divides it. . . . The serious division is the one that arises from the presence and absence of intellectual, moral, or religious conversion. For a man is his true self inasmuch as he is self-transcending."[99] Lonergan also speaks of alienation as "sin" because it alienates one from one's authentic being, which is self-transcendence, and justifies itself by ideology that in itself is destructive of community.[100]

In *Insight* Lonergan introduces the notion of "basic sin," which is a threat to CIT. Basic sin is quite different from physical or moral evil, and is a form of alienation. As intelligently and rationally conscious, the human person grasps and affirms what one ought to do and what one ought not to do. Basic sin is at the root of the irrational in a person's search for rational self-consciousness.[101] It is the human failure to choose a morally obligatory course of action when choosing such an action is demanded, or the failure to reject a morally

97. Nancy Ring, "Alienation and Reconciliation: The Theological Methods of Paul Tillich and Bernard Lonergan," in *Creativity and Method: Essays in Honor of Bernard Lonergan, SJ*, ed. Matthew Lamb (Milwaukee: Marquette University Press, 1981), 252.

98. Lonergan, *Method in Theology*, 55.

99. Ibid., 357.

100. Ibid., 364.

101. Bernard Lonergan, Collected Works of Bernard Lonergan: *Insight: A Study of Human Understanding*, eds. Frederick E. Crowe and Robert M. Doran (Toronto: University of Toronto, 1992), 689 [p.666 in the 1957 edition].

reprehensible course of action when such rejection is demanded.[102] It is the "choice of vacuum rather than value, and that vacuum destroys."[103] Basic sin is a result of the failure to reconcile knowing and doing. If a person wills, according to Lonergan, "he does what he ought; if he wills, he diverts his attention from proposals to do what he ought not; but if he fails to will, then the obligatory course of action is not executed; again if he fails to will, his attention remains on illicit proposals; the incompleteness of their intelligibility and the incoherence of their apparent reasonableness are disregarded."[104] Basic sin is therefore a contraction of consciousness that leads to performance of wrong action.[105] It is a form of alienation from oneself "and from the possibility of union with others and ultimately with God to the extent that one fails to realize one's *eros* [drive] toward knowledge and value. Alienation, for Lonergan, is experienced when one separates oneself from one's most fundamental orientation, when one engages, actively or passively, in the flight from understanding."[106] A person's transcendental subjectivity is mutilated or abolished unless that person is stretching toward the intelligible, the unconditioned, the good of value.[107] Accordingly, what is termed moral evil is nothing but the consequences of basic sin, the human freedom to frustrate oneself and deprive oneself of the possibility of realizing oneself in self-transcendence.[108] "From the basic sin of not willing what one ought to will, therefore, follow moral evils of omission and a heightening of the temptation in oneself or others to further basic sins. From the basic sin of not setting aside illicit proposals, there follows their execution and a more positive heightening of tension and temptation in oneself or in one's social milieu."[109]

---

102. Ibid.

103. Vernon Gregson, "The Faces of Evil and Our Response: Ricoeur, Lonergan, Moore" in *Religion in Context*, ed. Fallon and Riley, 135.

104. Lonergan, *Insight*, 689 [p. 666 in the 1957 edition].

105. Ibid.

106. Ring, "Alienation and Reconciliation," 256.

107. Lonergan, *Method in Theology*, 103.

108. Ring, "Alienation and Reconciliation," 256.

109. Lonergan, *Insight*, 666.

Basic sin is not an event, not something that positively occurs, but a failure to take a deliberate, responsible, and "reasonable response to an obligatory motive."[110] Basic sin is analogous to the process that led to the crucifixion of Jesus: "The refusal of Jesus' crucifiers of the personal transformation to which they were challenged by his message and his person is precisely what effected the crucifixion. Put simply, to respond to him they would have had to break through the categories which bound them, and they chose not to."[111]

CONCLUSION

Lonergan used his vocation as a Christian thinker to further the Catholic intellectual project. He made an immense contribution to CIT primarily because of his intellectual authenticity, integrating the old with the new. Intellectual authenticity was not just something he wrote about, but more fundamentally something he lived. He realized the dangers of classical culture to the Catholic tradition and worked indefatigably to bring this danger to an end, realizing that classical culture overlooked dimensions of human reality that have been brought to light, thematized, and elaborated by the empirical sciences. One way through which he overcame classicism was through renewal—not renewal as was understood in some Catholic circles at the time as "a return to the olden times of pristine virtue and deep wisdom," but renewal in John XXIII's sense of *aggiornamento*, bringing things up to date[112] (a requisite demand of authenticity). He knew that if Catholic education was to be brought up to date then it must have fallen behind the times. He wrote that to know what is to be done to bring it up to date "we must ascertain when it began to fall behind the times, in what respects it got out of touch, in what respects it failed to meet the issues and effect the developments that long ago were due and now are long overdue."[113] To know what to do and choose to do nothing is to be guilty of basic sin, a contraction of

---

110. Ibid., 667.

111. Gregson, "Faces of Evil," 135–36.

112. Bernard Lonergan, "Theology in its New Context," in *A Second Collection*, ed. Ryan and Tyrell, 55.

113. Ibid.

consciousness antithetical to the demands of authenticity. Authenticity "is not some pure quality, some serene freedom from all oversights, all misunderstanding, all mistakes, all sins. Rather, it consists in a withdrawal from unauthenticity, and the withdrawal is never a permanent achievement. It is ever precarious, ever to be achieved afresh, ever in great part a matter of uncovering still more oversights, acknowledging still further failures to understand, correcting still more mistakes, repenting more and more deeply hidden sins."[114]

Lonergan's recipe for intellectual authenticity is critical self-appropriation, which he saw as an adequate response to the problems of CIT. His concern was essentially a search for what it means to be oneself. "While it is true that the verbal expressions of the minds of great men shorten our labors, that like pygmies we stand on their shoulders, there can be an element of illusion regarding just how much shorter our labors are to be, just how authentic we stand."[115] In the human quest for autonomy the critical point is reached when one finds out for oneself that it is up to oneself to decide what to make of oneself.[116]

To be oneself is to seek that which is private and intimate, which at once is psychological, sociological, historical, philosophic, theological, religious, ascetic, and even mystical, because a person is all and involved in all.[117] Being oneself is a *Besinnung*, a becoming aware, a growth in self-consciousness, and a heightening of one's self appropriation.[118] What then is it to be oneself? For Lonergan *oneself* is the irreducibly individual element from which springs the choices of the decisive person. "What springs from the source is free; for it one is responsible. What results from that source is not only the sequence of activities but also the character of the man, what he is, the second nature, the essence or quasi-essence by which precariously one is what one is."[119] This is for Lonergan the meaning of the

114. Lonergan, *Method in Theology*, 252.

115. Philip McShane, "Systematics, Communications, Actual Contexts," in *Religion in Context,* ed. Fallon and Riley, 62.

116. Lonergan, *Philosophical and Theological Papers 1965–1980*, 315.

117. Ibid., 313–14.

118. Ibid., 314.

119. Lonergan, *Phenomenology and Logic*, 240.

existential subject that exists, the concrete individual, the *cor ad cor loquitor* (heart speaks to the heart) of Newman—a person who takes risks, freely chooses, and makes decisions that change his or her situation and those of others for good.[120]

Further Reading

Lonergan, Bernard. *A Third Collection: Papers by Bernard J. F. Lonergan SJ*. Edited by Frederick E. Crowe. Mahwah, New York: Paulist Press, 1985.

MacIntyre, Alasdair. *After Virtue*. Notre Dame, IN: Notre Dame University, 1981.

Metz, Johannes B. *Theology of the World*. Translated by William Glen-Doepel. New York: Herder and Herder, 1969.

Morelli, Mark. "Obstacles to the Implementation of Lonergan's Solution to the Contemporary Crisis of Meaning." In *The Importance of Insight: Essays in Honor of Michael Vertin*, edited by John Liptay, Jr. and David Liptay, 35. Toronto: University of Toronto Press, 2007.

Morelli, Mark, and Elizabeth Morelli. *The Lonergan Reader*. Toronto: University of Toronto, 1997.

---

120. Ibid.

CHAPTER 6

Understanding
and Learning Styles

Chapter 5 addressed the problem of authenticity in the intellectual appeal of Catholicism, i.e., how to be an autonomous person who makes a free and firm decision. Authenticity is a philosophical problem for experts in educational psychology to this day. In this chapter we explore Bernard Lonergan's thought on the subject by comparing it to that of the renowned contemporary specialist in human cognition and education, Howard Gardner. In working to bring CIT in line with modern science, Lonergan observed that the theology studied in a Catholic university is influenced by developments in psychology and the behavioral and social sciences.[1] His insistence that this influence be mutual—that theology can influence these sciences and incorporate what they contribute to learning—is part of his effort to vitalize CIT.

INTEGRATING DIVERSE LEARNING STYLES

Modern discussions about education in general are mired in parochial "debates that array one educational philosophy against another—traditionalists versus progressives, proponents of phonics

---

1. Donna Teevan, "Tradition and Innovation at Catholic Universities: Ideas from Bernard Lonergan," *Catholic Education* 7 (2004): 308–19, at 316.

versus advocates of 'whole language.'"[2] These debates, while not unimportant, skirt the most fundamental question,[3] lending credence to the claim that the history of educational innovations is littered with half-baked ideas.[4] Gardner's groundbreaking work, *Frames of Mind*, wherein he launched his theory of Multiple Intelligences (MI),[5] has since occupied a central place in educational reform movements worldwide. In this seminal work, Gardner broadens the scope of human potentials beyond the confines of the unitary concept of general intelligence (IQ score) to propose eight different intelligences.[6] Multiple intelligences refutes the idea that IQ alone should be the measure for success.[7] Gardner's theory has found popular support among educationists and has been effective in improving educational outcomes and personal achievement. Its popularity and increased acceptance has led to a fundamental reconsideration of the essential truth of the IQ concept.[8]

The IQ test has been hotly contested since its inception and development by Alfred Binet. Opposition to the test intensified after the 1970s.[9] The debate has centered on issues like: What is

---

2. Howard Gardner, *The Disciplined Mind: What All Students Should Understand* (New York: Simon and Schuster, 1999), 15. In hindsight, this chapter belongs to an old tradition of comparison that does not fit into the new context of *Method in Theology*'s view of Comparison; see Bernard Lonergan, *Method in Theology* (Toronto: University of Toronto Press, 1996), 250. At Philip McShane's suggestion, I leave it as a challenge to the reader to move into broad questions about the success of the old style as compared to the new scientific comparative work made possible by Lonergan's canons of hermeneutics. On the new view see Philip McShane, "The Future of Functional History," *www.philipmcshane.ca*, Fuse 15.

3. Gardner, *Disciplined Mind*, 15. Education, for Gardner, should be the education of all human beings. Debate on education should seek to answer why every society should devote monetary and human resources to the education of its young.

4. Branton Shearer, "Multiple Intelligences Theory after Twenty Years," *Teachers College Record* 106, no. 1 (2004): 2.

5. Howard Gardner, *Frames of Mind: The Theory of Multiple Intelligences* (New York: Basic Books, 1983).

6. Discussed below.

7. Pinar Ozdemir et. al., "Enhancing Learning through Multiple Intelligences," *Journal of Biological Education* 40, no. 2 (2006): 74.

8. Shearer, "Multiple Intelligences Theory after Twenty Years," 2.

9. Leona E. Tyler, "Testing the Test: What Tests Don't Measure," *Journal of Counseling and Development* 63 (1984): 48–50, at 48.

being tested? What, if anything, is measured? How is it measured? There is also the controversy regarding how intelligence is defined. "IQ tests do not purport to measure intelligence the way a ruler measures height (absolutely), but rather the way a race measures speed (relatively); IQ is described as a 'quotient' because, originally, it represented the ratio between a person's 'mental age' and actual chronological age. Likewise, IQ tests are generally designed to assess meaningfully learning discrepancies and deficiencies in comparison to relatively homogenous cultural groups."[10] But the test cannot measure unique characteristics of individuals, it only measures traits common to many people—a limitation that is often left unacknowledged by proponents of IQ testing.[11] "A score serves to show where a person stands in a distribution of scores of his or her peers. It does not provide evidence as to how a particular child thinks and feels"[12] People automatically tend to attach good and bad meanings to high and low test scores, forgetting that individual differences are for all intents and purposes neutral.[13] "The highness or lowness of a score is not a measure of an individual's worth or value to family, friends, or society at large. Each person functions in a unique way. . . . A person cannot be described as a combination of varying amounts of different traits. Trait labels such as IQ are misleading and can be insulting when applied to individuals."[14]

IQ tests have been used to determine and treat learning disabilities. "Variances between different component tests often indicate a person's performance on some component tests is limited by a neurological or other learning disability, who [sic] may be assisted by intensive educational intervention. Substantial test design and research focuses on the ability of a test component to predict later difficulties with reading and learning."[15] Some attribute variations in IQ between adults to genetic variation or environmental factors

10. See Robert Artmann, "The IQ Test Controversy," *http://www.iq-tests.eu/iq-test-Controversy-1200.html.*

11. Tyler, "Testing the Test," 48.

12. Ibid.

13. Ibid.

14. Ibid.

15. See Artmann, "The IQ Test Controversy."

not shared within families.[16] "In the United States, marked variation in IQ occurs within families, with siblings differing on average by 12 points."[17] Some statistical studies suggest "that income level, education level, nutrition level, race, and sex all correlate with IQ scores, but what this means is debated."[18] The extent to which nature or nurture affects the development of a person's intelligence remains hotly debated and probably will remain unresolved for a long time. There are some who are bent on using the IQ test as a definitive way of determining mental differences between the races; that was the position advocated by the late Harvard professor of psychology Richard Hernstein and his colleague Charles Murray in their controversial book *The Bell Curve*. In this work Hernstein and Murray highlighted racial differences in intelligence, suggesting also that there is a relationship between IQ and crime, welfare, poverty, unemployment, and other social ills.[19]

Critics of *The Bell Curve* see the thesis of the differential intelligence of whites and blacks as feeding into the prejudicial view of black mental inferiority and American prejudices against minority groups.[20] Even before *The Bell Curve*, Margaret Mead, a critic of earlier attempts in the 1920s to prove the mental inferiority or superiority of groups of people, has suggested extreme caution "in any attempt to draw conclusions concerning the relative intelligence of different racial or nationality groups on the basis of tests, unless careful consideration is given the factors of language, education, and social status, and further allowances made for an unknown amount of influence which may be logically attributed to different attitudes and different habits of thought."[21] While some scholars, like A. R. Jensen, hold tenaciously to the view that IQ tests are not biased against minorities and that the claimed cultural bias of IQ testing

16. Ibid.

17. Ibid.

18. Ibid.

19. See Richard J. Hernstein and Charles Murray, *The Bell Curve: Intelligence and Class Structure in American Life* (New York: Free Press, 1994).

20. Vernon J. Williams, Jr., "Fatalism: Anthropology, Psychology, Sociology and the IQ Controversy," *Journal of African American Studies* 13 (2009): 90–96, at 92.

21. Margaret Mead, "The Methodology of Racial Testing: Its Significance for Sociology," *American Journal of Sociology* 31 (1926): 218–24, at 224; cited in Williams, "Fatalism," 92.

is a farce,[22] most reputable social and cultural anthropologists, scientists, and psychologists agree that race is not a valid scientific concept and that IQ tests are culturally biased.[23] For example, a detailed study of three groups of identical twins who were reared apart found heritability of IQ to be nowhere "near substantial."[24]

Many opponents of the IQ test argue that, rather than measuring intelligence, the test measures the biases (intended outcome) of the makers of the test. Financial status, race, sex, class, and gender all contribute to convolute the test. In his helpful book, *Intelligence and Race*, Douglas Eckberg examined whether the IQ test really measures any gradient of one's mental ability and whether intelligence can be genetically determined. His conclusions rejected any notion of heritability of IQ. He further concluded that test scores cannot be used to predict one's socioeconomic status, nor can test scores be used to draw inferences regarding a person's intellectual ability.[25]

Psychologists and teachers who argue that schools should abandon the IQ test do so for reasons that are partly technical and partly practical.[26] The technical reasons have to do with "ambiguities in definition and with untenable assumptions which have been made regarding such matters as the contribution of heredity, the constancy of the I.Q. [and] the role of culture in defining intelligent behavior."[27] Some teachers and college professors—to say nothing of parents and students—still wrongly think of IQ tests as indications of innate intellectual capacities determined

---

22. See A. R. Jensen, "How Much Can We Boost IQ and Scholastic Achievement?" *Harvard Educational Review* 39 (1969): 1–123; *Educatability and Group Differences* (New York: Harper and Row, 1973); *The G Factor: The Science of Mental Ability* (Westport, CT: Praeger, 1998); *Individual Differences in Learning: Interference Factor* (Berkeley: University of California, 1964).

23. Williams, "Fatalism," 90.

24. Howard Taylor, *The IQ Game: A Methodological Inquiry into the Heredity–Environment Controversy* (New Brunswick, NJ: Rutgers University Press, 1980), 206.

25. See Douglas Lee Eckberg, *Intelligence and Race: The Origins and Dimensions of the IQ Controversy* (New York: Praeger, 1979).

26. A. Garth Sorenson, "The Use of Teaching Machines in Developing an Alternative to the Concept of Intelligence," *Educational and Psychological Measurement* 23 (1963): 323–29, at 323.

27. Ibid.

by heredity.[28] The practical reasons have to do with teachers who consciously or unconsciously assign students rigid tasks on the basis of test scores.[29] Studies in psychology and genetics have raised serious questions about the IQ test. The term "intelligence" has been assigned too many meanings, most of which still remain vague.[30] The argument for eliminating the IQ test is predicated on the idea that "concepts do have consequences, for people must act on their beliefs."[31] What people have erroneously believed about the concept of intelligence seem to damage the self-esteem of students and "have impaired the effectiveness of many teachers who, because they assume that a given test score proves that some of their students are unable to learn, give up trying to teach those students."[32]

CIT AND THE INTELLIGENCE DEBATE

While CIT is not directly concerned with the intelligence debate, the issues at stake hold important ramifications for CIT. CIT seeks an integrated whole in the act of organizing knowledge, while still paying attention to those limiting situations that can undermine knowledge. The existentialist philosopher Karl Jaspers (1883–1969) developed the concept of *Grenzsituationen* (limiting situations) to account for the day-to-day living experiences that confine us, such as suffering, guilt, pain, tragedy, and death. Indeed some experiences are unavoidable and do confine one's horizon or vision. Human beings always exist within a situation. "I can never step out of one situation without entering another."[33] Some day-to-day situations a person can change, if one is willing to change course. These include contingent situations, like where or when to send one's children to school. But *Grenzsituationen* are not contingent and therefore are unchangeable. "They are like a wall that we hit, and against which we fail. We cannot change them,

28. Ibid.
29. Ibid.
30. Ibid., 324
31. Ibid.
32. Ibid.
33. Karl Jaspers, *Philosophie Band II: Existenzerhellung* (Munich: Springer, 1932), 202.

but we only bring them to clarity."[34] This "wall" sometimes impacts how one absorbs information and affects how one learns.

In general terms, some situations are limiting, like a historical period or the social milieu of one's birth. For example, assume my parents have English heritage and I was born in Paris, France. My parents live in a German-speaking community of this French city where I had my elementary education. I may end up speaking French in school, German on the street, and English at home. That I end up speaking English, French, and German at a very early age is not something within my control. It was brought about by the circumstances of my birth that were entrusted to me: my limiting situation. Gender also makes a difference in one's life that one cannot control. But there are some limiting situations that may be totally within my control, such as how I navigate through life and how I handle suffering, death, and life's challenges. Some of these situations as well as my response to them may affect the way I process information and the way I learn. In the Catholic tradition, Lonergan was one of the first to pay attention to the way we learn and process knowledge.

A NATION AT RISK

Coincidentally, the year in which Gardner published his most famous work, *Frames of Mind: The Theory of Multiple Intelligences* (1983), was the same year that *A Nation at Risk* appeared, a document critical of American education. *A Nation at Risk* was the work of a commission of reputable scientists, policymakers, educators, and university presidents assembled by the United States Department of Education. The commission thought the American school system was losing "sight of the basic purposes of schooling, and of the high expectations and disciplined effort needed to attain them." They also reported, "that while we can take justifiable pride in what our schools and colleges have historically accomplished and contributed to the United States and the well-being of its people, the educational foundations of our society are presently being eroded by a rising tide of mediocrity

---

34. Ibid., 203.

that threatens our very future as a Nation and a people. What was unimaginable a generation ago has begun to occur—others are matching and surpassing our educational attainments."[35]

The commission identified a number of causes for concern, including a steady and dramatic decline in student performance, particularly vis-à-vis students in other countries; high rates of functional illiteracy; and a decline in level of achievement of high school and college graduates, with the result that business and military leaders were required to spend millions of dollars on costly remedial education and training programs in such basic skills as reading, writing, spelling, and computation.[36] These trends, in their view, threatened both children's opportunities and the nation's collective future.

Twenty-five years later, in 2008, the United States Department of Education revisited *A Nation at Risk* and published an anniversary document, *A Nation Accountable: Twenty-Five Years after a Nation at Risk* (2008), suggesting that we "remain a nation at risk but are also now a nation informed, a nation accountable, and a nation that recognizes there is much work to be done."[37] According to this twenty-fifth anniversary document, "if we were 'at risk' in 1983, we are at even greater risk now. The rising demands of our global economy, together with demographic shifts, require that we educate more students to higher levels than ever before. Yet our education system is not keeping pace with these growing demands. Of twenty children born in 1983, six did not graduate from high school on time in 2001. Of the fourteen who did, ten started college that fall, but only five earned a bachelor's degree by spring 2007."

According to *A Nation at Risk*, "the search for solutions to our educational problems must also include a commitment to life-long learning." The nation's goal, according to this landmark document, "must be to develop the talents of all to their fullest. Attaining that goal requires that we expect and assist all students to work to the limits of their capabilities. We should expect schools to have

35. See U.S. Department of Education, "A Nation at Risk," *http://www2.ed.gov/pubs/NatAtRisk/risk.html*.

36. Ibid.

37. See U.S. Department of Education, "A Nation Accountable: Twenty-Five Years after a Nation at Risk," *http://www.ed.gov/rschstat/research/pubs/accountable/index.html*.

genuinely high standards rather than minimum ones, and parents to support and encourage their children to make the most of their talents and abilities."[38] It recommended what it called a path to "authentic accomplishment"—that schools, colleges, and universities should adopt not only rigorous but also measurable standards for academic excellence and that four-year colleges and universities need to raise their requirements for admission. As part of this effort, the United States Congress passed the *Improving America's Schools Act of 1994*, which mandated state academic-content standards and tests, and the *Goals 2000: Educate America Act* (1994), which provided federal funds to aid states in writing those content standards. The movement toward standards culminated with George W. Bush's No Child Left Behind Act (2001). This is not the place to discuss the numerous problems with the No Child Left Behind Act; our point here is that the call for standards and accountability "has resulted in new transparency in student achievement—by grade, subgroup, and subject, and by school, district, and state. While we are finally capable of defining our difficulties, the full solutions to some of them have not yet been found."[39] This is where Lonergan's and Gardner's work offer help.

Lonergan was concerned with the act of organizing intelligence, specifically with the way that every human being experiences a spontaneous self-correcting process of learning in which ranges of skills are learned and perfected.[40] His emphasis on "nuanced acceptance of historical mindedness" and attempt to dialogue with colleagues in the field of theology led to the publication of his two massive works, *Insight: A Study of Human Understanding* (1957) and *Method in Theology* (1970). In these two works he laid out his cognitional method and showed how a person's unrestricted questioning opens one to self-transcendence. The implication of his ideas for Catholic higher education and its impact on the integration of knowledge that is central to CIT is immense.

---

38. Ibid.

39. Ibid.

40. Matthew Lamb, "The Social and Political Dimension of Lonergan's Theology," in *The Desires of the Human Heart: An Introduction to the Theology of Bernard Lonergan*, ed. Vernon Gregson (New York: Paulist Press, 1988), 255–84, at 257.

THE SCOPE OF HUMAN POTENTIAL IN GARDNER'S WORK

Gardner's MI follows and at the same time departs from the traditional view of psychometrics. The history of psychometrics has been traced to Charles Darwin, whose curiosity about the origin and development of psychological traits, including intellectual and emotional traits, led to his 1859 book on the evolution of species.[41] Working as a British naturalist and sailing around the world, Darwin observed physical differences among species of related living organisms. He noted, for instance, how some species of birds seemed to have evolved into other species. Darwin investigated why this happened and came up with the idea of transmutation (how some species transform into another), which in turn led him to his theory of "natural selection," i.e., that organisms that are best suited to their environment reproduce and survive more effectively, and dominate others. Speculations about intellectual differences across the species, following Darwin's theory, led Francis Galton (Darwin's cousin) to establish an anthropometric laboratory for the purpose of assembling empirical evidence of people's intellectual differences.[42] According to Gardner, the first intelligence test was developed by a French psychologist, Alfred Binet, and his colleague, Theodore Simon, when they were asked by the French Ministry of Education to devise some kind of measure that would successfully predict which Parisian children would succeed and which would fail in primary school. What they produced was later termed an "intelligence test," thanks to the efforts of the German psychologist Wilhelm Stern, whose 1912 work measures the ratio of one's mental age to one's chronological age, resulting in an "intelligent quotient" (IQ).

Gardner, like many critics of the IQ test, reasoned that one needs to "get away altogether from tests and correlations among tests and look instead at more naturalistic sources of information about how peoples around the world develop skills important to their way

---

41. Howard Gardner, *Intelligence Reframed: Multiple Intelligence for the Twenty-First Century* (New York: Basic Books, 1999), 11.

42. Ibid.

Howard Gardner

of life."[43] Gardner innovatively defined intelligence as the ability to solve problems or fashion products that are valued in one or more cultural settings.[44] In his earlier research on intelligence and cognition he discovered a number of different intellectual strengths or competencies, such as mathematical or musical intelligence, each of which may have its own developmental history.[45] Gardner argued that research in neurobiology lends credence to the idea that there are areas in the brain that correspond, at least roughly, to certain forms of cognition, implying a neural organization that proves hospitable

43. Howard Gardner, *The Development and Education of the Mind: The Selected Works of Howard Garner* (London: Routledge, 2005), 48.

44. Ibid.

45. Gardner, *Frames of Mind*, 59.

to the notion of different modes of information processing.[46] This led Gardner to conclude that "the zeitgeist," at least in the fields of psychology and neurobiology, "appears primed for the identification of several human intelligences."[47]

THE INTELLIGENCES CONSIDERED

Gardner formulated MI as a new kind of construct based on a unique definition of intelligences.[48] The theory suggests that only two intelligences—verbal linguistic and logical mathematical intelligence—have dominated in traditional schooling, while the other intelligences have often been neglected.[49] This neglect is based on the questionable assumption that one's success in all areas is predicated on one's development in these two areas. Gardner offered a more holistic accounting of individual talents and potentials.[50] His choice of the word "multiple" was deliberate, to stress an unknown number of separate human capacities. Thus he emphasized that these distinct human capacities are as fundamental as those historically captured within the IQ test.[51] He then defined intelligence as "a biopsychological potential to process information in certain ways, in order to solve problems or fashion products that are valued in a culture or community."[52] Sometimes cultural or individual choices determine whether a given intelligence can be creatively mobilized. Using about seven criteria (while leaving room for the possibility that there could be more), Gardner determined which sets of human capacities should be identified as a distinct form of intelligence.[53]

---

46. Ibid.

47. Ibid.

48. Shearer, "Multiple Intelligences Theory after Twenty Years," 3.

49. Ozdemir et. al., "Enhancing Learning through Multiple Intelligences," 74.

50. Dixon Hearne and Suki Stone, "Multiple Intelligences and Underachievement: Lessons from Individuals with Learning Disabilities," *Journal of Learning Disabilities* 26, no. 7 (1995): 441.

51. Howard Gardner, *Multiple Intelligences: The Theory in Practice* (New York: Basic Books, 1993), xii.

52. Shearer, "Multiple Intelligences Theory after Twenty Years," 3.

53. Ibid., 4.

- **Linguistic Intelligence:** The core features of linguistic intelligence include the ability to use words effectively for reading, writing, and speaking.[54] Gardner introduced linguistic intelligence through the perspective of the poet, who most fully exhibits this ability with language. To illustrate, he cited a correspondence between T. S. Eliot and a young British poet, Keith Douglas. The young poet had compared himself to a mouse only to later compare himself to a "pillar in a glass house." Elliot responded to the apparent inconsistency by pointing out that it is not useful to compare oneself to "a pillar and . . . a mouse in the same stanza."[55] Gardner used this illustration to show how the work of poets embodies core operations of language and sensitivity to the meaning of words. He argued that linguistic competence is the intelligence most widely shared across the human species. He also connected linguistic intelligence to musical and mathematical intelligence[56] and showed how human beings, both skilled and impaired, exploit their linguistic heritage for communicative and expressive purposes.[57]

- **Musical Intelligence:** Having its own developmental trajectory and neurological representation, musical intelligence includes "sensitivity to pitch, rhythm, and timbre and the emotional aspects of sound as pertaining to the functional areas of musical appreciation, singing, and playing an instrument."[58] Gardner cited Leonard Bernstein and Mozart as amply exemplifying this intelligence. Musical intelligence, which emerges early in life, is not isolated from other spheres of intelligence, but rather works cooperatively with them. This probably explains why in early

---

54. Ibid.

55. Gardner, *Frames of Mind*, 74.

56. Gardner points out four aspects of linguistic knowledge: (1) rhetorical aspect: the ability to use language to convince others of a course of action; (2) mnemonic potential: the ability to use language to help one remember information; (3) role of explanation: language as the optimal means for conveying ideas; and (4) metalinguistic analysis: the potential of language to explain its own activities.

57. Gardner, *Frames of Mind*, 97–98. Linguistic intelligence is not necessarily an auditory-oral form of intelligence.

58. Shearer, "Multiple Intelligences Theory after Twenty Years," 5.

twentieth-century Europe there was a fair amount of interest in the development of artistic abilities in children.[59]

- **Logical-Mathematical Intelligence:** Logical-mathematical intelligence involves skills in calculations as well as logical reasoning and problem solving.[60] In discovering that numerical thinking and high levels of logical thinking are transcultural, Gardner located the origins of logical-mathematical intelligence, not in the auditory-oral sphere (like musical and linguistic intelligence), but in one's encounter with the sensory world of objects. Gardner used developmental psychologist Jean Piaget's (1896–1980) anecdote of a child who grew up to be an accomplished mathematician to show that the origins of logical-mathematical intelligence lie in a child's interaction with the physical world, stemming from the child's manipulation of objects to the child's interiorized actions. Gardner used this to show that a child who very early in life interacts with physical objects soon begins to develop appreciation for numbers and begins to understand simple cause and effect.

- **Spatial Intelligence:** Spatial intelligence includes the "ability to perceive the visual world accurately and to perform transformations and modifications based on one's own initial perceptions via mental imagery."[61] Sailors, engineers, sculptors, surgeons, et al., have highly developed spatial intelligence because "central to spatial intelligence are the capacities to perceive the visual world accurately, to perform transformations and modifications upon one's initial perceptions, and to be able to re-create aspects of one's visual experience, even in the absence of relevant physical stimuli."[62] This intelligence, which is not inextricably linked to any particular sensory modality, entails a number of loosely related capacities, like the ability to conjure up mental imagery and then transform the imagery. With the exception of Piaget, who conducted several studies on the development of spatial intelligence in children, researchers tend to locate this

59. Gardner, *Frames of Mind*, 108.
60. Shearer, "Multiple Intelligences Theory after Twenty Years," 5.
61. Ibid.
62. Gardner, *Frames of Mind*, 173.

intelligence in adult subjects. Some have suggested that this might be due to the "gestalt" sensitivity (the ability to perceive the whole), which is central to this intelligence, and which in their view is more enhanced in adults.

- **Bodily-Kinesthetic Intelligence:** Languages can be expressed in means other than words. The masterful use of the body as a component of bodily-kinesthetic intelligence was mastered by the Greeks, who revered the beauty of the human form and sought harmony between mind and body by their athletic activities. Gardner considered how the body can be used as an object: dancers and athletes use their bodies as "mere" objects, while inventors and other workers use parts of the body—the hand in particular—to manipulate, arrange, and transform objects in the world. Gardner concluded that bodily-kinesthetic intelligence completes a trio of object-related intelligences: "logical-mathematical intelligence, which grows out of the patterning of objects into numerical arrays; spatial intelligence, which focuses on the individual's ability to transform objects within his environment and to make his way amidst a world of objects in space; and bodily intelligence, which focusing inward, is limited to the exercise of one's own body and, facing outward, entails physical actions on the objects in the world."[63]

- **Intrapersonal and Interpersonal intelligences:** Gardner identified two variants of personal intelligences: intrapersonal intelligence and interpersonal intelligence. Although Gardner discussed them together, these are two separate but related intelligences. Intrapersonal intelligence is the ability to understand oneself, to distinguish one's own feelings, e.g., pleasure versus pain. It is the ability to form an accurate, veridical (genuine or real) model of oneself and be able to use that model to live effectively.[64] Interpersonal intelligence is an "outward" turn in which one has the capacity to make distinctions between moods, temperaments, motivations, and intentions of others. Salespersons and politicians are more likely to have interpersonal intelligence.

---

63. Ibid., 235.

64. Gardner, *Multiple Intelligences*, 9.

After publishing *Frames of Mind*, Gardner added an eighth intelligence, naturalistic intelligence (the ability to understand patterns of relationship to nature) and left room for the possibility of a ninth, existential intelligence, which entails the proclivity to pose and ponder questions about life, death, and ultimate realities.[65]

Gardner was motivated by the need to refute earlier theories of human intelligence, which he thought undermined learning. These theories, in his view, mistakenly approached intelligence as a "black box" entity with which a person was born and which was likely not subject to change.[66] The claim in *The Bell Curve*, for instance, that it is difficult to change intelligence led "Richard Herrnstein and Charles Murray to conclude that there is little point in funding programs like Head Start, which attempt to enhance the intelligence of young children."[67] *The Bell Curve*, as Gardner saw it, envisions intelligence as "a single property distributed within the general population along a bell-shaped curve. That is, comparatively few people have very high intelligence (say, IQ over 130), comparatively few people have very low intelligence (IQ under 70), and most people are clumped together somewhere in between (IQ from 85 to 115)."[68]

Gardner rejected *The Bell Curve* for several reasons. First, Herrnstein and Murray claimed that intelligence is to a large extent inherited. Second, although they claimed to be "resolutely neutral" on the differences in black-white intelligence, they presented evidence to suggest a genetic basis for the disparity. Third, they used their theory to suggest that social pathology is due to low intelligence and that intelligence cannot be significantly changed through societal interventions.[69] Gardner, in challenging these claims, suggested that the wrong methods have been applied; new methods or new technologies might make it quite easy to raise intelligence significantly.[70]

---

65. Gardner, *Disciplined Mind*, 72.

66. Ibid., 68.

67. Ibid., 84. Herrnstein modified his position shortly before his death. He told Gardner that one can look at the same *Bell Curve* data and reach a different conclusion—that because it is not easy to alter intelligence more resources ought to be devoted to that end.

68. Gardner, *Intelligence Reframed*, 8.

69. Ibid., 8–9.

70. Gardner, *Disciplined Mind*, 84.

In Gardner's view, intelligence tests represent but the tip of the cognitive iceberg.[71] MI exposes the tendency of intelligence tests to conform to uniformity (materials are taught in the same way), a procedure Gardner thought offered an illusion of fairness.[72]

Even in the face of his call to move away from intelligence tests, Gardner did not describe how to apply MI. *Frames of Mind* offered only "six paragraphs of direct information on applications."[73] Aware that MI is not the kind of theory that can be proved correct or incorrect by a single study,[74] Gardner left the implementations of MI to other researchers. Further research did in fact follow and has yielded some useful results. For example, a 1994 study showed that the two dominant intelligences throughout elementary school are spatial and bodily-kinesthetic intelligence. Children in all elementary grades are strong in spatial intelligence, but lower in musical and interpersonal intelligences until high school. Although this study discovered that elementary students are strong in spatial intelligence, it by no means contradicted earlier research that adults are generally stronger in spatial intelligence than children. The most disturbing finding of the study, however, was that students enter elementary school strong in linguistic and logical-mathematical intelligences and leave high school with a sharp decline in both areas.[75] A follow-up study in 1996, also with the Teele Inventory for Multiple Intelligences designed to examine the dominant intelligences of students in all grades, confirmed that earlier in primary school the most dominant intelligences were spatial, bodily-kinesthetic, linguistic, and logical-mathematical, while upper elementary pupils were strong in spatial, bodily-kinesthetic, interpersonal, and musical intelligence. The study also revealed that "middle and high school students were strongest in interpersonal, bodily-kinesthetic, spatial and musical intelligences."[76]

---

71. Gardner, *Intelligence Reframed*, 3.

72. Gardner, *Disciplined* Mind, 72.

73. Mindy L. Kornhaber, "Multiple Intelligences: From the Ivory Tower to the Dusty Classroom—But Why?" *Teachers College Record* 106, no. 1 (2004): 67.

74. Howard Gardner, "Intelligences in Theory and Practice: A Response to Elliot W. Eisner, Robert J. Sternberg, and Henry M. Levin." *Teachers College Record* 95:4 (1994): 576–83, at 578.

75. Ozdemir et.al., "Enhancing Learning through Multiple Intelligences," 75.

76. Ibid.

GARDNER'S 8 INTELLIGENCES

1. Linguistic intelligence

2. Musical intelligence

3. Logical-Mathematical intelligence

4. Spatial intelligence

5. Bodily-Kinesthetic intelligence

6. Intrapersonal intelligence

7. Interpersonal intelligence

8. Naturalistic intelligence

THE SCOPE OF HUMAN POTENTIAL IN LONERGAN: COGNITIONAL METHOD

The foundation of Lonergan's Cognitional Method (CM) was laid in *Insight*. The goal of this groundbreaking work is tacitly evident in its opening statement: "In the ideal detective story the reader is given all the clues but fails to spot the criminal."[77] The goal of Lonergan's overall project is to convey "insight into insight" and by so doing "reach the act of organizing intelligence."[78] In this foundational work, Lonergan worked out a conception of human knowing as a structured set of related operations, reflected on the disposition of the human mind (the kind that led Archimedes to his famous discoveries),[79] and used the story of Archimedes to suggest that deep within every human person is a drive to know, to understand, to see why, to discover reason, to find the cause, and to explain—a drive

---

77. Bernard Lonergan, *Insight: A Study of Human Understanding* (London: Longman, 1957), ix.

78. Ibid.

79. William Mathews, *Lonergan's Quest: A Study of Desire in the Authoring of Insight* (Toronto: University of Toronto, 2005), 3.

that not only absorbs but is capable of sending one on "dangerous voyages of exploration."[80]

Archimedes (290/280–212/211 BCE) of Syracuse, a Greek city-state in Sicily, was a popular scientist, known for many inventions and for his formulation of a hydrostatic principle of displacement (the Archimedes principle).[81] While the story of his moment of discovery mixes truth and legend, it suggested to Lonergan a principle he would apply to CIT. The popular version is that the king of Syracuse wanted to know whether or not baser metal was added to the gold on his votive crown. Archimedes thought about the question day and night. Legend has it that the answer came to him while taking a bath; he was so excited about the solution that he jumped out of the water and ran naked through the streets of Syracuse, screaming *eureka*, "I found it!" Archimedes' *eureka* was to weigh the crown in water.

While the anecdote is likely fanciful, its significance was not lost on Lonergan: insight comes as a release from the tension of inquiry. When Archimedes went to the bath he did not know that he would find the solution in the waters of Syracuse, but it was there that his *eureka* moment came. From this Lonergan grasped that insight can come suddenly and unexpectedly. Archimedes' *eureka* moment came because he persistently thought about the question that was put to him. In other words, his inner disposition enabled his *eureka*. From this Lonergan deduced that insight is not a function of outer circumstances, but of inner disposition. With the Archimedes story, the intent of Lonergan's cognitional method (CM) is clear; that every human being to some extent experiences a spontaneous self-correcting process of learning in which ranges of skills are learned and perfected.[82] He pointed to the work of Piaget as exemplifying the earliest infant manifestations of the spontaneous self-correcting process of learning.[83]

In the quest to mobilize intelligence creatively, Lonergan proffered three basic but interrelated questions: What am I doing when

---

80. Lonergan, *Insight*, 4.

81. See *Encyclopedia Britannica Online*, s.v. "Archimedes," *http://www.britannica. com/EBchecked/topic/32808/Archimedes*.

82. Matthew Lamb, "The Social and Political Dimension of Lonergan's Theology," in *The Desires of the Human Heart*, ed. Vernon Gregson (New York: Paulist Press, 1988), 257.

83. Ibid.

I am knowing? Why is doing that knowing? What do I know when I do it? These suggest that cognitional process begins on the level of empirical or verifiable data that are contained in the transcendental imperatives: be attentive, be intelligent, be reasonable, and be responsible. When correlated with the fascinating opening statement of "the ideal detective story" in *Insight*, in which one is given all the clues but "fails to spot the criminal," it becomes clear that Lonergan has invited us to search with him, not for a criminal, but for our own dynamic power of inquiry.[84] The search for one's power of inquiry is not done by rote memory or by any recondite intuition but by a "distinct activity of organizing intelligence that places the full set of clues in a unique explanatory perspective."[85]

Knowing, for Lonergan, is dynamically structured. In CM the primacy is not in the known but in the structure of knowing and the knower. Lonergan used the analogy of a "whole" (say an orchestra) and its relation to its parts to buttress his argument. Despite its many parts, an orchestra possesses a unity. One cannot remove any of the parts without destroying its essential unity any more than one can add additional parts without seeming ludicrous. The set of internal relations in a "whole," such as an orchestra, is so significant that each part is what it is only by virtue of its functional relations to other parts. There is no part that is not determined by the exigencies of other parts.[86] In the same way, human knowing involves distinct and irreducible activities: seeing, hearing, smelling, touching, tasting, inquiring, imagining, understanding, conceiving, reflecting, weighing the evidence, and judging. No one of these activities alone and by itself constitutes knowing. "As merely seeing is not human knowing, so for the same reason merely hearing, merely smelling, merely touching, merely tasting may be parts, potential components, of human knowing, but they are not human knowing itself."[87] Just as knowing is not experience or understanding or judgment alone, it is at the same time not something totally apart from experience,

84. Gregson, "The Desire to Know," 16.

85. Lonergan, *Insight*, ix.

86. Bernard Lonergan, *Collection: Papers by Bernard Lonergan,* ed. F. E. Crowe (New York: Herder and Herder, 1967), 222.

87. Ibid.

understanding, and judgment. It is a materially dynamic structure. For Lonergan it is also a formally dynamic structure in the sense that knowing is not a single set of operations or activities but an operation that is self-assembling, self-constituting, one part summoning the next until the whole is reached. The parts of the structure are only functionally related to one another. Experience stimulates inquiry; inquiry is intelligence bringing itself to act.[88]

Lonergan referred to the pattern of inquiry as levels of consciousness. He distinguished four levels of consciousness that are related but qualitatively different, just as there are four levels of conscious intentionality: experiencing, understanding, judgment, and decision.[89] Knowledge comes to consciousness in four distinctive ways: in the scope of our experiencing, in the insight of our understanding, in the truth of our judging, and in the beauty of our deciding,[90] and hence the four imperatives: be attentive, be intelligent, be reasonable, and be responsible. On the first level of consciousness, the *empirical* level, we sense, perceive, imagine, feel, speak, and move, utilizing both our exterior and interior senses. On the second level, the *intellectual* level, we inquire, come to understand, express what we have understood, and work out the presuppositions and implications

LONERGAN'S FOUR LEVELS OF CONSCIOUSNESS

Four Levels of Consciousness	Four Transcendental Precepts	Four Operations of Consciousness
Empirical	Be Attentive	Experience
Intellectual	Be Intelligent	Understanding
Rational	Be Reasonable	Judgment
Responsible	Be Responsible	Decision

88. Ibid., 223.
89. Lonergan, *Method in Theology*, 9.
90. Gregson, "The Desire to Know," 16.

of our expression, performing operations necessary for understanding. The *rational* level is the level on which we reflect, marshal evidence, and pass judgment on the truth, falsity, or probability of a statement. Finally, on the *responsible* level we are concerned with ourselves, our goals, and we deliberate about possible courses of action, evaluate them, decide, and carry out our decisions.[91]

Lonergan's first level is a substratum for further activities: the data of sense provoke inquiry, inquiry leads to understanding, and understanding expresses itself in language.[92] This leads to the second (intellectual) level in which, as intelligent, we seek insight, which becomes evident in our speech, behavior, and grasp of situations. The second level in turn yields to the third (rational) level, in which we are both reflective and critically conscious, devoting our time primarily to the pursuit of truth. On the fourth (responsible) level we express our vertical exercise of freedom, becoming a person who has concern for values and acts accordingly. In the way Lonergan conceived them, the higher level always sublates the lower because the levels of consciousness are "successive stages in the unfolding of a single thrust, the eros of the human spirit."[93] The quality of our consciousness changes and develops as we move from level to level. "More of us is at stake, because more of us is involved, as we go from experiencing to understanding to judging to deciding."[94]

Although Lonergan claimed that all cognitional activities are conscious, only some may be known because human knowing is a structure of different activities and also because experience of human knowing is qualitatively differentiated. "When one is reflecting, weighing the evidence, judging, one is experiencing one's own rationality. When one is inquiring, understanding, conceiving, thinking, one is experiencing one's own intelligence."[95] Thus knowing for Lonergan means the assemblage of those cognitional activities in which the subject knows oneself as knowing. "There is material

---

91. Lonergan, *Method in Theology*, 9.

92. Ibid., 10.

93. Gregson, "The Desire to Know," 16.

94. Ibid., 20.

95. Lonergan, *Collection*, 225.

presence, in which no knowing is involved, and such is the presence of the statue in the courtyard. There is intentional presence, in which knowing is involved."[96] In CM intentional presence is the subject as empirically, intellectually, rationally, and morally conscious. The subject is empirically conscious in so far as the person is attentive, intellectually conscious in so far as the person is intelligent, rationally conscious in so far as the person is reasonable, and morally conscious in so far as the person is responsible. Intentional presence can be conceived as forms of intelligence. One who is intentionally present has intellectual proclivities and is a knower. Such intellectual proclivities are contained in the "intelligences" that Gardner identified in MI.

Just as Gardner spoke of eight intelligences, Lonergan spoke of eight functional specialties, corresponding to the four levels of conscious intentionality (and two distinct phases of theology): research,

FUNCTIONAL SPECIALTIES AND PHASES OF THEOLOGY

The chart divides eight functional specialties into groups to show how they correspond to the two phases of theology. It also correlates the functional specialties to Lonergan's four operations of consciousness.

Mediating Phase	Mediated Phase	Operations
Research	Communications	Experiencing
Interpretation	Systematics	Understanding
History	Doctrines	Judgment
Dialectic	Foundations	Decision

---

96. Ibid., 226.

interpretation, history, dialectic, foundations, doctrines, systematics, and communications.[97] Functional specializations arise "inasmuch as one operates on all four levels to achieve the end proper to some particular level."[98] Mindful of the different kinds of conscious operations that occur, Lonergan also distinguishes among the biological, aesthetic, intellectual, dramatic, practical, and worshipful patterns of experience.[99]

MI AND CM IN CONCERT

Gardner's innovative idea (the study of human potential beyond the confines of IQ) that revolutionized education is comparable to Lonergan's exploration of the dynamic power of the human mind in Cognitional Method (CM). Lonergan introduces his CM in *Insight*[100] and explores it further in *Method in Theology*. In these works Lonergan, like Gardner, explores the vibrant power of the mind with the aim of getting to the heart of human understanding. Brain research supports the fundamental ideas of CM, as it does MI; both theories are replete with educational implications.

Both Howard Gardner and Bernard Lonergan, rather than measuring all thought on the single axis of general intelligence, distinguish among several basic aspects of human thought. Although they divide up human thought in different ways, there are important parallels among aspects of their theories. MI is not geared toward producing a person's intellectual profile. Although MI has sometimes been criticized on theoretical, conceptual, empirical, and pedagogical grounds, there is no denying that MI has been a powerful catalyst in education,[101] just as Lonergan's CM has been a powerful catalyst

---

97. There are two distinct phases of theology: the mediating phase in which theology encounters the past, and the mediated phase in which theology confronts the future. See *Method in Theology*, 134–45.

98. Ibid., 134.

99. Ibid., 286.

100. Lonergan, *Insight*, ix.

101. Ozdemir et. al., "Enhancing Learning through Multiple Intelligences," 74. See also S. Kagan and M. Kagan, *Multiple Intelligences: The Complete Nil Book* (San Clemente, CA: Kagan Cooperative Learning, 1998), 23.

to CIT. Lonergan's CM can aid MI considerably in the task of educational reform, just as Gardner's MI can aid CM's view of human capacity for thought as ground for achieving self-transcendence, and by so doing further enrich the Catholic intellectual tradition.

The transcendental precepts (be attentive, be intelligent, be reasonable, and be responsible) are to Lonergan's CM what sensitivities to individual's talents and potentials are to Gardner's MI. In Lonergan the object in question is the subject-as-performing-subject, not subject-as-observed-object. In Gardner the object in question is the student-as-observed-object by the teacher. Intelligences as Gardner conceived them cannot be developed without making use of the transcendental precepts, whether they are identified as such or not. In other words, Lonergan's CM can enhance Gardner's MI. In Lonergan's schema each of the four levels of consciousness (though excellences in their own right) cannot stand alone but depend on the other levels, in the same way that in Gardner's schema the propensity to all the intelligences exists in everyone even though some may predominate. Bearing this in mind, a correlation of MI and CM might yield the following pattern:

- **Be attentive (empirical level):** musical intelligence (sensitivity to pitch, rhythm, and emotional aspects of sound) and bodily-kinesthetic intelligence (masterful use of the body)
- **Be intelligent (intellectual level):** linguistic intelligence (ability to use words effectively) and logical-mathematical intelligence (logical reasoning)
- **Be reasonable (rational level):** logical-mathematical intelligence (skills in calculation, logical reasoning, and problem solving) and spatial intelligence (ability to perceive accurately the visual world)
- **Be responsible (responsible level):** intrapersonal intelligence (ability to understand oneself) and interpersonal intelligence (ability to understand others)

While Lonergan did not conceive of the four levels of conscious intentionality as independent modes of cognition as did Gardner, he did speak of each level as having "its own proper achievement and end. So the proper achievement and end of the first level, experiencing, is the apprehension of data; that of the second level, understanding, is insight into the apprehended data; that of the third level, judgment, is the acceptance or rejection of the hypotheses and theories put forward by understanding to account for the data; that of the fourth level, decision, the acknowledgment of values and the selection of the methods or other means that lead to their realization."[102] Thus one can argue that each of Lonergan's four levels can, like MI, depending on the individual, be more developed in one person than in another. For example, while one person may have more strength and competencies in Lonergan's third level, judgment, another may have more strength and competencies on the fourth level, decision.[103] In that way they may be said to possess different modes of information processing. One can also correlate MI with Lonergan's pattern of experience to yield the following pattern:

1. Linguistic intelligence	Practical pattern of experience
2. Musical intelligence	Aesthetic pattern of experience
3. Logical-Mathematical intelligence	Intellectual pattern of experience
4. Spatial intelligence	Dramatic pattern of experience
5. Bodily-Kinesthetic intelligence	Dramatic pattern of experience
6. Intrapersonal intelligence	Dramatic pattern of experience
7. Interpersonal intelligence	Dramatic pattern of experience
8. Naturalistic intelligence	Dramatic pattern of experience
9. Existential intelligence	Worshipful pattern of experience

102. Lonergan, *Method in Theology*, 133.

103. Of course, one must bear in mind that Lonergan conceived of his levels as successive, one progressing to the next, while Gardner's are essentially independent one from another.

MI and CM belong to the same trajectory of attempts to organize human intelligence with the goal of reaching acts of understanding. Both are unmistakably clear that the process of acquiring knowledge is laborious.[104] They not only depart from the traditional unitary view of intelligence but also embrace a more radical multiple vision of the human mind. MI envisions a pluralistic view of the mind that recognizes different and discrete facets of cognition, acknowledging that people have different cognitive strengths and contrasting cognitive styles.[105] CM, while not stressing the unique cognitive styles of individual persons, identifies the deep cognitive strength from which can emerge solutions to pressing educational problems. CM envisions groundbreaking ideas as things that pass through the habitual texture of the human mind. One learns as one is able to add new ideas to existing ones, inasmuch as the new does not exclude the old but complements and combines with it.[106]

The implications of MI and CM for education are manifold. The quest to determine who is intelligent, as far as schools are concerned, and to do it as early as possible, is hardly going to disappear.[107] MI "offers a richly diversified way of understanding and categorizing human cognitive abilities, and combinations of abilities, heightening our awareness of what makes learning possible for individualized students."[108] This can be correlated with CM's claim that learning is a relentless pursuit that occurs slowly and gradually. Lonergan was clear that learning is a vast undertaking that calls for relentless perseverance. "The process of learning is marked by an initial period of darkness in which one gropes about insecurely, in which one cannot see where one is going, in which one cannot grasp what the fuss is about; and only gradually, as one begins to catch on, does the initial darkness yield to a subsequent period of increasing light, confidence, interest, absorption."[109] When one has persevered,

---

104. Lonergan, *Insight*, 6.

105. Gardner, *Multiple Intelligences*, 6.

106. Lonergan, *Insight*, 6.

107. Gardner, *Intelligence Reframed*, 3.

108. B. A. Haggarty, *Nurturing Multiple Intelligences: A Guide to Multiple Intelligences Theory and Teaching* (New York: Addison Wesley, 1995), 49; cited in Ozdemir et.al., "Enhancing Learning through Multiple Intelligences," 74.

109. Lonergan, *Insight*, 6.

the "mysterious and foggy realms" that had once characterized learning yield to "modest self-confidence" that makes knowledge seem much more simple and obvious.[110]

Just as Gardner was reluctant to identify other intelligences, Lonergan was cautious to determine intelligence. In MI the intelligences are differentiated and are conceived as personal endowments. In CM consciousness is differentiated and is conceived "as a style of developing intelligence."[111] Just as Lonergan spoke of the need to constantly ask questions that would heighten consciousness, Gardner spoke of the need for essential questions: "On my educational landscape, questions are more important than answers; knowledge and, more importantly understanding should evolve from constant probing of such questions."[112] The heightening of consciousness, as Lonergan pointed out, is "something that each one, ultimately, has to do in himself and for himself."[113] One does this in the measure that he or she is attentive, intelligent, reasonable, and responsible. Gardner's analysis can contribute to a more realistic education for the person, making the person more human in that one makes full use of all external and internal sensory organs. Lonergan would agree with this but would go a step further, that when one gives oneself over to the transcendental imperatives, one chooses the truth and the good. In these acts of self-transcendence one opens oneself to the transcendent—which is a goal of CIT.

CONCLUSION

Catholic colleges and universities are established principally to cultivate the intellectual aspect of the Church's identity.[114] Catholic schools do not fulfill their mission if they fail to be places of rigorous and vital intellectual inquiry.[115] Lonergan, speaking within

---

110. Ibid.

111. Lonergan, *Method in Theology*, 272.

112. Gardner, *Disciplined Mind*, 24.

113. Lonergan, *Method in Theology*, 14.

114. See William J. Cahoy, "The Catholic Intellectual Tradition: What Is It? Why Should I Care?," *http://www1.csbsju.edu/catholicidentity/values/billcahoy.htm*.

115. Ibid.

the tradition, showed how such rigorous intellectual activity can be undertaken. He showed how a relentless search for knowledge is basic to the self-reflection necessary to the Catholic intellectual tradition. His endeavor in this regard sheds light, not only on how Catholic intellectual tradition is rooted in mystery, tradition, and a spirituality that is relational (not individualistic) but also on how properly it is a product of a community of learners who blend heart and mind in their search for truth.[116]

In previous chapters, we alluded to some of the Catholic Church's anti-intellectual or "darker moments"—the church's undermining of the concept of individual responsibility, the tendency to act irrationally even in the face of advances in science, failure to rise to the challenges of the modern world, espousing teachings not always in harmony with reason, and the Church's slow evolution in relation to gender equality, to mention a few. These are issues that not only militate against the ideals of a Catholic university but also contradict what that intellectual tradition stands for. As someone who lived and worked at the time of some of the "darker moments" of modern Church life, Lonergan, through his CM, offers correctives. CM shows that the fundamental task of education, and of a Catholic university in particular, to which all other tasks must remain subservient, is the preserving, nurturing, and cultivating of a person's mysterious desire to respond to a transcendent summons that calls one to move beyond the limits imposed on us by our respective limiting situations.

Lonergan's CM, like the scientific revolutions of Newton and Copernicus that, in their age, cleared up confusion in methods of inquiry, serves for our time as a new kind of paradigm for inquiry and knowing.[117] Gardner's MI augments Lonergan's CM in providing for us a different but complementary paradigm. Gardner's groundbreaking work on MI supports the growing body of research that calls for revision of our views about intelligence.[118] Gardner conceives education as a far broader endeavor than simply cultivating or rewarding

116. See Dennis Doyle, "The Trinity and Catholic Intellectual Life," in *As Leaven in the World: Catholic Perspectives on Faith, Vocation, and the Intellectual Life*, ed. Thomas M. Landy (Franklin, WI: Sheed and Ward, 2001), 151.

117. See Hugo Meynell, *The Theology of Bernard Lonergan*, American Academy of Religion Studies in Religion (Atlanta: Scholars Press, 1986), xi.

118. Hearne and Stone, "Multiple Intelligences and Underachievement," 441.

a narrowly defined intelligence, an endeavor involving motivation, emotions, and social and moral practices and values. Gardner cautions that unless these facets of the person are incorporated into daily practice, education is likely to be ineffective—or worse, to yield individuals who clash with our notion of humanity.[119] Like Gardner, Lonergan also saw education as a far broader endeavor than the antiquated model assumed by IQ tests, acknowledging the polymorphism of the human mind as a rich resource worth developing. As Gardner cautioned against an ineffective education that yields individuals who clash with "our notion of humanity," Lonergan similarly cautioned against a narrow classicist education that denies pluralistic education. Classicist education is based, not on an empirical notion of culture, but on a normative notion that assumed that there was only one culture for all people and all places and all times. Lonergan, however, recognized that individuals differ from one another, not only in their characters and ways of life but also in their mentalities and the way they learn. Human concepts and courses of action are products and expressions of acts of understanding that develop over time. To assume that there is one way of learning (classicist) or one way of acquiring knowledge, which transcends time and place, is to miss the whole point about education. To reclaim its preeminent position in education, the Catholic Church "needs to foster scientific inquiry because scientific inquiry raises serious questions about ultimacy and because it has a passion for truth. A faith not fed by these scientific questions and this passion is a faith diminished."[120]

The psychologist in Gardner alludes to three important concerns that should animate education, concerns that have names and histories "that extend far back into the past. There is the realm of *truth*— and its underside, what is false or indeterminable. There is the realm of *beauty*—and its absence in experiences or objects that are ugly or kitschy. And there is the realm of *morality*—what we consider to be good, and what we consider to be evil."[121] Lonergan would agree with

---

119. Gardner, *Disciplined Mind*, 22.

120. Cahoy, "The Catholic Intellectual Tradition"; paraphrasing Michael Buckley, "The Catholic University and the Promise Inherent in Its Identity," in *Catholic Universities in Church and Society: A Dialogue on* Ex Corde Ecclesiae, ed. John P. Langan, SJ (Washington, DC: Georgetown University Press, 1993), 74–89.

121. Gardner, *Disciplined Mind*, 16.

Gardner because in CM the levels of intentionality and consciousness are directed to an infinite God who is One, True, Good, Righteous, and supreme Beauty; through the knowledge of this God the individual's values are transformed. Moreover, if one follows the transcendental precepts (be attentive, be intelligent, be reasonable, and be responsible), the result is something true and valuable; it is authenticity, which one achieves in self-transcendence because the "desires and longings which we have for what is beautiful, for what makes sense, for what is true, for what has value, and for what has ultimate value are at the heart of what it means to be human."[122] The unrestricted questioning of the human spirit also leads to God because through knowledge the human person is intellectually self-transcendent; morally self-transcendent in so far as one chooses what is worthwhile and what is truly good, and affectively transcendent in as much as one spontaneously functions not just for oneself but for others as well.[123] Thus the rationale for Catholic intellectual tradition is realized when everyone—scientists, poets, musicians, playwrights, accountants, teachers, cooks, coaches, et al.— are good at what they do. Equally important is the fact that one need not necessarily be a member of the Catholic Church to participate in this mission. One only needs "a passion for truth and an openness to the ultimacy such a passion raises."[124]

Further Reading

Armstrong, Thomas. *Multiple Intelligences in the Classroom.* 3d ed. Alexandria, VA: Association for Supervision and Curriculum Development, 2009.

Gardner, Howard. *Five Minds for the Future.* Boston: Harvard Business School, 2009.

——————. *Multiple Intelligences: New Horizons in Theory and Practice.* New York: Basic Books, 2006.

——————. *Truth, Beauty, and Goodness Reframed: Educating for Virtues in the Twenty-First Century.* New York: Basic Books, 2011.

Ulrich, Cynthia. *The Way They Learn.* Bemidji, MN: Focus, 1998.

---

122. Gregson, "The Desire to Know," 16–17.

123. Lonergan, *Method in Theology,* 289.

124. Cahoy, "The Catholic Intellectual Tradition."

CHAPTER 7

Modules and Implementation of Lonergan's Plans for CIT

Our earlier chapters offered, at best, a tentative and incomplete description of Catholic intellectual tradition (CIT). Rather than risk a one-sided or lopsided definition, we have opted to consider CIT in its all-embracing and all-encompassing sense. For this reason, we find it helpful to show the place and significance of Lonergan's work for CIT.

In our concluding remarks in chapter 2 we suggested that CIT resembles a palimpsest, an ancient, vellum manuscript, handwritten and subsequently erased and reused to fresh purpose, but through which faint traces of the original writing may yet be seen.[1] Likewise in Lonergan's contribution to CIT one can discern traces of the treasures of the past. Lonergan was nurtured in the Catholic tradition. His fidelity to that tradition was never in doubt. He worked tirelessly to maintain and sustain it throughout his life, insisting on the preeminent place of Catholic schools and respect for the community of Catholic scholars.[2] One of his early scholarly papers (April 28, 1935) was the *Panton Anakephalaiosis*[3] article, the very theme of the papal

---

1. Patrick Brown, "Insight as Palimpsest: The Economic Manuscripts in the Text of *Insight*" (paper presented at the Twenty-Fifth Annual WCMI Lonergan Conference, Loyola Marymount University, Los Angeles, April 8–10, 2010).

2. Frederick Crowe, *Christ and History: The Christology of Bernard Lonergan from 1935 to 1982* (Ottawa: Novalis, 2005), 23.

3. "The gathering up of all things" or "The Restoration of all things [in Christ];" a phrase adapted from Eph. 1:10, "To gather up all things in him [Christ]." Published as *Panton Anakephalaiosis* [The Restoration of All Things] *Method: Journal of Lonergan Studies*, vol. 9: 2, ed. F.E. Crowe and R. M. Doran (Boston: Boston College, 1991): 134–72.

encyclical for renewal in Catholic studies,[4] the same theme Pius X (1903–1914) adopted as his papal motto in Lonergan's boyhood days.[5] The *Panton* article, a mini treatise on the historical causality of Christ, was the context in which Lonergan worked out his Christology and the wider context of his renewal of Catholic thought.[6] Having devoted his entire career to nurturing the CIT, Lonergan produced works that are now considered classics in this tradition.

DOES LONERGAN OFFER A SOLUTION?

Generally speaking, education is currently moving in a direction that makes it difficult for Catholic colleges and universities to maintain "the old way" of teaching and learning. Lonergan summarizes three important factors driving general education today. First is what he called the problem of the masses—how to educate everyone. Second is what he termed the new learning, which is not merely an addition to old subjects but their transformation in one way or another. This transformation may take different forms and work out differently, depending on the discipline.[7] Finally, there is the problem of specialization—the new knowledge to be imparted is mountainous, divided, and unassimilated, requiring functional specialization.[8] Catholic education must attend to these issues or risk being out of date. Lonergan insisted on reforming Catholic education by consistently speaking of the need to embrace the new learning, which, he insists, "is not simply secularist."[9] Rather it only requires that one take seriously the context of contemporary learning.[10]

---

4. See *Aeterni Patris* (1879) of Leo XIII at *http://www.vatican.va/holy_father/leo_xiii/encyclicals/documents/hf_l-xiii_enc_04081879_aeterni-patris_en.html*.

5. Crowe, *Christ and History*, 24.

6. Ibid., 30.

7. Here Lonergan is hinting at the generalized empirical method he is about to introduce, which has cross-disciplinary appeal.

8. Bernard Lonergan, *Topics in Education*, vol. 10 of *Collected Works of Bernard Lonergan*, ed. Robert M. Doran and Frederick E. Crowe (Toronto: University of Toronto Press, 1993), 14–18.

9. Ibid., 14.

10. Ibid., 3.

Lonergan's new learning seeks to overcome ideologies that undermine education (skepticism, fideism, rationalism, etc.). Sir Walter Moberly spoke in the mid-twentieth century about the need for educational institutions in general to "repent,"[11] by which he meant a "reorientation" or "reconstitution."[12] Lonergan was adept at "reconstitution," which he saw as the only way to move CIT forward. He thought that in every human reality there are two components: human nature, given at birth, and human "historicity," what one makes of oneself. Human historicity is of fundamental importance in the educational process,[13] for what one has constructed one can also reconstruct.[14] His work of "reconstitution" is future oriented. Because it draws from the existing tradition and goes beyond it, reconstitution offers a way that guides the faithful handing-on of CIT. There are eight key steps in Lonergan's program of "reconstitution." Because these are modules of what ought to characterize CIT, we shall give a general description of each module before proceeding to show its place in Lonergan's life and work.

MODULE 1: CIT IS BUILT ON AUTHENTICITY

The modern secular world is still very much characterized by the *verum-factum* principle that was fully developed in the seventeenth century—that only what is constructed by humanity has truth and value.[15] Although this idea has led to the development of new knowledge in mathematics, it has "also led over time to the diminishing respect for what is already given: God, nature, tradition,

11. Nels Frere, *Christian Faith and Higher Education* (New York: Harper and Brothers, 1954), 10, citing Walter Moberly, *The Crisis in the University* (London: S.C.M. Press, 1949), 212.

12. See Mobley, *The Crisis in the University*, 112; cited in Frere, *Christian Faith and Higher Education*, 10.

13. Bernard Lonergan, "Natural Right and Historical Mindedness," in *A Third Collection: Papers by Bernard J. F. Lonergan, SJ*, ed. Frederick Crowe (New York: Paulist Press, 1985), 170.

14. Bernard Lonergan, "The Ongoing Genesis of Methods," in *A Third Collection*, 155.

15. Mark W. Roche, *The Intellectual Appeal of Catholicism and the Idea of a Catholic University* (Notre Dame, IN: University of Notre Dame Press, 2003), 17.

other selves, and an ideal sphere of meaning. Seeing all positions as human constructions, this perspective ultimately negates every objective order and, with it, any moment of higher meaning or transcendence."[16] The Catholic tradition, in contrast, affirms a sacramental vision that finds God in and through the world, showing not only how divine truth, beauty, and goodness are reflected in the world but also how, in spite of original sin, humanity can still come to a knowledge of God and by so doing draw closer to God.[17] This Catholic view serves as a corrective—or at least an alternative—to the dominant secular view that every position is a construction that has neither intrinsic value nor a claim on objective reality.[18] The sacramental vision, according to Roche, elevates what *is*, and measures it against a higher ideal. It also "gives greater dignity to the university enterprise than the current secular framework that reduces science and engineering to merely technical reason and reduces the social sciences, the humanities, and law to the merely contingent and the merely critical, severing in each case any connection to the transcendent."[19] A sacramental vision in a Catholic university particularly ennobles the arts. This is because art is not only inexhaustible, but makes the ideal real. It expresses truth and beauty, and like the sacraments, not only gives a window onto the transcendent but leaves one with a sense of mystery and multivalence.[20]

The Catholic sacramental vision that is fostered in Catholic colleges and universities requires authenticity, a *sine qua non* for grasping transcendent reality. Authenticity—being true to oneself and internalizing what one has truly uncovered—is the key to genuine education or scholarship. The most conspicuous (yet often forgotten) characteristic of human education is that it is something that happens between persons, particularly between the teacher and student.[21] Teaching and learning are, in the final analysis, a continuous

16. Ibid., 18.

17. Ibid., 19.

18. Ibid., 21.

19. Ibid., 22.

20. Ibid., 22–23.

21. Emil Piscitelli, "The Fundamental Attitudes of the Liberally Educated Person: Foundational Dialectics," in *Lonergan Workshop*, ed. Frederick Lawrence (Chico, CA: Scholars Press, 1985), 5:289.

and unified activity, requiring authenticity in order to be successful. Authenticity can easily be lost in the process for the student, between studying to get a good grade, in order to excel in one's major, and in order to ensure a good job after college. Authenticity can also be lost in the process for the teacher, between teaching in order to meet the institutions' requirements and efforts to get tenure and promotion in order to climb the ladder of advancement (careerism).

All knowledge comes from learning and no learning can take place without the internalization of an ideal worthwhile for its own sake. Without such an ideal learning and scholarship become insignificant pastimes.[22] This raises the question of the self-authenticating objectives of human teaching and learning and the commitment that guides both teacher and student in the learning process.[23] In other words, how do we help students internalize and appropriate what they have learned? And how do students, on their part, translate theory into practice? Catholic tradition regards teaching as a vocation; teachers are called to this vocation in the same way priests are called to the ministry. Teachers have a special power to fashion or mold students in the image of the wise or of a fool, in the image of a free or a bound person.[24] By their scholarship teachers assist others and themselves in seeking the truth and appropriating what is real, important, useful, and satisfying.[25] Thus teaching is the art of "offering to others, with discrimination, what we are, know, and believe, the more mature members sharing with the less mature."[26] This is attainable only to the extent that one is authentic.

Authenticity is achieved through unwavering fidelity to the exigencies of one's intelligence, reasonableness, and conscience. The business of molding minds is predicated on authenticity. Without authenticity the shortcomings of the individual teacher or the one in authority can become the accepted practice of the school or group; and the accepted practice of the school or group in turn becomes

---

22. Ibid., 292.

23. Ibid.

24. Bernard Lonergan, *Method in Theology* (Toronto: University of Toronto Press, 1996), 99.

25. Frere, *Christian Faith and Higher Education*, 15.

26. Ibid.

the tradition accepted in good faith by succeeding generations. "The evil can spread to debase and corrupt what is more vulnerable while it prostitutes to unworthy ends what otherwise is sound and sane. Then the authentic, if any have survived, are alienated from their society and their culture. The courageous look about for remedies but find none that even appear equal to the task. The average man, who knows he was not born to be a hero, decides he has no choice but to go along with things as they are. And the more numerous the people who concur with that decision, the less is the hope of recovery from unauthenticity, the greater the risk of the disintegration and the decay of a civilization."[27]

Lonergan's Pursuit of Authenticity

We have already discussed the role of authenticity in Lonergan's work in chapter 5; but a few points should be reiterated in the present context. The crucial question for Lonergan, as relates to authenticity, is this: how can one tell that one is not appropriating a tradition that has become unauthentic?[28] For him, "love, loyalty and faith can all be questioned. When they are authentic, readily they are esteemed beyond price. But so easily they are unauthentic, whether from the failures of the individual or, tragically, from the individual's authentic appropriation of an unauthentic tradition."[29] This means that the question of authenticity, as it pertains to CIT, emerges in two ways. First there is the authenticity of the individual as he or she relates to the accepted tradition; and second, there is the authenticity of "that tradition itself which becomes questionable when the failures of individuals become the rule rather than the exception, when vital reinterpretation is corrupted by rationalization, when heartfelt allegiance more and more gives way to alienation."[30]

27. Lonergan, "The Ongoing Genesis of Methods," 151–52.

28. Bernard Lonergan, "Religious Knowledge," in *Lonergan Workshop*, ed. Lawrence, 1:310–11.

29. Ibid., 314.

30. Ibid., 310.

MODULE 2: CIT ATTENDS TO DIVERSITY AND INCULTURATION

The Catholic tradition is as Efik as it is Greek. It is as Hausa as it is English, as Twi as it is French, as Wolof as it is Spanish, as Ibo as it is German, as Yoruba as it is Dutch, as Swahili as it is Polish, as Kikuyu as it is Flemish, as Mexican as it is Canadian, as Anglo as it is Saxon, and as African as it is European. CIT is not merely a tradition of diverse languages and cultures; it is nourished and sustained by diversity. A Catholic school is a melting pot of diverse people of diverse cultures and diverse languages, signifying in reality the root meaning of the word "catholicity" (universality in the sense of "throughout the whole world").

A Catholic institution of higher learning strives to build an authentic Christian community where people of different backgrounds may feel welcome. Sadly, the concept of community today critically needs rehabilitation, largely because natural communities of the past have been weakened by many influences, such as urbanization and suburbanization.[31] Where a living and vibrant community is lacking there is bound to be racial and ethnic tension. A Catholic school meets this challenge through its commitment to community and development of social skills and virtues needed to overcome ethnic and racial fragmentation.[32] "Participation together in the liturgy and in paraliturgical activities and spiritual exercises can effectively foster community among students and faculty. Since the Gospel spirit is one of peace, love, patience and respect for others, a school rooted in these principles ought to explore ways to deepen its students' concern for and skill in peacemaking and the achievement of justice."[33]

The educational mission of the Church is an integrated ministry, consisting of three important and interlocking dimensions: *didachē*, i.e., teaching, the revealed message that the Church proclaims; *koinōnia*, i.e., fellowship in the life of the Spirit, and *diakonia*, i.e., service to the Christian community as well as to the entire human community. The integration of religious truth and life values distinguishes a Catholic

---

31. USCCB, *To Teach as Jesus Did* (Washington, DC: USCCB, 1973), 30.

32. Ibid.

33. Ibid., 30–31.

school from other schools. Even where Catholic and non-Catholic schools share values, a Catholic school is unique "because it is distinguished by its commitment to the threefold purpose of Christian education [*didachē*, *koinōnia*, and *diakonia*] and by its total design and operation which foster the integration of religion with the rest of learning and living."[34] It is also contemporary because "it enables students to address with Christian insight the multiple problems which face individuals and society today."[35] And it is oriented to Christian service because "it helps students acquire skills, virtues, and habits of heart and mind required for effective service to others."[36]

Catholic intellectual tradition, for these reasons, pays attention to cultural pluralism and fosters inculturation, encouraging all those under its umbrella to make incarnate meanings derived from their learning. It helps them to transpose meaning grasped within one cultural context into another seemingly different cultural context. "As a multicultural tradition, its richness is in proportion to its appropriation of the distinctive gifts of many cultures—some literary, some liturgical, some artistic, some anthropological, etc."[37] CIT mediates "what Christians believe as true and value as good, not so much with a relatively stable set of cultural meanings and values as with an emergent and potentially more differentiated set adequate to a global social order."[38]

Lonergan's Sensitivity to Cultural Pluralism

The terms *meaning* and *mystery* taken together define Lonergan's life and work. When Lonergan speaks of meaning he is thinking about historicity and inculturation.[39] He understood culture as a set of

---

34. Ibid., 29.

35. Ibid.

36. Ibid., 30.

37. John Haughey, SJ, *Where Is Knowing Going? Horizons of the Knowing Subject* (Washington, DC: Georgetown University Press, 2009), 88.

38. Robert M. Doran, *Theological Foundations: Theology and Culture*, vol. 2 (Milwaukee: Marquette University Press, 1995), 525.

39. Frederick Crowe, "From Kerygma to Inculturation: The Odyssey of Gospel Meaning," in *Developing the Lonergan Legacy: Historical, Theoretical, and Existential Themes*, ed., Michael Vertin (Toronto: University of Toronto Press, 2004), 21–22.

meanings and values embodied in a people's way of life and their attunement with the deepest exigencies of human liberty.[40] He spent a great deal of time reflecting on how to effect a shift from classicist to modern culture. In the classicist view of culture the Church was a *societas perfecta* (perfect society) endowed with all the powers neces-sary for its autonomy. In a *societas perfecta*, a classicist thinks of him-self or herself as conferring a double benefit on those to whom he or she is reaching: the gospel and the "riches" of the one and only true culture. In debunking this myth, Lonergan shows how the Church, like the state or any society, is not a perfect society, but a *Selbstvoll-zug*, an ongoing process of self-realization "in which the constitutive, the effective, and the cognitive meaning of Christianity is continu-ously in ever changing situations."[41]

In Lonergan's distinction between a society and community, five key elements are contained in the notion of society: intersub-jective spontaneity, technological institutions, the economic system, the political order, and culture. These elements are interrelated. The more complex a society is, the more differentiated the elements.[42] Culture is the clue to the ethos of a society (tone, character, quality of life, and style) and sets the horizon within which the specific prob-lems of political agreement are to be resolved.[43] It is the operative set of meanings and values that govern a society's way of life, "an histori-cally transmitted pattern of meanings embodied in symbols, a system of inherited conceptions expressed in symbolic forms by means of which men communicate, perpetuate and develop their knowledge about and attitudes towards life."[44]

---

40. Lonergan, *Method in Theology*, xi. See also Frederick Lawrence, "Lonergan as a Political Theologian," in *Religion in Context: Recent Studies in Lonergan*, ed. Timothy Fallon and Philip Riley (Lanham, MD: University Press of America, 1988), 12.

41. Bernard Lonergan, "Revolution in Catholic Theology," in *A Second Collection: Papers by Bernard J. F. Lonergan, SJ*, ed. William Ryan and Bernard Tyrell (Toronto: University of Toronto Press, 1974), 233–34.

42. Bernard Lonergan, *Insight: A Study of Human Understanding*, in *Collected Works*, 3:237–38.

43. Doran, *Theological Foundations*, 2:234–35.

44. Ibid., quoting Clifford Geertz, *The Interpretation of Cultures* (New York: Basic Books 1973), 89.

One of the key functions of culture is to reverse decline.[45] Human living, informed by meanings, is a product of intelligence, which not only develops cumulatively over time but also differs (in its development) in different histories.[46] This development goes through three stages or realms of meaning. There is the realm of common sense, the realm of theory, and the realm of interiority. The realm of common sense is learning in its infancy. Not much thought is involved. One merely depends on what the senses provide. The realm of theory is a progressive development of the realm of common sense. Here one begins to grasp concepts and ideas. The progressive development from the level of common sense to theory is analogous to what Paul described: "When I was a child, I spoke like a child, I thought like a child, I reasoned like a child; when I became an adult, I put an end to childish ways" (1 Cor. 13:11). The third level is the realm of interiority, when one begins to make one's own what one has learned; one no longer makes decisions and choices on the evidence of others, but on one's own. In Paul's words, "when the complete [or 'perfect'] comes, the partial will come to an end" (1 Cor. 13:10); the third stage approaches "perfection."

It is essential for Lonergan that human cultures move into a third stage of meaning. While it may not be the responsibility of CIT to help cultures move from one stage of meaning to another, Catholic institutions of higher learning can play a significant part in the process if CIT works from an empirical notion of culture and acknowledges that there are varieties of human mentalities. An empirical culture acknowledges a multiplicity of cultural traditions and the possibility of diverse human mentalities.[47] In these vast differentiations, once the Christian doctrine has been successfully introduced into a culture its subsequent development calls for further exploitation of the resources of that culture. Simply to use the resources of one's own culture is not to communicate with the other but to remain locked up in one's own.[48] The meanings of the

---

45. Doran, *Theological Foundations*, 2:63.

46. Lonergan, *Method in Theology*, xi.

47. Bernard Lonergan, *Philosophical and Theological Papers 1965–1980*, in *Collected Works*, 72.

48. Lonergan, *Method in Theology*, 300.

Christian message must be diligently and creatively reconstructed to a people of a particular time and a particular place using the resources of that culture, discovering in the process, not only accurate but also effective manners of conceptualizing the message.[49] "If interpretation of the faith of the early church is a problem precisely because the early church expressed its faith in a way of thinking that is foreign to us, then presumably there will be a similar problem when we go on to express Catholic doctrine in the equally foreign categories of the various particular cultures of the world."[50] Creative employment of the resources of the culture makes it possible to say in that culture what as yet had not been said.[51]

The demand Lonergan makes on CIT to embrace an empirical notion of culture must have been the fruit of the seed planted by his reading of Christopher Dawson's *The Age of the Gods* in the 1930s.[52] Dawson's book was providential for Lonergan in that it corrected early in his formative years his hitherto normative or classicist notion of culture and made him embrace an anthropological or modern culture.[53] "Reflections on race, environment, economics, and mind, the main influences that shape a culture, lead Dawson to ask, what is progress? He is concerned with understanding the world order by means of which, empirically, a succession of cultures emerge, flourish, atrophy, and decay into extinction or are reborn."[54] Dawson shows how progress does not follow a single uniform law, but is attainable by a series of possible types of social and cultural change.[55] Dawson's book raised for Lonergan the questions of economic and cultural progress and decline, questions Lonergan would ponder for many years and would apply to contemporary discussion of culture as it relates to CIT.

---

49. Lonergan, *Philosophical and Theological Papers 1965–1980*, 72.

50. Frederick Crowe, "The Spectrum of 'Communication' in Lonergan," in *Developing the Lonergan Legacy*, ed. Vertin, 70–71.

51. Lonergan, *Philosophical and Theological Papers 1965–1980*, 72.

52. Crowe, "From Kerygma to Inculturation," 28–29.

53. Frederick Crowe, *Lonergan* (London: Geoffrey Chapman, 1992), 18.

54. William Mathews, *Lonergan's Quest: A Study of Desire in the Authoring of Insight* (Toronto: University of Toronto Press, 2005). 50.

55. Ibid.

By addressing the problem of contemporary culture, Lonergan in effect addresses the challenge facing contemporary philosophy of education. It was for him an epochal problem,[56] comparable to the crisis leading up to the Greek discovery of the mind.[57] The Greek discovery of the mind marked the transition from the first stage of meaning (the world of common sense) to the second (the world mediated by meaning). "The Greek historical experience was limited to the breakdown of myth. It was an experience of the collapse of an unreflective, spontaneous mediation of meaning."[58] The breakdown of the classical mediation of meaning is a breakdown of a reflectively achieved effort to control meaning. "As the Greeks completed and consolidated the transition from the mythic mentality to the logical mentality, we must complete and consolidate the transition from the logical mentality to the methodical mentality."[59] Lonergan's mediation of the transcultural constituents of integrity would lead to a world-cultural humanity.[60] It is a realm of authenticity or genuineness in which one makes choices and decisions on the evidence of intellectually satisfying answers that one has reached on one's own.

MODULE 3: CIT RESPECTS UNITY OF REASON AND FAITH

Earlier we pointed out that we need to distinguish the Catholic intellectual tradition from the Church's sacred tradition. This distinction is helpful in understanding the relationship between faith and reason. It also "helps both faith and reason develop a mature, mutual respect for one another, as well as mutual dependence. It is also this

---

56. Mark Morelli, "Obstacles to the Implementation of Lonergan's Solution to the Contemporary Crisis of Meaning," in *The Importance of Insight: Essays in Honor of Michael Vertin*, ed. John Liptay Jr. and David Liptay (Toronto: University of Toronto Press, 2007), 22.

57. Lonergan, *Method in Theology*, 90. See also Bruno Snell, *The Discovery of the Mind* (New York: Harper Torchbook, 1960).

58. Morelli, "Obstacles," 22–23.

59. Ibid., 23.

60. Doran, *Theological Foundations*, 2:200.

interdependence that makes the Church effective in human affairs. It can bring a history of reasoning to such affairs that few other memories or traditions of reason are able to."[61] The unity of reason and faith is a central pillar in Catholic thought.[62] Contrary to the anti-intellectual perception of the Church in some quarters, what makes the Catholic tradition intellectual and distinguishes it from other traditions is its profound integration of Hellenic thought and its emphasis through the centuries on philosophical argument and historical tradition.[63] In *Fides et Ratio* (1998) John Paul II draws from the rich Catholic tradition of integration of faith and reason, showing how the human quest for truth, particularly transcendent truth, is a quest for human self-understanding, including the place of humanity in the natural world.[64] The elevation of tradition and reason mandates that Catholic universities retain requirements in philosophy and theology, whereas other institutions abandon them or give these disciplines a less privileged position.[65] The elevation of reason suggests that the Catholic intellectual is open to learning from other traditions and eager to pursue alternative understandings, either to ensure that one's positions measure up to reason or to adjust them accordingly.[66] The elevation of faith suggests that faith, rather than contradicting the rigorous use of reason, enriches one's grasp of the mystery and inexhaustible potential of truth.[67] "Catholic students tend to be at ease with tradition, which makes them more stable, a potential virtue in a world of flux; being anchored in super-temporal values, they may be more resistant to the faddishness of the age."[68]

---

61. Haughey, *Where Is Knowing Going?* 94.

62. Paula Powell Sapienza, "Catholic Intellectual Life: An Opportunity for the Church to Continue to Learn," in *As Leaven in the World: Catholic Perspectives on Faith, Vocation, and the Intellectual Life*, ed. Thomas M. Landy (Franklin, WI: Sheed and Ward, 2001), 19.

63. Roche, *Intellectual Appeal*, 24–25.

64. Sapienza, "Catholic Intellectual Life," 19.

65. Roche, *Intellectual Appeal*, 25.

66. Ibid., 27.

67. Ibid., 26.

68. Ibid., 31.

Lonergan's Integration of Reason and Faith

Lonergan carefully distinguishes between faith and belief and treats both as a form of knowledge.[69] Some contemporary philosophers and theologians tend to regard reliance on belief as uncritical because in belief one accepts the conclusions of others rather than what one has arrived at immanently oneself.[70] While Lonergan accepts that belief is not immanently generated knowledge, he insists that belief is a form of knowledge because it is rooted in one's reasonable judgment of value. Belief is based upon a judgment of value by which one accepts the judgments of fact and the judgments of value that are handed on through a religious tradition.[71] In Lonergan's description of "the usual process of coming to know something, understanding will precede judgment. In this regard, questions of meaning precede questions of truth. When it comes to belief, however, the reverse is the case. One accepts as true something which one does not know for oneself. Lonergan emphasized that belief, including religious belief . . . is a kind of knowledge in which the embrace of truth is basically prior to achieving a fuller understanding."[72]

For Lonergan, human minds "are not isolated faculties lost in a vast cosmic loneliness but are ultimately orientations toward Infinite Intelligence and Infinite Love."[73] He used what he retrieved from Aquinas on the relationship of human intelligence and freedom vis-à-vis infinite Intelligence-Love to dispel the myth of opposition between divine grace and human freedom.[74] The question of free will was debated by the ancient Greek philosophers, i.e., to what extent are humans free to make moral decisions and to what extent are their actions determined by forces beyond their control. This question took center stage in the fifth century in Augustine's debate with the Manicheans, who denied freedom of the will, and later in the rancorous debate between the Dominican school of theology in

---

69. See Lonergan, *Method in Theology*, 41, and *Insight*, 703–18.

70. Dennis M. Doyle, "Jesus' Founding of the Church," forthcoming.

71. Ibid.

72. Ibid.

73. Matthew Lamb, "Foreword," in *Creativity and Method: Essays in Honor of Bernard Lonergan, SJ*, ed. Matthew Lamb (Milwaukee: Marquette University Press, 1981), vii–viii.

74. Ibid., viii.

Salamanca, Spain, and their Jesuit counterparts. It resurfaced in the sixteenth-century Reformation with Luther and Calvin's denial of human free will—that humans can do no good works except when they are moved by God's grace.

Faith is knowledge born of religious love.[75] It is a further knowledge by which people acknowledge the love of God and apprehend transcendent value. It enables them to measure all other values against the transcendent value of truth, unity, goodness, and beauty. Transcendent value, as a measure of all other values, transforms all other values.[76] Faith liberates reason from its ideological prisons and can undo decline brought about by human inattention, oversights, irrationality, and unreasonableness. It gives confident assurance to one's undertakings.[77] Thus Lonergan's treatment of faith as a form of knowledge helps overcome fragmentation in modern consciousness, without imposition of extrinsic limitations on creativity that stifles openness to the new and unexpected.[78]

MODULE 4: CIT IS HISTORICALLY MINDED

Historical mindedness or historical consciousness runs counter to a normative conception of culture. Classicists who cling to the idea that there is only one culture (their own), which is valid for all peoples and all times, have a normative conception of history. Their idea of history is linear. But the modern idea of culture, thanks to the social and behavioral sciences, is not monolithic, but pluriform. It understands that history is not linear, but multidimensional and that sensitivities to times, places, circumstances, etc., have merit. To illustrate this point, as this manuscript was being prepared, news media reported about a high school history teacher in Georgia in trouble over a class project assignment in which he asked some students to dress like the Ku Klux Klan (KKK). When those unaware of the project saw "Klansmen" on campus, they became alarmed, unaware that these were fellow students dressed for a history project. The

---

75. Lonergan, *Method in Theology*, 115.

76. Ibid., 116.

77. Ibid., 117.

78. Lamb, "Foreword," viii.

good intention of the history teacher notwithstanding, he had erred in judgment and in historical mindedness, ultimately leading to his suspension as the matter was investigated.

Catholic colleges and universities strive to produce students with a global perspective (world citizens). World citizens need knowledge of history and social fact.[79] Being historical minded is to be aware of the past. As we have seen, some who question the very idea of a Catholic university do so on the premise that it is not clear whether one can genuinely speak of a Catholic university in the face of the darker moments in the Catholic tradition, notably the Church's tendency to undermine individual responsibility, to act irrationally regarding certain advances of science, to espouse teachings not always in harmony with reason, and to evolve only slowly in relation to gender equality.[80]

History, as Lonergan conceives it, is a triadic movement of progress-decline-redemption. There are in Church history ample examples that whenever Church leaders abandon rationality for myopia, the tradition suffers, and whenever they enlarge their horizons the intellectual tradition prospers.[81] The suppression of Galileo and the crusades of the Middle Ages, to cite two examples, continue to haunt the Church as dark moments that could have been avoided had the Church sought a higher viewpoint in the lessons of history. Compare that to the ecumenical spirit that prevailed at Vatican II, however, when the Church was willing to listen to different viewpoints and consider different voices, Catholic and non-Catholic alike. This ecumenical spirit has greatly enriched the Catholic intellectual tradition.

Historical Mindedness in Lonergan's Life and Work

Lonergan understood the value of historical mindedness to CIT. There were two great shifts that immensely influenced Lonergan's

---

79. Martha C. Nussbaum, *Cultivating Humanity: A Classical Defense of Reform in Liberal Education* (Cambridge, MA: Harvard University Press, 1997), 85. See also M. C. Nussbaum, *Poetic Justice: The Literary Imagination in Public Life* (Boston: Beacon Press, 1996).

80. Roche, *Intellectual Appeal*, 2.

81. Haughey, *Where Is Knowing Going?* 82.

thinking and convinced him that the thought of St. Thomas needed a radical rethinking. The first was the scientific revolution that effected a shift from Aristotelian to modern science (a shift in the world of theory). While the Aristotelian science was individualistic and permanent in its achievements, modern science is ongoing, collaborative, and open to further development.[82] "Aristotelian science wanted to be a Thucydidean[83] possession for all time. . . . But modern science claims no more for its positive achievements than probability. The ideal has ceased to be a definitive achievement; it has become ongoing advance."[84] It was the influence of this shift in Lonergan's thinking that culminated in the *Verbum* articles published in *Theological Studies* (1946–1949).[85] The second shift that influenced Lonergan was the critical movement in philosophy that was begun by Descartes, Hume, Kant, and Hegel. This critical movement led him to embark on a critical study of modern philosophy. His study of Kant and Hegel led him to the realization that every search for knowledge is a heuristic search for an unknown.[86] He would derive from this a relation or ongoing dynamism between questioning and answering. While the questioner does not know the answer, he or she at least intends it, for the question itself sets the standard that leads to the rejection of insufficient answers.[87] It was this recognition that made Lonergan take seriously what Alan Richardson termed *historical mindedness*[88] when he came in contact with the German Historical School when he returned to Rome in 1953 to teach at the

---

82. Nelson Falcao, *"Knowing" According to Bernard Lonergan* (Rome: Urbaniana University Press, 1987), 17–21.

83. Thucydides (460–400 BCE) was a Greek historian who wrote about the history of the Peloponnesian War (the war between Sparta and Athens in the fifth century). The information we have about this important war solely derives from Thucydides. Thucydides thought that the facts he revealed in his book should be regarded as the general principles that ought to govern human behavior.

84. Bernard Lonergan, "Aquinas Today: Tradition and Innovation," *Journal of Religion* 55 (1975): 171.

85. See Bernard Lonergan, *Verbum: Word and Idea in Aquinas*, ed. David Burrell (Notre Dame, IN: Darton, Longman and Todd, 1967).

86. Falcao, *"Knowing" According to Bernard Lonergan*, 25.

87. Bernard Lonergan, "A Post-Hegelian Philosophy of Religion," in *Lonergan Workshop*, ed. Lawrence, 3:181.

88. See Alan Richardson, *History Sacred and Profane* (London: S.C.M., 1964), 32.

Gregorian. To be clear, it was not Hegel, but the German Historical School that was a strong agent in the shift in Lonergan's thinking, particularly the change in his thinking after *Insight*.[89] The influence of this school would lead him to speak of historicity and history as related and to agree with the school, in their massive effort to comprehend the human person, not in the abstract, but in its concrete self-realization, that the goal of history is "the interpretative reconstruction of the constructions of the human spirit."[90]

Lonergan would write later that "to understand men and their institutions we have to study their history. For it is in history that man's making of man occurs, that it progresses and regresses, that through such changes there may be discerned a certain unity in an otherwise disconcerting multiplicity."[91] He would much later speak of the emergence of a new historical thinking in CIT quite different from what obtained in the past. He would credit this new broad historical thinking to Arnold Toynbee's *A Study of History* (1934–1961) and Eric Voegelin's *Order and History* (1956–1987). Lonergan appreciated the fact that Voegelin's interpretation of history is sympathetic to religion.[92]

MODULE 5: CIT APPRECIATES THE UPPER BLADE OF HISTORY

A contemporary Catholic education cannot overlook the value of history. The distinguished English historian, Herbert Butterfield, was once asked what difference it would make if people knew no history at all. His answer was that if people knew no history at all they could probably get along well in their public and private lives.[93] " 'The trouble is,' says Butterfield, 'there is a great deal of history that is bad history, that has disastrous effects in all directions, and this makes history a matter of the greatest practical importance:

89. Crowe, *Christ and History*, 90.

90. Lonergan, "Natural Right and Historical Mindedness," 171.

91. Ibid., 171.

92. Lonergan, *Topics in Education*, 16–17.

93. Ibid., 4, referencing Herbert Butterfield, *History and Human Relations* (London: Collins, 1951), 171–72.

bad history must be replaced with a good history.'"[94] There is a tendency in our educational curriculum, unfortunate though it seems, to simply present history as a story or chronicle of past events that students need to be aware of lest history repeats itself. Noticeably absent in the way history is taught is the nature of historical insight and its relation to historical consciousness or historical mindedness. This absence reduces historical thinking and historical consciousness to a set of benchmarks or psychological processes, failing to situate historical thinkers or events being studied in their proper personal, political, and social contexts.[95]

Rather than a story of the past, CIT approaches history as a form of inquiry. It helps students "make sense of who they are, where they stand, and what they can do—as individuals, as members of multiple, intersecting groups, and as citizens with roles and responsibilities in relation to nations and states in a complex, conflict-ridden, and rapidly changing world."[96] There are six generally accepted procedural concepts or core issues to be taken into account if history is to be presented, not as a story of the past, but as a form of critical inquiry. The first is the concept of historical significance, "an acknowledgment that historians do not produce chronicles about everything that happened in the past; that embedded into the creation of historical narratives or representations are judgments about what is important about the past."[97] The second is historical epistemology and evidence—understanding the basis for claiming to know about the past.[98] The third is continuity and change—that change is continuous and occurs in different rates and affects people in different ways.[99] The fourth is progress and decline—that situations

94. Lonergan, *Topics in Education*, 4.

95. Lance Grigg and Amy von Heyking, "Lonergan and Current Research on Historical Thinking in Education: A Dialogue" (paper presented at the Twenty-Fifth Annual Fallon Memorial Lonergan Symposium WCMI, Loyola Marymount University, Los Angeles, April 8–10, 2010).

96. Ibid; quoting Peter Seixas, "What Is Historical Consciousness?" in *To the Past: History Education, Public Memory, and Citizenship in Canada*, ed. Ruth Sandwell (Toronto: University of Toronto Press, 2006), 21.

97. Grigg and Heyking, "Lonergan and Current Research."

98. Ibid.

99. Ibid.

can improve or worsen over time, depending on the choices and decisions that are made.[100] Fifth is historical agency—that economic, political, social, and cultural factors can and do contribute to change.[101] Finally, there is the concept of historical empathy—that historical imagination or appreciation of historical perspective "requires that when students are drawing conclusions about the past and about representations of the past, they are informed about and remain conscious of the values, beliefs and worldviews of the time and of their own."[102]

Lonergan and the Challenge of History

Lonergan's life's work may be summed up as "introducing history into Catholic theology," a history set within the wider context of the Second Vatican Council, because Vatican II was for him also "the acknowledgment of history."[103] As a discipline to be studied, Lonergan regarded history as something totally different, at least pedagogically, from other disciplines or subjects in that it does not easily lend itself to the formation of a scientific mentality; it does not help in the training of a student's critical power, at least in its early stages. Yet, for Lonergan, "reflection on history is one of the richest, profoundest, and most significant things there is."[104]

Lonergan introduced history into Catholic thought by first introducing it into his own thinking, making history intelligible in the context of theology that was strong on tradition.[105] When he embarked on a study of the speculative development of thought on grace from Augustine to Aquinas, Lonergan knew the study had to be historical without at the same time yielding to the positivist principles, the arid debates that dragged on interminably between the

100. Ibid.

101. Ibid.

102. Ibid.; paraphrasing O. L. Davis Jr., Elizabeth Ann Yeager, and Stuart J. Foster, eds., *Historical Empathy and Perspective Taking in the Social Studies* (Lanham, MD: Rowman and Littlefield, 2001).

103. Frederick Crowe, "All My Work Has Been Introducing History into Catholic Theology," in *Developing the Lonergan Legacy*, ed. Vertin, 78.

104. Lonergan, *Topics in Education*, 233.

105. Crowe, "All My Work," 80.

Spanish Jesuits and the Dominicans that stymied the development of Aquinas's position on the matter.[106] He found a middle course in the construction of an "a priori scheme that is capable of synthesizing any possible set of historical data irrespective of their place and time, just as the science of mathematics constructs a generic scheme capable of synthesizing any possible set of quantitative phenomena."[107] The scheme referenced here is the general form of the speculative movement on the nature of grace from Augustine to Aquinas that follows the general form of any speculative development that oscillates between the general and particular.[108] Crowe explains it as follows: "We have an insight on a specific point; we generalize it and make it the whole explanation; we learn it is insufficient for a complete explanation, so we go behind it to a more general factor; we make this in its turn the whole explanation, only to discover that it too is insufficient by itself; we go back to our first insight, the specific one, but now we make a synthesis of the general and specific, and have a better approximation to a complete explanation."[109] This is the self-correcting process of learning in which one comes to know, not by applying scientific methods, but by insights as they gradually accumulate, coalesce, qualify, and correct one another, until a point is reached when one is able to meet new situations as they arise and size them up by adding a few more insights to the acquired store.[110] Thus, using his dialectic of particular and general discoveries, Lonergan, knowing full well that he was dealing with actual history, was able to find an intelligible order in the works of greats like Augustine, Abelard, Bernard Clairvaux, Peter Lombard, Alexander of Hales, Albert the Great, and Thomas Aquinas.[111]

In *Insight* Lonergan spoke of his heuristic structure in terms of the metaphor of a scissors: upper blade and lower blade.[112] In the metaphor, the lower blade is the accumulation and collection of data

---

106. Ibid., 83.
107. Ibid., 84.
108. Ibid.
109. Ibid.
110. Lonergan, *Method in Theology*, 81.
111. Crowe, "All My Work," 85.
112. Lonergan, *Insight*, 337 and 546.

and the upper blade is the structure in which the data is ordered.[113] Using the scissors metaphor analogously for Lonergan's life work in general, without specifying the lower blade, Crowe thinks the upper blade is surely history because history was a dominant theme in Lonergan's own life work.[114] History was also a unifying theme that captured his early interest.[115] Lonergan, according to Crowe, remarked that the "whole problem in modern theology, Protestant and Catholic, is the introduction of historical scholarship."[116] Crowe suggests that we make a distinction in Lonergan's thinking between the history that is written and "the history that is written about" and argues that though both types of history engaged Lonergan's interest, it was the latter, the history that is written about, that Lonergan regarded as the real problem. Granted that the history that is written is closely linked with the history that is written about,[117] Lonergan was troubled by historical positivism, truth claims that ridicule faith or do not adequately take faith into consideration.[118] "The history that is written is a second-order category that emerged as a scientific study with the German Historical School in the 1800s (Leopold von Ranke, 1795–1886); it became a challenge to Lonergan and an object of his special study with his transfer to Rome in 1953."[119] The need to understand the history that happens and move it forward is a chief characteristic to be found in Lonergan's writing, including *Insight* and *Method in Theology*.[120]

What is termed *the underlying structure of history* ranks very high in Lonergan's thinking. The structure, which includes the triads of progress, decline, and redemption, was supposed to be the title of the

---

113. See Neil Ormerod, "Charles Taylor in Conversation with Lonergan and Doran: On Upper and Lower Blades," in *Meaning and History in Systematic Theology: Essays in Honor of Robert M. Doran, SJ*, ed., John D. Dadosky (Milwaukee: Marquette University Press, 2009), 449–63, at 450; see footnote 3.

114. Crowe, *Christ and History*, 12.

115. Ibid., 166.

116. Crowe, "All My Work," 78.

117. Crowe, *Christ and History*, 168.

118. Crowe, "All My Work," 83.

119. Crowe, *Christ and History*, 168.

120. Ibid., 168–69.

final chapter of *Insight* before Lonergan abandoned the idea.[121] But the triad of progress, decline, and redemption was never abandoned because the triad is "a permanent and constitutive feature of human life, always operative in human affairs, a continual dialectic at work within the human subject: we are always at one and the same time making progress, falling into decline, and being renewed."[122] Crowe thinks this three-fold structure, later worked out ordinarily in the context of history, is that which carries human affairs forward, not in historical succession of events, but in the ongoing dialectic of growth.[123] "The shape and form of human knowledge, work, social organization, cultural achievement, communication, community, personal development," Lonergan writes, "are involved in meaning. Meaning has its invariant structures and elements but the contents in the structures are subject to cumulative development and cumulative decline."[124] Crowe thinks this is better described as a theology of history.[125] History, for Lonergan, is that cultural change that rendered scholasticism irrelevant and demands the development of a new theological method and style that, though continuous with the old, meets all the genuine exigencies both of Christian religion and of up-to-date philosophy, science, and scholarship.[126] "So it is that man stands outside the rest of nature, that he is a historical being, that each man shapes his own life but does so only in interaction with the traditions of the communities in which he happens to have been born and, in turn, these traditions themselves are but the deposit left him by the lives of his predecessors."[127] It is in history that what one makes of oneself takes place and in history that a person progresses and regresses.[128] When Lonergan speaks of his life work being that of introducing history into Catholic

---

121. Frederick Crowe, "The Future: Charting the Unknown with Lonergan," in *Developing the Lonergan Legacy*, ed. Vertin, 354.

122. Ibid., 354–55.

123. Ibid., 355.

124. Lonergan, *Method in Theology*, 81.

125. Crowe, "The Future," 355.

126. Bernard Lonergan, "Unity and Plurality: The Coherence of Christian Truth," in *A Third Collection*, 247.

127. Lonergan, *Method in Theology*, 81.

128. Bernard Lonergan, "Natural Right and Historical Mindedness,"171.

theology, he is attempting, as it were, "to combine changing history and permanent dogma, to have a view of things that is broad enough and deep enough and strong enough to allow one to acknowledge history and retain traditional faith."[129]

Crowe cites Aquinas's *Summa Theologiae* (1–2, q.109, a.8) where Aquinas, referencing Aristotle's *Ethica* (3, c.8, 117a 18–22) agrees with Aristotle that character is manifested *ex repentinis*, i.e., in sudden reaction to the unexpected. Crowe suggests that it is in the nature of Lonergan to think in terms of change, development, and history, and that some phrases in Lonergan's writings suggest this fact. Such phrases include: "on the move," "ongoing," "transition," "emergence," "from . . . to," "systems on the move," "ongoing discovery of mind," the "long transition from primitive fruit-gatherers, hunters, and fishers to the large-scale agriculture of the temple states," and "how is there effected the transition from one level or stage in human culture to another later level or stage."[130] The point of all this is to show Lonergan's theological analysis of God's entry into human history and how all history is brought to unity in Christ.[131] Lonergan's theological analysis of history is based on three main approximations: first, that humans always do what is intelligent and reasonable, the implication being an ever increasing progress; second, the radical inverse insight that people can be biased and so unintelligent and unreasonable in their choices and decisions, thus leading to decline; third, the redemptive process resulting from God's gift of grace to individuals and the manifestation of God's love in Christ Jesus.[132]

MODULE 6: CIT FOSTERS UNITY OF KNOWLEDGE AND METHOD

A Catholic university emphasizes the unity of knowledge. Such emphasis calls for the development of method. CIT today, unlike in the past, acknowledges the fundamental role of method in the unity

---

129. Crowe, "All My Work," 104.

130. Crowe, *Christ and History*, 169.

131. Ibid., 172.

132. Bernard Lonergan, "Insight Revisited," in *A Second Collection*, 272.

of knowledge. In the past a single value served as an overarching framework for different spheres of life. For example, the idea of God provided such a framework in the Middle Ages.[133] The modern secular culture is, "characterized by a splintering of the spheres of life into autonomous subsystems, each of which has its own inner logic."[134] The fatal outcome of this is disintegration of knowledge, which has led modern culture to view the diverse subsystems of modern life as autonomous and beyond moral judgment.[135] The Catholic tradition, inspired by the ideal of integrative knowledge, "seeks in contrast to cultivate meaningful and integrative thought across the disciplines and argues that morality is not one sphere separate from the others but that it infuses all spheres: one can and should ask moral questions of architecture, art, business, engineering, law, politics, science, society, even religion."[136] What this means is that theoretically there is no area of rational human inquiry that cannot inform faith and there is no aspect of faith that cannot impact our efforts to reason and make sense of our experiences.[137] The ideal of unity of knowledge might seem foreign or strange to the modern mind, but an ideal that promotes fragmentation or disjointing of knowledge is hardly defensible.[138] "The lost ideal of holistic knowledge provides, precisely in its foreignness, a valuable antidote to some of the weaknesses of the modern age and of the contemporary university. . . . This ideal can help address a broader crisis in higher education and in contemporary culture, a crisis that calls out for alternative models."[139]

In chapter six, where we compared Lonergan's cognitional method (CM) with the multiple intelligence (MI) theory of Howard Gardner, we saw that human learning calls for multiple differentiations of consciousness because of the self-transcending and unrestricted nature of "knowing." One of the reasons for the comparisons was to show that the unlimited possibility in the act of knowing

133. Roche, *Intellectual Appeal*, 33.

134. Ibid.

135. Ibid., 34.

136. Ibid., 35.

137. Sapienza, "Catholic Intellectual Life," 18.

138. Roche, *Intellectual Appeal*, 41.

139. Ibid.

necessarily calls for a development of method, even though far too many educational institutions either do not have method or ignore its possibility. "With regard to the Catholic intellectual tradition, the temptation that has to be stared down and avoided is to ignore method, and to look instead for contents that have already been established, on the assumption that to be faithful to this tradition, one's findings must somehow or other be isomorphic with or deduced from contents already arrived at by this tradition."[140] When Aquinas, for example, used Aristotelian philosophy to explain Christian teaching, at first it drew the ire of Church authorities who thought only the Platonism of the Fathers was compatible with Christian teaching. The Archbishop of Paris condemned Aquinas and ordered his work to be destroyed. But the same Aquinas a few years later was proclaimed *doctor ecclesiae* (doctor of the Church)—one of only four persons on whom the Church had bestowed this title up to that time. On August 4, 1880 Leo XIII proclaimed Aquinas to be patron of Catholic schools, all because his method, which was once vilified, with the benefit of hindsight was seen to be revolutionary.

There is another compelling reason why the existence of CIT calls for a development of method. Most institutions of learning, whether Catholic, Protestant, or secular, pride themselves particularly in their mission statements of educating the whole person—without, however, indicating the method or means of arriving at this goal. Educating the whole person requires "a systematic and programmatic attention to the four realms of meaning: common sense, theory, interiority, and transcendence. Common sense and theory are the bread and butter of any school. . . . But understanding of the education of the whole person would require faculty and administrators to care for students' own unique interiorities, by teaching and modeling what it means to be attentive, intelligent, reasonable, and responsible."[141]

Lonergan's Approach to Method

For Lonergan, the question of human knowledge calls for a development of method. History of inquiry in all fields of human endeavor

---

140. Haughey, *Where Is Knowing Going?* 91.

141. Ibid., 84.

in the last two thousand years shows how advances in knowledge came only after the development of methods that served to clarify certain basic questions. Before Galileo there was no well-developed method for science. But science became successful with Galileo only because he helped scientists at the time develop a new methodical procedure. The human sciences became successful in the nineteenth century only after they developed their own method. Descartes invented the methodic doubt in response to the crisis resulting from the breakaway of the natural sciences from philosophy.[142] For Lonergan, therefore, the question of human identity can be resolved methodically, in so far as the principles of the method are not based on Aristotelian logical propositions but on concrete realities of a sensitive, intellectual, rational, and morally conscious subject.[143] "The shift from abstract premises to concrete subjects is not privation but enrichment. A basis in cognitional theory is not a negation of metaphysics but the establishment of a critically structured metaphysics. To replace faculty psychology by intentionality analysis is to set aside a jejune and ambiguous scheme in favor of a wealth of ordered fact."[144] When he embraced the *aggiornamento* program of John XXIII Lonergan was convinced that if Thomism was to remain relevant and continue its mediating function in contemporary theology a serious modification of the Aristotelian philosophy on which Thomism was built was needed.[145] Such modification calls for a clearly distinguished method as solution to disarray in contemporary theology, since contemporary theology was beginning to denote "not some well-defined form of thought but rather an aggregate of quite different and often quite nebulous forms."[146]

Lonergan concurred with Herbert Butterfield[147] that the scientific revolution of the sixteenth and seventeenth centuries that

---

142. Joseph Flanagan, *Quest for Self-Knowledge: An Essay in Lonergan's Philosophy* (Toronto: University of Toronto Press, 1997), 4.

143. Lonergan, "Aquinas Today," 46.

144. Ibid.

145. Ibid., 44.

146. Lonergan, "Third Lecture: The Ongoing Genesis of Methods," in *A Third Collection*, 146.

147. See Herbert Butterfield, *The Origins of Modern Science*, rev. ed. (New York: Free Press, 1997).

upturned the scientific views held up to the Middle Ages was the most significant discovery since the beginning of Christianity. The new scientific discovery called not only for the rejection of earlier held traditions but also for a new method that would replace that of the Middle Ages that relied heavily on Aristotelian science. "Where the Aristotelian placed his reliance on first principles he considered necessary, the modern scientist places his reliance ultimately not on the basic laws and principles but on his method. It was the method that brought forth the laws and principles in the first place, and it will be the method that revises them if and when the time for revision comes."[148] Thus, in contrast to the Aristotelian static view of the nature of the sciences and their relations to one another, Lonergan proposes a method that is not static but dynamic, not fixed once for all but that keeps developing and differentiating as the exigencies of progress demand.[149]

While method does not guarantee success, its discovery changes the way a knower proceeds and significantly alters the chances of success. There is a mistaken tendency, in scientific and ordinary forms of knowing, to assume that reality is already known and that it is known infinitely and absolutely. But there is a foundational difference between what we know immediately and what we know mediately through our operations of knowing; scientists may be aware of what they are doing, but awareness is not knowing. It is only a condition of knowing.[150] To achieve a methodical understanding of our philosophical identity as human beings we need to shift our attention away from what we know about ourselves or reality and pay attention to the conscious operations by which we know. "The foundational problem in this journey of self-discovery is to realize that we do not know the reality of anything, including ourselves, immediately. The reality that we do know is known in and through the mediating operations of knowing. This implies that we do not know reality, infinity, space, time, or any other basic constituent of reality, except in a very limited way."[151]

---

148. Lonergan, "The Ongoing Genesis of Methods," 149.

149. Ibid., 146.

150. Flanagan, *Quest for Self-Knowledge*, 5–7.

151. Ibid., 8–9.

MODULE 7: CIT USES THE GENERALIZED EMPIRICAL METHOD

Method, although difficult to develop, is indispensable for integration or unity of knowledge. Module 7 may serve as an alternative to module 6 where there is a struggle to develop one's own method. Methods, generally, can be adapted to any field of human endeavor and undergo revision and adaptation before they become specialized.

Lonergan and Generalized Empirical Method

Lonergan's solution to the problem of understanding was the generalized empirical method (transcendental method), a method that critiques not only basic assumptions but also provides a lens to evaluate our formulations of reality.[152] There are three practical elements of the generalized empirical method that are relevant to the Catholic university. The first is a two-pole movement: "One may ascend the levels from experience to values in the way of achievement, but equal in importance, indeed more fundamental and chronologically prior, is the descent in the other direction, the way of heritage, from love through values, truth, and understanding to a more mature and perceptive experience."[153] Second is the often neglected role of community. The way of heritage is possible only in community and is rendered actual only in community. "Even the way of achievement, where individuals must develop their own personal understanding, judgment, and set of values, even this way requires the community of pupil and teacher in the schools, and the collaboration of scientists and scholars in the academic community."[154] Third is the historical side of development. Although the levels of consciousness give us a structure, the history of the individual and that of the human race are also a record of what happens within a given structure. "Here we have room for all the differentiations of consciousness that pertain to the

---

152. Jacob Dumestre, PhD diss., "The Contribution of Bernard Lonergan toward the Recovery of a Catholic Philosophy of Education" (Vanderbilt University, 1990), 91.

153. Frederick E. Crowe, "Lonergan's Vocation as a Christian Thinker," in *Developing the Lonergan Legacy*, ed. Vertin, 3–20, at 13.

154. Ibid., 14.

human race: the artistic, the scholarly, the theoretic, the philosophic, the religious, the mystic. Here too are the various degrees in which we become authentic human beings or fail to become authentic, the various responses or failures to respond to the conversions proper to a fallen human race—intellectual, moral, religious."[155]

The content of knowledge, according to Lonergan, is so extensive that it mocks encyclopedias and overflows libraries.[156] In the dialectic of openness to truth, between the position of the naïve and the counterposition of the skeptic and between the position of the dogmatist and the counterposition of the relativist "there is not only something true but also something false in so far as the question for reflection (is it so?) requires both reflective understanding (against dogmatism) and the judgment based upon sufficient, not exhaustive, evidence (against relativism)."[157] To avoid the inherent dangers in the naïve and skeptic's positions and in the dogmatist and the relativist's positions, Lonergan insists that anyone intent on achieving self-transcendence cannot but be aware of their own shortcomings.[158] He makes a helpful distinction between "inner conviction" and "objective truth." Inner conviction is subjective. But objective truth, in principle, can be tested by anyone and is always beyond doubt or question.[159] By inner conviction is not meant passion or stubbornness or willful blindness, but "the fruit of self-transcendence, of being attentive, intelligent, reasonable, responsible; in brief of being ruled by the inner norms that constitute the exigencies for authenticity in the human person."[160] Inner conviction is the conviction that the norms of attentiveness, intelligence, reasonableness, responsibility have been satisfied. And satisfying those norms is the high road to the objectivity to be attained in a world mediated by meaning and motivated by values."[161] Lonergan probes whether inner conviction bears any relation to objective truth and concludes that science "yields not

155. Ibid.

156. Lonergan, *Insight*, 12.

157. Piscitelli, "Fundamental Attitudes," 312.

158. Lonergan, "Religious Knowledge," 314.

159. Ibid., 315.

160. Ibid., 327.

161. Ibid.

objective truth, but the best available opinion of the day."[162] Since science does not give us objective truth Lonergan recommends generalized empirical method as a solution to the dialectic of truth.

Generalized empirical method invites one to be at the level of one's time and leads one to the appreciation of how limited one's knowledge is and how such a limited knowledge is itself an instance of the limited achieved good. The content of knowledge is too vast to be grasped by only one individual person or one individual discipline—say history, or biology, or sociology. Lonergan's generalized empirical method challenges one to abandon such fragmentations of knowledge and seek in their place an integration of knowledge—dialogue with all the disciplines, including the natural and human sciences. Lonergan gave an example of this in his Halifax lectures where he recounted the story of Christopher Columbus defending himself on charges brought against him by the grandees of Spain. In his defense, Columbus cited the greatness of his discovery of America, to which the grandees responded that there was nothing great about it because all he (Columbus) did was simply sail west until he hit land. To further buttress his point, Columbus asked if any of the grandees could make an egg stand on its end. They tried, but to no avail. When it was Columbus's turn, he gave the egg a simple tap, and it stood on its end. The grandees, rather than hail Columbus, exclaimed, "Well, that is easy!" Columbus replied, "It's easy when you know how."[163]

MODULE 8: CIT CALLS FOR CONVERSION

Mark Roche identified, as a distinguishing mark of a Catholic university, the stress on universalist principle, i.e., on community of love.[164] This emphasis on community of love might be termed (moral) conversion in a loose sense. Roche sees many reasons—like

---

162. Ibid., 322.

163. See Bernard Lonergan, *Understanding and Being: An Introduction and Companion to Insight: The Halifax Lectures*, ed. E. A. Morelli and M. D. Morelli (New York: Mellon Press, 1987), 1, cited in Dumestre, "Contribution," 88.

164. Roche, *Intellectual Appeal*, 11. When I wrote this section I had not as yet adverted to the sophisticated notion of conversion—indeed a genetics of conversions that belongs to a developing collaboration. On this see "Fuse Series" on *www.philipmcshane.ca*, fuses 15–20, on the dialectic and the foundations of sequences of refined conversions.

the American Bill of Rights that stresses individuality and personal autonomy, and the influence of Protestantism—for concluding that America is fertile ground for the elevation of individuality. But Catholicism's emphasis on universals offers, in contradistinction to this American emphasis on individuality, a super-temporal value that balances the excesses of our culture and our age.[165] Anthony Bryk and Barbara Schneider, in their helpful study of school reform in Chicago in the 1990s,[166] offer empirical evidence that shows how schools are less likely to grow where there is no moral agency and peer community.[167] They wanted to find out why some Chicago schools were much better at educating children during the 1990s than others. After examining the curriculum, technique, professional development support, models of governance, and budgets of the schools they were studying they discovered that none of these variables significantly predicted who would succeed and who would not. The only variable that made a huge difference, according to their finding, was what they called "relational trust." Schools with high levels of relational trust had better chances of educating children than schools with lower levels of relational trust.[168] "Significantly, this correlation between relational trust and educational success held strong no matter what happened with those other, external variables; e.g., having the money to do what's needed does not overcome the distrust that keeps us from doing it."[169] What lies behind the relational trust is moral agency, the personal capacity to sideline one's ego for the common good (collegial community).[170]

A narrow conception of human values that stresses the individual dimension at the detriment of the communal dimension constitutes *reductive distortion*,[171] to the extent that the other dimensions

---

165. Roche, *Intellectual Appeal*, 12.

166. See A. S. Bryk and B. Schneider, *Trust in Schools: A Core Resource for Improvement* (New York: Russell Sage Foundation, 2002).

167. Parker Palmer, "On the Edge: Have the Courage to Lead with Soul," *National Staff Development Council* 29, no. 2 (2008): 13.

168. Ibid.

169. Ibid., 13–14.

170. Ibid., 14.

171. Dennis M. Doyle, *Communion Ecclesiology* (Maryknoll, NY: Orbis, 2000), 14.

of the human person, who is multidimensional, are disparaged or left unacknowledged. "Individualism is the insistence that the individual is the basic unit of human reality and that all types of community are secondary and accidental."[172] But the Catholic sense of community is primal in that it places community at the center of activity. It is nourished by a vibrant liturgical life. There is also devotion to the common good and to the poor and needy. Roche is quick to admit that Catholic universities are not alone in this task of moral education and community involvement as these can be found in non-Catholic universities as well. "What makes Catholic universities distinctive, however, is the explicit institutional commitment to these values, which tends to be less explicit and therefore increasingly less secure at secular universities."[173]

Knowing is not an activity that is fixed and unchangeable. It is a self-correcting process. Admittedly CIT is a continuous tradition that cannot be blown away by changing tides or wind, but it is self-correcting in the sense that it can revise its understandings as new evidence of its limitations emerges.[174] The attainment of knowledge calls for differentiation of consciousness: common sense, theory, interiority, and transcendence. A person may be operating in the realm of common sense and theory, but not in the realm of interiority. Such a person will not have the kind of understanding one operating in the realm of interiority would have. The latter would not only understand more but would also know how to relate the several realms to one another and would shift from one realm to another by consciously changing procedures in pursuit of truth. For such a person, knowledge would appear easy—in contrast to a person without a differentiated consciousness, for whom things would appear fuzzy and mysterious.[175] A further level is required, the realm of transcendence, which makes conversion imperative. Conversion is not only intellectual but also moral, religious, and affective. Conversion helps in overcoming fundamental conflicts in the human person who, in "a community of selves in conflict or tension," is involved

172. Ibid.

173. Roche, *Intellectual Appeal*, 16.

174. Haughey, *Where Is Knowing Going?* 88.

175. Lonergan, *Method in Theology*, 84.

in a self-conscious dialectical process.[176] A self-conscious authenticated human person is a being-in-the-world who understands that it is far from always true that the world in which we live is a world that really exists. Such a person not only thinks of the universe but also attempts to know what the universe really is.[177]

A good human education seeks to achieve, in the teacher and in the student, the fundamental attitudes of openness to understanding, knowing, and meaningful true human good. Self-knowledge, with truth as its specifying object; self-understanding, with meaning as its specifying object; and moral excellence, with the good as its specifying object, are the self-authenticating objectives of human education.[178] As understanding intends meaning, and knowing intends truth, and moral excellence intends the good, the self-authenticating objectives of human education make unavoidable the question of fundamental attitudes and basic orientation of the human person,[179] attitudes that orient a person toward self-transcendence.[180] Self-transcendence is that by which a person becomes authentically human. One fully realizes oneself because one has learned to surrender oneself through a religious experience.[181] The Auschwitz survivor and psychologist, Viktor Frankl (1905–1927), makes a compelling argument in *Man's Search for Meaning* that life is not something vague and that questions about the meaning of life cannot be answered by sweeping simplistic statements. Rather, life is something real and concrete.[182] It is for this reason that human beings are always searching for personal identity and meaning. Meaning can be found in the context of family and culture. Our families, community, culture, and social context influence the persons we are, the way we perceive ourselves, and our roles in the world.[183] It is also in the context of searching for

---

176. Piscitelli, "Fundamental Attitudes," 293.

177. Lonergan, "Religious Knowledge," 312.

178. Piscitelli, "Fundamental Attitudes," 292.

179. Ibid., 293.

180. Lonergan, "Religious Knowledge," 311.

181. Lonergan, *Method in Theology*, 104.

182. Viktor Frankl, *Man's Search for Meaning* (New York: Pocket Books, 1984), 98.

183. Margaret Huff and Ann Wetherilt, *Religion: A Search for Meaning* (Boston: McGraw Hill, 2005), 9–13.

meaning in our community and culture that we experience God, for as people experience their limitations as human beings they begin to realize that there is a reality beyond them. In this experience of limitation they begin to grasp the mystery of human existence and begin to transcend themselves. In this transcendental experience they experience God and begin to find out who they truly are.[184]

Conversion helps resolve the polarity of naiveté versus skepticism. Naïve persons exploit the "natural" belief that is part of their human spontaneity and willfully refuse to think intelligently. They seek security by depending on others for answers they can discover on their own. Paradoxically the more they depend on others the more insecure they become.[185] "Security is never a terminal value, understanding always is. Questions make the naïve uncomfortable so that what they do understand tends to become a set of fixed answers rather than a motive for further understanding."[186] No one, however, can live perpetually in a naïve world, a world where personal reflective thinking is outsourced to others. There would ensue an inevitable crisis that brings the naïve to the realization that unthought-out answers are no longer adequate.[187] Juxtaposed with the naïve attitude is that of the skeptic. Skepticism itself is a reaction to the naïve attitude to trust in the answers of others. "In its positive moment the attitude of skepticism is the power of questioning, for behind every doubt is a possible fruitful question; but the skeptic makes every question into a doubt and every doubt into a weapon of 'self-defense.'"[188] The skeptic, defining himself or herself in opposition to the naïve person, does not see meaning in human experience or intelligibility, thereby assuming that human experience and the intelligibility of the world collapse under the weight of his or her doubt.[189]

Apart from the differences they share in how and why the project of human understanding might be impossible, the naïve person

184. Karl Rahner, *Foundations of Christian Faith: An Introduction to the Idea of Christianity* (New York: Crossroads, 1997), 44–71.

185. Piscitelli, "Fundamental Attitudes," 297.

186. Ibid.

187. Ibid., 298.

188. Ibid.

189. Ibid.

and the skeptic share certain commonalities.[190] While the naïve person basks in the illusionary security of unthought-out answers and uncritically appropriated beliefs, the skeptic uses the well thought-out answers and beliefs of others as ground for unbelief. "Both seek security instead of understanding: naiveté, the security of unexamined beliefs; skepticism, the 'security' of empty self-reliance."[191] The naïve person's opposition to belief and knowledge, i.e., unthought-out answers, is the counterposition of the skeptic's opposition to knowledge and belief, i.e., self-reliance. Neither can be maintained without self-contradiction and neither is viable because they exclude the attitude of openness to understanding; both are impossible for authentic human selfhood and orientation to meaning.[192] "Self-transcendence is the eagerly sought goal not only of our sensitivity, not only our intelligent and rational knowing, not only of our freedom and responsibility but first of all of our flesh and blood that through nerves and brain have come spontaneously to live out symbolic meanings and to carry out symbolic demands."[193] In many indigenous societies, particularly African and Asian cultures, religion and culture are often inseparable because their cultural symbols also carry with them religious meanings and participation in religious practices is considered part of what it means to be a member of the community. What we call "religion" in the West (i.e., our Enlightenment critique of religion that separates religion from culture) would be for them part and parcel of a normal way of life and part of a person's search for identity and meaning.

Conversion also helps resolve the relativism versus dogmatism polarity. The dogmatist identifies the human orientation to truth with the dogmatist's own apprehension of the perceived truth. Dogmatists falsely identify the absolute expressed in true human discourse with the absolute truth intended by human discourse.[194] The dogmatist's false ideal of human knowledge tries to absolutely preserve and defend the dogmatist's unthought-out and unevidenced

190. Ibid., 299.

191. Ibid.

192. Ibid.

193. Lonergan, "Religious Knowledge," 313–14.

194. Piscitelli, "Fundamental Attitudes," 310.

quest for certainty—a self-defense mechanism. "The dogmatist feared being 'wrong' just as the naïve person feared being 'mistaken.' As she gives up the false ideal of certainty without giving up the fear of being wrong she begins to use a new defensive strategy: if she cannot preserve her certainty with her unthought-out, unevidenced judgments because one by one they are struck down by intelligent criticism, then the way she thinks she can protect herself from being wrong will be to suspend all judgments."[195]

Closely related but somewhat opposed to the unreasonable judgments of the dogmatist in the dialectic of openness to truth is the relativist who refuses to make judgment until all available evidence is examined. The relativist denies that anyone can know anything until the relativist ascertains that such knowledge has been reached.[196] The relativist reduces the question about truth (is it so?) to the question of understanding (what is it?). "These questions obviously cannot be reduced to each other. It is true that all human understanding involves some relativity, since direct understanding involves a grasp of things in relation to us (description) or of things in relation to one another (explanation), while reflective understanding involves a grasp of the relation between evidence and the fulfillment of the conditions in the virtually unconditioned—a relative absolute. Nevertheless, when we say that something is in fact the case, knowing always goes beyond the relativity of understanding and the conditions of the unconditioned."[197]

The relativist and dogmatist share a number of commonalities. The dogmatist is uncritical because of his or her tendency to make judgment without sufficient evidence. The relativist is uncritical because of his or her tendency to avoid making judgment until absolute certainty is reached.[198] The dogmatist suppresses questions for reflection, the relativist ignores the reflective act of human understanding by insisting on an infinite act of understanding, which is impossible.[199] The dogmatist and relativist both confuse a genuinely

---

195. Ibid.

196. Ibid., 311.

197. Ibid.

198. Ibid.

199. Ibid.

self-transcending quest for truth with a quest for certainty devoid of self-transcendence and tailored toward their own self-defensive mechanism.[200] "Just as the dogmatist falsely believes that his own human mind is already in possession of an absolute divine truth, so the relativist falsely thinks that a human mind cannot know anything that is true until it becomes an absolute divine mind which it can never become."[201]

Lonergan on Conversion

Lonergan was not unfamiliar with challenges. He was in his youth when the modernist crisis was tearing the Church apart. It is not easy to trace the history or origin of modernism, but the Catholic Church saw this nineteenth- and twentieth-century phenomenon as a threat to the faith. All modernists cannot be grouped together because there are variations in their teachings. But in general, those who were considered modernists, like George Tyrrell (1861–1909), an Anglo-Irish ex-Jesuit who became a principal modernist figure, were critical of the Church's teaching and attempted to explain the truth of human life solely through reason (science). The modernist crisis reached a new height when Alfred Loisy (1857–1940), a diocesan priest in France, published his *L'Evangile et L'Eglise*, denouncing the idea of God as a human attempt to project human personality on the divine. His book, like many others that were considered a threat to the Christian faith, was placed in the Index of Forbidden Books (books that Catholics were forbidden to read) by the Vatican in 1903. Modernism was condemned by a decree from the (Vatican) Holy Office known as *Lamentabili* in 1907. In the same year, Pius X also condemned modernism in the encyclical *Pascendi Dominici Gregis* (1907), declaring modernism a synthesis of all heresies. Fearful of the influence of modernist heresies among the clergy, in 1910 the Vatican came up with an Oath against Modernism that candidates for the priesthood were required to take. The oath remained in force until it was abolished in 1967 by Paul VI.[202]

---

200. Ibid.

201. Ibid., 312.

202. See Marvin R. O'Connell, *Critics on Trial: An Introduction to the Catholic Modernist Crisis* (Washington, DC: Catholic University of America Press, 1994).

As a theology professor in the 1940s, Lonergan had to interrupt his lectures on Christology to give his students a historical summary of the movements or forces that came together to birth modernism.[203] His effort to combat modernism was not an isolated event, but followed the same trajectory of ideas he developed to reform Catholic philosophy and theology. Catholic education could not be reformed unless errors such as those latent in modernism were combated. He would combat modernism following the steps laid down by the papal encyclical on modernism, *Pascendi Dominici Gregis*. While he was excited by the progress brought about by modernity, he was disappointed by the fact that the same modern development was susceptible to a monster of heresy that went by the name of modernism. What Lonergan did was accept features (modern science, modern philosophy, and modern scholarship) that belong to modernity and reject those that he thought turned modernity into the heresy of modernism.[204] Some modernists had accepted the findings of modern science, which they thought could be applied to Scripture. Lonergan accepted some of their positions, only to the extent that they were right. Scientific findings, for examples, can help shed light on one's understanding of Scripture, and Lonergan had no problem accepting that. But modernists' obtuse denial of faith was, for Lonergan, unacceptable. It was this denial that in part turned modernism into a heresy. Lonergan accepted the dogma of the Church as true. He saw truth as transcendent and having the character of the unconditioned, the absolute, and not tied to some determinate context.[205]

Similarly, Lonergan saw the challenge facing CIT as well as the contemporary crisis of meaning as analogous to the challenges faced by the Greeks in their transition from mythic mentality to logical mentality, and he sought ways to meet the challenge. In searching for cognitional foundations, the question for him was not whether knowledge exists but what precisely is its nature: when can one ascertain that one has acquired knowledge? His proposed solution would be, not a logical foundation in the classicist sense, but a "methodical

---

203. Crowe, *Christ and History*, 95.

204. Ibid.

205. Ibid., 98.

foundation in the distinctively modern fashion."[206] In the old Aristotelian-Thomistic distinction between *priora quod nos* (reality as it is known to us) and *priora quod se* (reality as it is in itself) only two stages of meaning were recognized: common sense and theory. But Lonergan recognized a third stage of meaning and offered a new starting point, moving away from faculty psychology to intentionality analysis.[207] In *Method*, where the break from faculty psychology becomes more explicit, rather than speak of intellect and will, Lonergan chose to speak of the second, third, and fourth levels of conscious intending: intelligent grasp (understanding), critical reflection (judgment), and evaluation and love (decision). This transcendental method would ensure a person's engagement in the acts of experiencing, understanding, and judging. "When people get to know something they do so precisely by performing these very operations, thereby using them as the foundation or point of departure for their knowledge."[208] Lonergan insisted that conscious and intentional operations "exist and anyone that cares to deny their existence is merely disqualifying himself as a non-responsible, non-reasonable, non-intelligent somnambulist."[209]

The fourth level of conscious intentionality—the level of deliberation, evaluation, and decision—is crucial in human consciousness. Lonergan identified the pure desire to know, described in *Insight*, with a pure detached desire for value because of the eminent place of value (in *Insight* the notion of being) as a fourth level of consciousness: decision.[210] Value, like being, is a transcendental notion. As being is a dynamic principle that moves one closer to a fuller comprehension of being, so value dynamically moves one closer to fuller realization of what is good and worthwhile.[211] Religious experience also

206. Morelli, "Obstacles," 23.

207. See Lonergan, *Method in Theology*, 76–78. Referenced also in Michael Morrissey, *Consciousness and Transcendence: The Theology of Eric Voegelin* (Notre Dame, IN: University of Notre Dame Press, 1994), 120.

208. Ulf Jonsson, *Foundations for Knowing God: Bernard Lonergan's Foundations for Knowledge of God and the Challenge from Antifoundationalism* (Frankfurt am Main: Peter Lang, 1999), 308.

209. Lonergan, *Method in Theology*, 17.

210. Ryan and Tyrell, eds., *A Second Collection*, viii.

211. Bernard Lonergan, "The Subject," in *A Second Collection*, 82.

belongs to the fourth level of conscious intentionality (decision). The foundations of religious experience lie in the intellectual, moral, religious, and affective development of a person. As functional specialties, foundations and dialectic correspond to the fourth level of consciousness in that they deal with religious experience and conversion.[212] Knowledge, in a nutshell, is acquired through a rigorous and critical process—requiring that one performs the functional specialties. The eight functional specialties, divided into two equal parts, correspond to the four levels of conscious intentionality. The first four, the mediating phase—research, interpretation, history, and dialectics—are akin to experience, understanding, judgment, and decision. The second four—foundations, doctrines, systematics, and communications—in reverse order correspond to decision, judgment, understanding, and experience. They constitute the mediated phase of the process by which knowledge is acquired. These are grounded on conversion, an about-face in which one discovers what is inauthentic in oneself and seeks a higher viewpoint to remedy it. Conversion is not a personal or private matter alone; it is also communal. It can happen to an individual student just as it can happen to an entire body or learning community. Conversion is not a onetime event that is attained once and for all. It is rather a reaching out, an ongoing process.

Lonergan spoke of conversion as intellectual, moral, religious, and even affective. To speak of fourfold conversion is to acknowledge that there are two variants of conversion: authentic conversion and inauthentic conversion. Inauthentic conversion is marked by flight from understanding. Authentic conversion is attentive, reasonable, and responsible. When a group attains conversion they usually form a community to sustain one another in their self-transformation.[213] Such authentic conversion becomes communal and historical when it passes from one generation to another, spreading from one cultural milieu to another, and adapts to new situations and changing circumstance of each time period.[214]

---

212. Morrissey, *Consciousness and Transcendence*, 198. The four levels of consciousness (empirical, intellectual, rational, and reasonable) correspond to the transcendental precepts (be attentive, be intelligent, be reasonable, be responsible).

213. Bernard Lonergan, "Theology in Its New Context," in *A Second Collection*, 55–68, at 66.

214. Ibid.

CONCLUSION

Often missing in the educational curriculum of a Catholic university is an agenda for intellectual conversion. An explicit program of intellectual self-transcendence is today a real need if universities are to produce students who are more than what Lonergan calls "a weekend celebrity,"[215] i.e, a person who has an opinion about everything but lacks depth of knowledge. The models we highlighted in this chapter ought to be the backbone of such a program in a Catholic university. Students need, not just knowledge, but the right kind of knowledge that comes from intellectual conversion. Knowledge is not something to be trifled with, but a vast undertaking that calls for relentless perseverance. One's living is more or less constantly absorbed by the desire to understand.[216] Intellectual conversion eliminates myth about reality, knowledge, and objectivity, i.e., "the myth is that knowing is like looking, that objectivity is seeing what is there to be seen and not seeing what is not there, and that the real is what is out there now to be looked at."[217] Lonergan offered a program— or more properly a set of exercises—on how to acquire intellectual conversion. His book *Insight* "provides a set of exercises for those that wish to find out what goes on in their own black boxes."[218] One may perform the exercises and still fail. But what counts is doing them and doing them repeatedly.[219] "As long as one is content to be guided by one's common sense, to disregard the pundits of every class whether scientific or cultural or religious, one need not learn what goes on in one's black box. But when one moves beyond the limits of commonsense competence, when one wishes to have an opinion of one's own on larger issues, then one had best know just what one is doing. Otherwise one too easily would be duped and too readily exploited."[220]

215. Lonergan, *Insight*, 210.

216. Ibid.

217. Lonergan, *Method in Theology*, 238.

218. See Philip McShane, "The Psychological Present of the Academic Community," in *Lonergan Workshop, Vol.1*, ed. Frederick Lawrence (Chico, CA: Scholars Press, 1978), 27–68, at 57.

219. Ibid.

220. Ibid.

Intellectual conversion is a process by which one becomes more fully aware of the cognitive structure already operative in oneself, enabling one to arrive at a personal appropriation of that structure, i.e., learning how to live with the inherent demands of the human mind by being attentive, intelligent, and reasonable.[221] An intellectual conversion translates into a moral conversion when it helps one to choose the truly good and changes one's decisions and choices from satisfactions to values. To cite a helpful example from Frederick Crowe, "Most of our remote ancestors saw nothing wrong in the practice of slavery. Then someone, somewhere, at some time achieved a new understanding of human dignity and human rights; the cause of abolition of slavery became 'connatural' to that person; and from this as a center it spread through the civilized world. Today abhorrence of slavery is 'connatural' to most of the human race."[222] Our capacity for knowledge, in other words, helps to redress the distortions or deformations of our shared humanity. As one's insight increases because of one's desire to know and to understand, one stands in a better position to make good judgments and sound moral decisions. Gerard Manley Hopkins, according to Lonergan, characterizes this as "the different self-taste, on the successive levels: the spontaneous vitality of our sensitivity, the shrewd intelligence of our inquiring, the detached rationality of our demand for evidence, the peace of a good conscience and the disquiet released by memory of words wrongly said or deeds wrongly done. Yet together they form a single stream, and we live its unity long before we have the leisure, the training, the patience to discern in our own lives its several strands."[223]

Lonergan saw self-transcendence as that which gives meaning to each of the multilayered levels of human reality and as that which gives meaning to the whole; and the meaning of the whole, when concretely realized, can be conceived as utter falling in love with God, i.e., religious conversion.[224] Religious conversion is being

221. Jonsson, *Foundations for Knowing God*, 308.

222. Frederick Crowe, "Rhyme and Reason," in *Developing the Lonergan Legacy*, ed. Vertin, 314–31, at 328–29.

223. Lonergan, "Religious Knowledge," 313.

224. Ibid., 314.

grasped by ultimate concern. It is being-in-love with God, which is the basic fulfillment of the human person's conscious intentionality. "That fulfillment is not the product of our knowledge and choice. On the contrary, it dismantles and abolishes the horizon in which our knowing and choosing went on and it sets up a new horizon in which the love of God will transvalue our values and the eyes of that love will transform our knowing."[225] Thus religious conversion is an experience of fulfillment, of complete integration and self-actualization from which flows abundance of good will and good deeds.[226]

Further Reading

Benders, Alison Mearns. "Renewing the Identity of Catholic Colleges: Implementing Lonergan's Method for Education." *Teaching Theology and Religion* 10, no. 4 (2007): 215–22.

Carmody, Brendan. "A Context for the Catholic Philosophy of Education." *Lumen Vitae* 36 (1981): 45–61.

Conn, Walter. "Affectivity in Kohlberg and Fowler." *Religious Education* 76 (1981): 33–48.

Crysdale, Cynthia S. W. "Development, Conversion, and Religious Education." *Horizons* 17 (1990): 30–46.

Duddy, Marie. "'Liberation' in Religious Education: The Application of Bernard Lonergan's Educational Philosophical Thinking to the 'Education of Faith' as an Experience of Liberation and Self-Transcendence." *Milltown Studies* 24 (Autumn 1989): 113–41.

Helminiak, Daniel A. "Self-Esteem, Sexual Self-Acceptance and Spirituality." *Journal of Sex Education and Therapy* 15 (1989) 200–210.

Kerr, Fergus. *Twentieth-Century Catholic Theologians: From Neoscholasticism to Nuptial Mysticism* (Oxford: Basil Blackwell, 2007).

McGuckian, Michael C. "The Role of Faith in Theology: A Critique of Lonergan's Method." *Irish Theological Quarterly* 71 (2006): 242–59.

---

225. Lonergan, *Method in Theology*, 106.
226. Lonergan, "Religious Knowledge," 314.

Piscitelli, Emil J. "Fundamental Attitudes of the Liberally Educated Person." In *The Questions Behind the Answers*, edited by Donald Gregory, 51–71. Washington, DC: University Press of America, 1982.

Ries, John C. "From 'What' to 'How' . . . and Back: Reflections on Be(com)ing a Catholic Liberal Arts College in the Light of Bernard Lonergan." *Current Issues in Catholic Higher Education* 25, no. 2 (2006): 157–68.

CHAPTER 8

Final Reflection: Group Dynamics and Identity Formation in CIT

The question of identity is complex and involves a wide range of issues. It must be approached empirically rather than normatively, because identity, like mission, changes over time.[1] The issue of identity of Catholic colleges and universities is central to CIT. The behavioral and social sciences can shed light on this question of identity and thus illumine our discussion of CIT.

In his own day, Lonergan engaged the sciences in dialogue as part of his personal *aggiornamento*—his *vetera novis augere et percifere* (completing the old with the new) to bring Catholic thought up to contemporary standards. Integral to Lonergan's reform efforts is the cross-disciplinary, generalized empirical method that he developed to help contemporary educators advert to cultural development in the education of the mind.[2] The generalized empirical method is geared toward helping a person attend to the conflict arising from one's need to exist authentically as well as the conflict arising from the objective situation in which one finds oneself.[3] It is fitting then to conclude this reflection on CIT by putting Lonergan in dialogue with the social and behavioral sciences.

---

1. See Neil Ormerod, "Identity and Mission in Catholic Organizations," *Australasian Catholic Record* 87 (2010): 430–39, at 432.

2. See Bernard Lonergan, "Gilbert Keith Chesterton," in *Collected Works of Bernard Lonergan*, vol. 20, *Shorter Papers*, ed. Robert Croken, Robert Doran, and H. Daniel Monsour (Toronto: University of Toronto Press, 2007), 55–56.

3. Bernard Lonergan, "Existential Crisis," in *Shorter Papers*, 259.

A SHARED IDENTITY
OF CATHOLIC INSTITUTIONS

Although Lonergan did not speak of *identity* in the same way psychologists and sociologists use the term, and although he did not lay down specific guidelines for identity construction in the way social and behavioral scientists like Erik Erikson do, he shared with social and behavioral scientists an interest in the progress and development of individual persons and groups or communities and the way group dynamics enhance or inhibit one's ability to realize one's full potential (a life of self-transcendence). Research in identity formation in the first half of the twentieth century was indebted to the psychological works of Erikson, who saw identity development as a problem for the individual.[4] Erikson reflected on the shaping influences of a person's identity, i.e., one's cultural, historical, and institutional contexts. What Erikson calls "institutional context" is what Lonergan calls "community."

Lonergan agrees with Erikson that the community (institutional context) is a great force in identity construction. It is within a given community that individuals are reared and nurtured, grow in experience, understanding, and judgment, and attain common meanings.[5] No identity can be forged outside of a community. Identity is "a form of action that is first and foremost rhetorical, concerned with persuading others (and oneself) about who one is and what one values to meet different purposes: express or create solidarity, opposition, difference, similarity, love, friendship, and so on."[6] It is the business of all institutions of higher learning to help in the identity or personality development of their students. A primary value in the vocation of Catholic colleges and universities is the true meaning of human life and the ultimate destiny of the human person. This value entails the challenge of how to create in Catholic institutions of learning an

---

4. See E. H. Erikson, *Young Man Luther* (New York: Norton, 1958), *Childhood and Society* (New York: Norton, 1963), *Insight and Responsibility* (New York: Norton, 1964), and *Identity: Youth and Crisis* (New York: Norton, 1968).

5. Bernard Lonergan, *Method in Theology* (Toronto: University of Toronto Press, 1996), 79.

6. William R. Penuel and James V. Wertsch, "Vygostky and Identity Formation: A Sociocultural Approach," *Educational Psychologist* 30 (1995): 83–92, at 91.

environment that is conducive to the formation of a Catholic identity while respecting the diversity and religious freedom of all students, regardless of religious affiliation or belief. This can be understood as developing perspectives and values that are foundational to CIT. Again, authenticity comes into play.

Constructing identity, in Lonerganian terms, comes down to communal and individual authenticity. Communal authenticity involves the Catholic college and the university, i.e., their fidelity to the Catholic tradition. Individual authenticity involves individual students, faculty, and staff at these colleges and universities that are nourished by the tradition. The individual might be authentic in appropriating the tradition handed to him or her by the institution. But if the institution is lacking in authenticity in its fidelity to that tradition, its inauthenticity undermines the authenticity of the individual students, faculty, and staff at the institution.

A collective identity is "developed as the result of external forces and the collective's response to them."[7] It is formed "by producing *new* meaning from an *existing* knowledge set of political, social, economic, and cultural experiences shared by multiple persons."[8] An inquiry into what is CIT, in sociological terms, is an inquiry into the shared "we-perspective" or "we-feeling" of the tradition that binds Catholic institutions of higher learning. It is an investigation of the extent to which these institutions of learning in the Catholic tradition have embraced the "collective intentionality," or the collective commitment or the group ethos[9] that is called Catholicism. The Catholic Church is an identity-focused organization. Identity-focused organizations tend to create shared meanings to enhance their collective identity.[10] "These meanings are a foundation from which [they] define boundaries and a sense of belonging, binding individuals together and giving them the tools to engage with

---

7. Jennifer A. Jones, "Who Are We? Producing Group Identity through Every Day Practices of Conflict and Discourse," *Sociological Perspectives* 54, no. 2 (2011): 139–61, at 142.

8. Ibid., 140.

9. Raimo Tuomela, *The Philosophy of Sociality: The Shared Point of View* (Oxford: Oxford University Press, 2007), 3.

10. Jones, "Who Are We?" 142, paraphrasing Lewis A. Coser, *The Functions of Social Conflict* (New York: The Free Press, 1956), 93.

external threats."[11] When a group is lacking in basic consensus it generally suffers apathy and disintegration.[12] "Weak shared identities cause organizations to fail."[13] All Church-related agencies and organizations in some respects partake in the identity and mission of the Church, albeit in different ways.[14] As an agency of the Church's teaching mission, individual Catholic colleges and universities are members of a wider organization or group with a shared meaning and common way of understanding that is intrinsic to Catholicism.

One of the fundamental problems of human existence is the tension between the need for individuality and community, i.e., the need to be apart from the community and a part of the community. In other words, identities separate and connect. While some aspects of our identity connect us with others, the merging of all aspects of our identities makes us unique.[15] How we navigate these borders is extremely significant.[16] As institutions of learning under the umbrella of the Catholic Church, Catholic colleges and universities are members of a community of (Catholic) scholars. Yet each one is autonomous because each has the institutional autonomy and academic freedom that are necessary for the rigors of academic scholarship. The tension between the institution's need to be a part of the Catholic community and apart from it is a positive good. How the institution navigates these borders is the challenge. Lonergan, referring to the question posed by Kierkegaard regarding whether he was a genuine Christian, wonders to what extent Catholics are "genuine[ly] Catholic."[17] An institution may declare itself genuinely Catholic and be correct,

---

11. Jones, "Who Are We?" 142. See also Alberto Melucci, *Nomads of the Present: Social Movement and Identity Needs in Contemporary Society*, ed. J. Keane and P. Mier (Philadelphia: Temple University Press, 1989), and Francesca Polleta and James M. Jasper, "Collective Identity and Social Movements," *Annual Review of Sociology* 27 (2001): 283–305.

12. Jones, "Who Are We?" 142.

13. Ibid., 141.

14. Ormerod, "Identity and Mission in Catholic Organizations," 431.

15. Ibid., 49, paraphrasing Amin Maalouf, *In the Name of Identity: Violence and the Need to Belong* (New York: Arcade Publishing, 2011).

16. Eleanor Hunter, "Beyond the Shadows of Cohousing: Cultivating Idealism, Identity, Borders, and Trust" (PhD diss., Pacifica Graduate Institute, 2006), ii.

17. Lonergan, *Method in Theology*, 80.

or it may be mistaken. If mistaken, it may not be because the institution is deceptive, but because it is not truly authentic.[18] There exists "a series of points" in which one is "what the ideals of the tradition demand,"[19] and another series in which one diverges from what the tradition demands either from "a selective inattention, or from a failure to understand or from an undetected rationalization."[20]

Achievements of common meaning, like CIT, are not fixed and permanent.[21] They are always ongoing, requiring further development. In all facets of identity construction, there are principles of growth and development; the trajectory of change is shaped by various forces, internal and external.[22] Erikson viewed identity as "a subjective sense of an invigorating sameness and continuity"[23] because the dynamic tension of sameness and continuity has no guarantee of permanent stability.[24] Pertaining to the Catholic tradition, it is important for its vitality and growth "that through the full variety of structures and institutions which emerge from its life all aspects of its identity and mission be expressed."[25]

Lonergan's principles of operators and integrators can help to explain how the process of growth and development coalesce in shaping identity:

> Lonergan speaks of process of development (as distinct from just change) involving principles of transformation (which he calls operators) and principles of limitation (which he calls integrators). The opposed but linked principles constitute a dialectic structure which he claims is operative in any process of genuine development. As the operator "operates" it produces a change "in, not of," the identity of the

---

18. Ibid.

19. Ibid.

20. Ibid.

21. Donna Teevan, "Tradition and Innovation at Catholic Universities: Ideas from Bernard Lonergan," *Catholic Education* 7 (2004): 308–19, at 309.

22. Ormerod, "Identity and Mission and Catholic Organizations," 431.

23. Erikson, *Identity*, 19; cited in Penuel and Wertsch, "Vygostky and Identity Formation," 87.

24. Penuel and Wertsch, "Vygostky and Identity Formation," 87.

25. Ormerod, "Identity and Mission in Catholic Organizations," 431.

developing reality. This transformed identity becomes the new base from which all further developments will occur. For example the growth of a tree might be stunted by a particularly cold summer; this event will continue to shape its future possibilities for all further growth. It has an indelible impact on the development and identity of the tree.[26]

CATHOLIC UNIVERSITIES AS GROUP WITH A COMMON MEANING

In theology the term *group* is rarely used, and when used is sometimes poorly understood. In one of his rare uses of the term Lonergan employed it while discussing the distortion of a person's intellectual development, which occurs in four principal ways: the bias of unconscious motivation, bias of individual egoism, general bias of common sense, and what he calls the more powerful and blinder bias of group egoism. Even in such rare usage, Lonergan acknowledged that the term *group* properly belongs to those sciences that organize "evidence on group behavior."[27] While still not averse to using this sociological term to formulate theories that further social ends, Lonergan's preference is for the more theologically nuanced term *community*, which, for him, is not just an aggregate of people within a geographical frontier, but an achievement of common meaning.[28] In this chapter, the term *group* is used more or less interchangeably with the term *community* to reinforce Lonergan's preference.

In group dynamics, often the distinction is made between what behavioral scientists call "in-group" and "out-group" behavior. An

---

26. Ibid., 431–32. See Bernard J. F. Lonergan, *Insight: A Study of Human Understanding*, in *Collected Works of Bernard Lonergan*, ed. Frederick E. Crowe and Robert M. Doran (Toronto: University of Toronto Press, 1992), 3:489–92.

27. Bias of unconscious motivation is what Lonergan called "love of darkness" or the repression of understanding that makes one flee from understanding. Individual bias is a scotoma or blind spot that causes an individual to act irrationally in the face of knowledge. Group bias is the distortion of the intellectual development of a group or social class. General bias of common sense arises when a person seeks a short-term quick-fix solution to a complex problem. See Lonergan, *Method in Theology*, 231. See also *Insight*, chapter 6.

28. Lonergan, *Method in Theology*, 79.

in-group is a group to which one belongs and with which one identi-fies, while an out-group is a group to which one does not belong and with which one does not identify.[29] Social and behavioral scientists also speak of a *we-mode* or *we-perspective* of a group, i.e., "group-involving states and processes that the group itself has at least partly conceptually and ontologically constructed for itself."[30] A group in we-mode is a group in which members profess a collective commit-ment to abide by the group's ethos. A member acting in we-mode does so for "a collectively constructed group reason,"[31] because his or her way of acting presupposes an explicit acceptance of the group's ethos and goals.[32] Individuals with collective identity or common interests often collaborate (collective action) to further those inter-ests and by so doing enhance the common good of the group.[33]

The sociological term *group*, understood as "a collectivity of indi-viduals with a common goal or, equivalently, with a common inter-est,"[34] helps our understanding of the theological term *community* as it pertains to CIT vis-à-vis forging a Catholic identity of Catho-lic colleges and universities. The shared meaning or goal that unites members of a group suggests they have a "common understanding" and have made some "common judgments" and "common commit-ments." A group or community "coheres or divides, begins or ends, just where the common field of experience, common understand-ing, common judgment, common commitments begin and end."[35] Schools that are under the umbrella of the Catholic Church are a good example of this kind of group. As a community of Catholic and other scholars, they are a group with a common goal, common inter-ests, common judgment, and common meaning. Each scholar tries to authentically appropriate what is good in CIT and make the best of their collective identity under the umbrella that is CIT.

---

29. See G. S. Gregg, *Self-Representation: Life Narrative Studies in Identity and Ide-ology* (New York: Greenwood Press, 1991).

30. Tuomela, *The Philosophy of Sociality*, 3.

31. Ibid.

32. Ibid., 4.

33. Karl-Dieter Opp, *Theories of Political Protests and Social Movements: A Multi-disciplinary Introduction, Critique, and Synthesis* (London: Routledge, 2009), 48.

34. Ibid.

35. Lonergan, *Method in Theology*, 79.

A collective identity is "an interactive and shared definition produced by several individuals and concerned with the orientations of action and the field of opportunities and constraints in which the action takes place."[36] As a process, collective identity is always evolving. Its evolution includes "(1) formulating cognitive frameworks concerning the ends, means, and the field of action, (2) activating relationships between the actors, who interact, communicate, influence each other, negotiate, and make decisions, (3) making emotional investments, which enable individuals to recognize themselves."[37] CIT is analogously a collective identity that Catholic colleges and universities share. Because collective identity is "a process in which the actors produce the common cognitive frameworks that enable them to assess the environment and to calculate the costs and benefits of the action,"[38] the process by which individual Catholic schools navigate their common Catholic identity needs to be negotiated. We shall return to this process of negotiation later.

The point here is to reinforce the argument that CIT does not derive from a particular individual and is not a product of a particular generation, but that it is the work of different individuals in the particularities of their age, time, and custom. CIT is a collection of individual meanings that in due time have become a common meaning. The question then is, since the common meaning (CIT) is the work of isolated individuals spread out over a period of many generations, how can Catholic colleges and universities form a generation of students that can both contribute to and carry the legacy forward? Every Catholic college or university has a stake in CIT and, like individual actors in a group, is interested in the well-being of the (Catholic) tradition to which they belong.

In group dynamics, as demonstrated earlier, acting in the interest of the group generally benefits the group; the reverse is also true.[39] To

---

36. See Alberto Melucci, "Getting Involved: Identity and Mobilization in Social Movements," in *International Social Movement Research*, ed. B. Klandermans, H. Kriesi, and S. Tarrow (Greenwich, CT: JAI Press), 1:329–48, at 342, cited in Opp, *Theories of Political Protests and Social Movements*, 208–9.

37. Melucci, "Getting Involved," 343; cited in Opp, *Theories of Political Protests and Social Movements*, 209.

38. Melucci, "Getting Involved," 343.

39. Opp, *Theories of Political Protests and Social Movements*, 232.

act in a group's interest is "to act intentionally within the group's realm of concern, promoting (furthering) the satisfaction and maintenance of the ethos—the central, constitutive goals, values, standards, beliefs, norms, and/or elements of the history of the group."[40] The degree to which one does this depends on the extent to which one is authentic, i.e., the degree to which one works to further the interest of the group—or, conversely, the degree to which one is inauthentic, i.e., selfishly pursuing personal interests to the detriment of the group. Common meanings, though they have histories, are meant to be clarified, expressed, formulated, deepened, enriched, and transformed in due time.[41] The authenticity of Catholic schools will depend on the degree to which common meanings are fostered in this way. Catholic schools may be authentic in either their faithfulness to the common meaning that has been preserved down through the rich history of the Catholic Church that they seek to carry forward, or in the way they embody and promote conversion.[42]

CIT is a common meaning that has been realized in the course of centuries not only by the decisions, choices, and permanent dedication and loyalty of the Church's many members but also by the faith and love of all who have contributed to the tradition. Catholicism engenders a habit of mind and imagination that suggests a hopeful intelligence. "Hope inspires and sustains its own kind of intelligence in regard to the direction of history, the meaning of the good society, the destiny of the universe. It bears on the ultimate worthwhile-ness of the values we most cherish—including the value of intelligence and truth itself."[43] In Catholicism, hope conditions the way individual Catholics understand and amplify the scope of their common meaning[44] because Catholic ideals (e.g., sacramentality and communion) inform all facets of life. It is also hope that, together with faith, liberates reason from its ideological prison, strengthening new understanding with

---

40. Tuomela, *The Philosophy of Sociality*, 23.

41. Lonergan, *Method in Theology*, 78–79.

42. Teevan, "Tradition and Innovation at Catholic Universities," 309.

43. Anthony J. Kelly, "A Tradition of Hopeful Intelligence: The Catholic Intellectual Tradition," *Australian EJournal of Theology* 5 (August 2005), no page numbers.

44. Ibid.

confidence.[45] Thus a university in the Catholic tradition that fails to uphold the common meaning may be said to be "out of touch"[46] in so far as it acts contrary to the in-group ethos of Catholicism. This in-group ethos is by no means a finished product. Hopeful intelligence puts CIT in a frame that leaves it open to consider new questions, understanding that issues of human life are not once and for all settled, but open to new ways of exploration, new ways of understanding, new ways of conception, and new ways of conversation.[47]

INSTITUTIONAL IDENTITIES AND CHARACTERISTICS OF A CATHOLIC UNIVERSITY

For behavioral and social scientists, as mentioned already, identities are "contested, negotiated, and mediated through different institutional and discursive universes."[48] Individual actors involved in collective identity are expected to negotiate continually and renegotiate all aspects of their action,[49] and in the process come to a determination of their own sameness with or difference from the group. Thus identity construction is a dynamic process that involves negotiations among members of the group.[50] Some of the issues to be negotiated may include desired goals and strategies, i.e., means of achieving these goals. For example, the question of mission and identity is widely discussed at Catholic colleges and universities. It is part of the self-assessment and self-determination that is integral to CIT. These schools desire to know the extent to which they have been faithful to and reflective of CIT. They recognize, even if implicitly, that to be in the Catholic tradition a college or university must exhibit, to the greatest degree possible, these five marks or characteristics:

---

45. Ibid.

46. Lonergan, *Method in Theology*, 79.

47. Ibid.

48. Barbara Hobson, "Introduction," in *Recognition Struggles and Social Movements: Contested Identities, Agency and Power*, ed. Barbara Hobson (Cambridge: Cambridge University Press, 2003), 1–17, at 5.

49. Melucci, "Getting Involved," 333.

50. Alberto Melucci, *Challenging Codes: Collective Action in the Information Age* (Cambridge: Cambridge University Press, 1996), 78.

1. act as a beacon of hope or inspiration for their individual members (faculty, staff, and students) and the entire cultural community (local, national, and international)

2. contribute to the stock of human knowledge through research that is grounded in the Christian principles of faith, hope, and love

3. remain faithful to the Christian message and Catholic ideals

4. serve not only their local community but the entire human family[51]

5. collaborate with the Church and the network of Catholic colleges and universities

Individual actors negotiate strategies mindful that in a shared *we-perspective* one is still governed by the ethos of the larger group. Since "a group ontologically consists of its members functioning as group members with collective commitment to its ethos,"[52] its intending, believing, and acting is realized in the intending, believing, and acting of its conglomerate members. Individual Catholic colleges and universities address the question of their mission and identity without losing sight of the mission and identity of their conglomerate members. Their margin of success depends on the extent to which these colleges and universities have drawn upon those members. Bernard of Chartres (d. c. 1126–1130) remarked, "We are like dwarfs sitting on the shoulders of giants; we see more things, and more far-off ones, than they did, not because our sight is better, nor because we are taller than they were, but because they raise us up and add to our height by their gigantic loftiness."[53] It is because Catholic colleges and universities owe a great deal to the past that they are better able to articulate their self-understanding of the collective identity. The past (mediating phase) and the present (mediated phase) are to be understood, not as disjunction or alternatives

---

51. See *Ex Corde Ecclesia*, part 1, no. 13.

52. Tuomela, *The Philosophy of Sociality*, 124.

53. Cited in Frederick E. Crowe, *Old Things and New: A Strategy for Education* (Atlanta: Scholars Press, 1985), 63. According to Crowe, who relied on the evidence of Etienne Gilson, the quote occurs in John of Salisbury's *Metalogicon* III. See also Etienne Gilson, *History of Christian Philosophy in the Middle Ages* (New York: Random House, 1955), 140.

(either/or), but as a unit of close relationship (both/and); the new does not arise *ex nihilo* but derives from a transposition and interiorization of the past.[54]

Furthermore, because the concept of collective identity can be "surprisingly vague,"[55] individual institutions can explicate their self-understanding of their Catholic identity in a way that reflects their own appropriation of the common meaning. Lonergan gave as one example of appropriating the Catholic imagination for one's own time—Ignatius of Loyola (1491–1556) and the tradition of Jesuit higher education. Ignatius's capacity for reflection and introspection enabled him to draw from the existing tradition and beyond to work out a methodic set of principles that became the *Spiritual Exercises*.[56] Ignatius applied his practical wisdom to produce a thirty-day masterpiece (commonly termed a *retreat*)[57] that facilitated Jesuit entry into the field of education and made it easy for the Jesuits "to dominate in the secondary schools of Catholic Europe, turning out the audience if not all the writers of the Grand Siècle of French literature."[58] When the medieval Church became embroiled in the crisis of the Reformation it was through the masterpiece worked out by Ignatius that his followers were able to offer concrete solutions by opening up "schools that were not merely models of efficiency but as well educational syntheses combining and intertwining the triple cord of Europe's heritage: the Gospel, articulated thought, and balanced humanism."[59] Lonergan observes further,

> If there is any "power and secret" to the Jesuits, it is [Ignatius's] *Spiritual Exercises*, his method of coaching cooperation with the grace of God. They alone explain the Society's record of two doctors of the Church, twenty-four saints, one hundred and forty-nine blessed, one hundred and forty-eight officially recognized martyrs, one hundred and

---

54. Ibid.

55. Opp, *Theories of Political Protests and Social Movements*, 215.

56. See Bernard Lonergan, "Quatercentenary," in *Shorter Papers*, 83–88.

57. Lonergan thinks it is a misnomer to call it a "retreat."

58. Lonergan, "Quatercentenary," 86.

59. Ibid., 87–88.

eighty-five revered with the title of venerable. They alone have enabled the Society to live and die, and live again through wave upon wave of slander, confiscation, expulsion, and persecution. They alone can infuse some measure of, some approximation to, a common way of thought and character into the novices that enter today in Tokyo and Melbourne, Madura and Madagascar, Warsaw and Berlin, Lyons and London, Bogota and Guelph. And if the Jesuits of today succeed in making any contribution to the solution of the present problems, then it will be, as in the past, because each man finds himself in a framework hoisting him to the level of his better self, the spiritual framework conceived by Ignatius.[60]

The Society of Jesus (Jesuits) is not alone in working out a successful educational plan that has enriched CIT. Most Catholic colleges were founded by religious orders and congregations, including several in the United States that have crafted a successful academic plan that has enriched CIT. For example, Dominicans provide an educational program in the Catholic and Dominican tradition; Franciscans provide education in the Catholic and Franciscan tradition; Benedictines provide education in the Catholic and Benedictine tradition; Salesians provide education in the Catholic and Salesian tradition, and Marianists provide education in the Catholic and Marianist tradition. Working within the Catholic tradition, all Catholic colleges and universities bring their own unique perspectives and charisms (gifts) of their respective orders and congregations to Catholic education, the ideals of a university education in the Catholic tradition. They pass on to their students their own unique emphasis of the Catholic tradition. For example, some may emphasize, in addition to academic excellence, service and outreach to the poor, others may emphasize community or spirituality. The imprint (identity) they want to leave on their students would, to great extent, be driven by these emphases.

---

60. Ibid., 88.

BUILDING PERSONAL IDENTITIES

Personal identity is not a mere philosophical or psychological construct, but a major sociocultural educational issue in culturally diverse societies like the United States.[61] The Cartesian *cogito* that led to the conception of the self "as individualized, ahistorical, noncultural, disembodied, and centralized,"[62] is no longer tenable in either theology or the social sciences. Social and behavioral scientists, as well as philosophers and theologians, have taken issue with Cartesian dualism, criticizing it for distorting the unity of self and body.[63] This dualism is a disservice, not only to the unity of mind and body but also to the unity of self and the other in the social process.[64]

Psychologists have an abiding interest in the role of the individual in the social process and human development. For some psychologists, identity is synonymous with self and refers to the individual as a whole.[65] In sociology the theoretical problem of identity is traditionally framed as the question "Who am I?"[66] As pointed out already, Lonergan did not use the term *identity* in the way social and behavioral scientists do. As an abstraction, *identity*, when used in theology, can never fully capture the ever-changing practices of human self-constitution.[67] But Lonergan was concerned, like sociologists and behavioral scientists, with the problem

61. Thomas Wren and Carmen Mendoza, "Cultural Identity and Personal Identity: Philosophical Reflections on the Identity Discourse of Social Psychology," in *Moral Development, Self, and Identity*, ed. Daniel K. Lapsley and Darcia Narvaez (Mahwah, NJ: Lawrence Erlbaum Associates, 2004), 239–66, at 239.

62. Hurbert J. M. Hermans, "The Construction and Reconstruction of a Dialogical Self," *Journal of Constructivist Psychology* 16 (2003): 89–130, at 89.

63. Ibid., 92.

64. Ibid. See also E. W. Straus, "Aesthesiology and Hallucinations," in *Existence: A New Dimension in Psychiatry and Psychology* , ed. R. May, E. Angel, and H. F. Ellenberger (New York: Basic Books, 1958), 139–69.

65. See Jonathan Luckhurst, "A Constructivist Approach to Identity and How to Combine Different Levels of Analysis" (paper presented in panel, "Combining Methodologies to Contextualize 'Postnational' Identity: Overcoming the 'Levels of Analysis Problem'" at the International Studies Association Annual Convention, San Francisco, March 26–29, 2008), 1–18, at 3.

66. Hermans, "The Construction and Reconstruction of a Dialogical Self," 104.

67. Luckhurst, "A Constructivist Approach," 6.

of how individuals constitute themselves as subjects and how they adapt to their social context and changing life situations. Granted that *subject* is not a synonym for *identity* because "the concept of subject refers to a series of particular configurations of what (or who) a self or identity is,"[68] nonetheless, when properly nuanced, *identity* and *subject* can refer to the same reality. Lonergan's preferred term, *person-as-subject*, makes sense in light of the findings of the social sciences—that "self-knowledge concerns not the self as object but the self as project: the self-in-relation-to-the-other is a form of social exploration and discovery as part of an unfinished dialogue, both external with the actual other and internal with the imagined other."[69]

Personal identity, like group identity, is forged in a social context. There is a dialogical relationship between the individual and the society that nurtures him or her. From the perspective of the dialogical self, the question, "Who am I?" can be rephrased as, "Who am I in relation to the other?" and "Who is the other in relation to me?"[70] Individuals are not the sole creators of their own identity. Erikson distanced himself from psychologists like Sigmund Freud (1856–1939) who considered identity solely in personal terms. For Erikson, identity must be integrated inside of culture.[71] Identity is "a form of action that is first and foremost rhetorical, concerned with persuading others (and oneself) about who one is and what one values to meet different purposes: express or create solidarity, opposition, difference, similarity, love, friendship, and so on."[72] Self-knowledge is "the discovery of the alterity of the other, and by consequence, my self-knowledge increases when the alterity of the other is admitted and explored as part of the external domain of myself."[73] One who is conscious of the alterity of the other is able to make a clear distinction between his or her personal interest and the interest of the other and is other-minded. He

---

68. Ibid., 4, quoting Alan Finlayson, *Making Sense of New Labor* (London: Lawrence and Wishart, 2003), 145.

69. Hermans, "The Construction and Reconstruction of a Dialogical Self," 104.

70. Ibid.

71. Penuel and Wertsch, "Vygostky and Identity Formation," 87.

72. Ibid., 91.

73. Hermans, "The Construction and Reconstruction of a Dialogical Self," 104.

or she is less conscious of him or herself and more mindful of others. Thus there is "no determinate, de facto 'hidden self' that . . . suddenly reveals itself when conditions are right."[74]

Because identities are not things but narratives that are fashioned in specific institutional and historical contexts,[75] schools play a large role in helping individuals shape their identities. In general, schools have a profound influence on moral and social development as well as the academic success of their students.[76] Education in the Catholic tradition, for example, strives not only to educate students in order to form them for the faith but also to help them deal with and effect change.[77] The decline of religious orders in the United States in the decades following the Second Vatican Council not only affected the pastoral life, politics, and collective intelligence of the Catholic Church in the United States[78] but also its collective identity. "The explosion of Latino and new immigrant Catholicism, especially in regions outside the northeast and middle west . . . and the slow but steady erosion of pastoral leadership and creativity in those historical urban centers of American Catholic life,"[79] also combined to alter or reshape Catholic collective identity in the United States.

Countless external forces are at play in various aspects of identity construction. Psychologists speak of "the interplay of family background, personality, moral cognitions and attitudes, self-perceptions and moral emotions, and social relationships and interactions with social institutions"[80] as the context for moral identity development.

74. Wren and Mendoza, "Cultural Identity and Personal Identity," 242.

75. Ibid.

76. Robert Atkins, Daniel Hart, and Thomas M. Donnelly, "Moral Identity Development and School Attachment," in *Moral Development, Self, and Identity*, ed. Lapsley and Narvaez, 65–82, at 65.

77. James Heft, SM, "The Open Circle: The Culture of the Catholic University," *Australian Ejournal of Theology* 2 (February 2004), no page numbers.

78. David J. O'Brien, "The Renewal of American Catholicism: A Retrospect," *The U.S. Catholic Historian* 23 (2005): 83–94, at 83.

79. Ibid.

80. Daniel Hart and M. Kyle Matsuba, "Urban Neighborhoods as Contexts for Moral Identity Development," in *Personality, Identity, and Character: Explorations in Moral Psychology*, ed. Darcia Narvaez and Daniel K. Lapsley (Cambridge: Cambridge University Press, 2009), 214–31, at 228.

Thus schools are highly influential in helping individuals form their own identity.[81] They help students develop a self-image and moral goals that advance their welfare and the welfare of others.

Given that identity is a "continuous activity of construction and deconstruction, of developing, maintaining, and evaluating personal commitments to values, persons, and practices,"[82] the denominational identity of a school can help students form their own personal identity.[83] The way denominational schools, like Catholic universities and colleges, interpret their own position and mission within the larger scheme of the institutional identity of the group to which they belong can be either helpful or problematic in achieving the goal of helping students develop personal identity.[84] Education is "ultimately *not* just about the acquisition of knowledge and skills, *not* just about building cognitive and emotional maps of the world. [It is] about learning to see oneself as a possible participant and contributor to cultural practices and traditions, as somebody who has a commitment to such practices and their inherent values." [85] The real goal of education is, ultimately, "the enhancement of identity processes in their relation to cultural processes and traditions."[86]

The institutional identity or culture of Catholic universities guides or shapes the identity of students in these schools, notwithstanding the fact that the larger culture validates the identity of the individual. For Erikson, "without some validation of identity, neurosis, or even pathology, develops in the individual."[87] When personal identities are shaped and constructed they can then have, as Lonergan observed, "a grave responsibility for the future of man."[88]

---

81. Willem Wardekker and Siebren Miedema, "Denominational School Identity and the Formation of Personal Identity," *Religious Education* 96 (2001): 36–48, at 36.

82. Ibid., 37.

83. Ibid., 36.

84. Ibid.

85. Ibid., 38.

86. Ibid.

87. Penuel and Wertsch, "Vygostky and Identity Formation," 87.

88. Bernard Lonergan, "Theology and Man's Future," in *Collection: Papers by Bernard J. F. Lonergan*, ed. William Ryan and Bernard Tyrell (London: Darton, Longman, and Todd, 1974), 135.

The university is no longer "a storehouse whence traditional wisdom and knowledge are dispensed. It is a center in which ever-increasing knowledge is disseminated to bring about ever-increasing social and cultural change."[89]

CONCLUSION

In medieval Catholic Europe where the idea of university first emerged, following Aristotle's distinction between form and matter, intellectuals argued about the *what* and *why* of a thing. In this old distinction, there is a sense in which *what* has the same meaning as *why*. To ask in the same question *what* a thing is, in effect asks *why* it is so.[90] Similarly the question *what* is CIT has the same meaning as *why* CIT. The burden of this text has been to clarify not only the question *what* and *why* CIT but also to show the place of CIT in the Church and the relationship of this learning tradition to Catholic colleges and universities in general. In describing *what* CIT means we have, in effect, also offered an answer to the *why* CIT question. We have done this by uncovering how CIT exists, not as a neatly packed box that can be opened and tucked away at whim, but in individuals across the ages who have embraced a higher viewpoint in the search for truth and knowledge. One such person was the Canadian Jesuit, Bernard Lonergan. As a contributor to CIT, Lonergan demonstrated how it is in the nature of CIT to grow—that CIT is not like a train whose sole purpose is to get to its destination, but rather that each moment is its own self-justification.[91]

Lonergan scholarship enhances both the quest to understand the relationship of Catholic colleges and universities to CIT and *why* one should care about the identity of Catholic colleges and universities. Generally speaking, a university is a reproductive organ of a

89. Ibid.

90. Bernard Lonergan, *Collected Works of Bernard Lonergan*, vol. 10, *Topics in Education*, ed. Robert M. Doran and Frederick E. Crowe (Toronto: University of Toronto, 1993), 171.

91. See Herbert Butterfield, *Christianity and History* (London: Collins Books, 1957), 91, cited in Frederick Crowe, *Christ and History: The Christology of Bernard Lonergan from 1935 to 1982* (Ottawa: Novalis, 2005), 13.

cultural community whose constitutive element lies, not in the magnificence of its buildings or the size of its endowments, but in the intellectual investment of its faculty and students. The central function of any university is the fostering of intellectual development.[92] Catholic and non-Catholic (as well as secular) universities all communicate intellectual development. If Catholic and secular universities exercise the same function, then why a Catholic university? Of what relevance is a Catholic university? What difference does a Catholic university make to learning?

Although Catholic and secular universities exercise the same function, they do so under different conditions.

1. The secular university world is still "firmly rooted in the Enlightenment with its secularizing tendencies and its disregard for the particular in favor of the universal and whatever can be broadly standardized."[93]

2. The secular university is caught in the ambiguities of civil and cultural development-and-decline and yields to the aberrations of the modern secular world.[94]

Catholic education offers the following advantages:

1. Although Catholic colleges and universities, like the secular university, are caught in the ambiguities of civil and cultural development-and-decline, they do not yield to the aberrations of the modern secular world because they are strengthened by the theological virtues of faith, hope, and charity,[95] which they openly profess as colleges and universities in the Catholic tradition. While Catholic colleges and universities take pride in and maximize the religiosity of their institutions, secular universities often trivialize religion or consider it unimportant.

---

92. Bernard Lonergan, "The Role of a Catholic University in the Modern World," in *Collection: Collected Works of Bernard Lonergan*, 4:108–13, at 111.

93. Monika Hellwig, "The Catholic Intellectual Tradition in the Catholic University," in *Examining the Catholic Intellectual Tradition*, ed. Anthony J. Cernera and Oliver J. Morgan (Fairfield, CT: Sacred Heart University Press, 2000), 1–18, at 15.

94. Lonergan, "The Role of a Catholic University in the Modern World," 111.

95. Ibid.

Secular universities, in fact, are "most zealous in guarding our public institutions against explicit religious influences."[96] Since the secular university sees the spiritual and human realms as opposed, they push religion to the private sphere, which results in fragmenting knowledge. A net result of this is that in public discourse citizens are asked "to split their public and private selves."[97] But the Catholic university sees the secular and human realms as complementary and as two sides of the same reality, which leads to unity of knowledge. The secular university seeks only what can be verified by reason, saying in essence: "I believe because I have a verifiable reason." The Catholic university seeks both the truth that reason can prove and truth beyond reason, saying in essence: "I believe in order that I may understand." For the Catholic university faith or belief is a form of knowledge.

Catholic tradition understands faith, together with hope and charity, as supernatural virtues that orient a person to God. These virtues also have a profound social significance: "Against the perpetuation of explosive tensions that would result from the strict application of retributive justice, there is the power of charity to wipe out old grievances and make a fresh start possible. Against the economic determinism that would result were egoistic practicality given free reign, there is the liberating power of hope that seeks first the kingdom of God. Against the dialectic discernible in the history of philosophy and in the development-and-decline of civil and cultural communities, there is the liberation of human reason through divine faith; for men of faith are not shifted about by every wind and doctrine."[98]

2. Because Catholic colleges and universities seek to integrate revelation with human reason, they are "more capable of conducting an impartial search for truth, a search that is neither subordinated to nor conditioned by particular interests of any kind" (*Ex Corde Ecclesia*, 7).

---

96. Stephen L. Carter, *The Culture of Disbelief: How American Law and Politics Trivialize Religious Devotion* (New York: Anchor Books, 1994), 8.

97. Ibid.

98. Lonergan, "The Role of a Catholic University in the Modern World," 111–12.

3. Catholic colleges and universities hold a distinctive notion of the good.[99] Because it seeks the whole truth (not partial truth), a Catholic university fosters a universal humanism. By dedicating itself completely and without reservation to the cause of truth, exploring the mysteries of human life, and clarifying them in light of revealed truth, a Catholic university promotes at one and the same time the dignity of the human person and the good of the Church (*Ex Corde Ecclesia*, 4). CIT exists for the human good and the good of Catholicism. It studies the human person in all its particularities: physical, spiritual, emotional, psychological, etc, and promotes human progress; it also helps in the development and dissemination of Christian culture.

4. Although Catholic colleges and universities do not have a monopoly on education, as "trustees of Catholic learning," the demands of faith, hope, and charity that they publicly profess means that Catholic institutions of higher learning strive to offer something more.[100] CIT, in other words, engenders several qualities or habits of mind in individuals and institutions that embrace the unique Catholic "way of doing things."[101] The Catholic way of doing things in a Catholic college or university, for example, engenders research that includes (a) the search for an integration of knowledge, (b) a dialogue between faith and reason, (c) an ethical concern, and (d) a theological perspective.[102]

5. CIT is rich, not only in intellectual, religious, and aesthetic treasury but also in hallowed names: "From the great treatises of the Patristic writers, such as Clement, Origen, and Gregory, to the works of the Doctors of the Church, such as Bonaventure, Theresa, and Catherine of Sienna; from Augustine's *Confessions* to Pope John XXIII's *Journal of a Soul* and Thomas Merton's *Seven Story Mountain*, from the philosophical theologies of Thomas Aquinas and Don Scotus to the more

99. Lonergan, *Topics in Education*, 69.

100. Hellwig, "The Catholic Intellectual Tradition in the Catholic University," 10.

101. Anthony J. Cernera and Oliver J. Morgan, "The Catholic Intellectual Tradition: Some Characteristics, Implications, and Future Directions," in *Examining the Catholic Intellectual Tradition*, ed. Cernera and Morgan, 199–222, at 203.

102. See *Ex Corde Ecclesia*, part 1, no. 15

contemporary theologies of Karl Rahner, Bernard Lonergan, and Hans Urs von Balthasar."[103]

In sum, there is such a thing as a Catholic sensibility—a way of looking at reality from a Catholic viewpoint that makes Catholic education highly desirable.[104] Catholic sensibility is not mere feelings or emotions but "a feeling for life, a way of taking events and making experience, a ground for life-style and at last for morality."[105] In view of this uniquely Catholic sensibility, i.e., a Catholic way of doing and acting, a Catholic university communicates intellectual development in ways different from secular universities because it is aided by the supernatural or theological virtues of faith, hope, and charity. "Though a Catholic university does not dispense the grace of God, though it is not entrusted with Christ's mission to teach, though it must see to the conservation and transmission of acquired knowledge before it can turn to its extension and development, still it is the normal center in which both the need for intellectual integration is felt and the way toward that integration is prepared."[106]

We conclude the *what* and *why* of Catholic intellectual tradition with a story Lonergan told about the dangers of limited vision. It is a story about the colonial administration of nineteenth-century British India. At that time communication was not as sophisticated as it is today. The people who administered India from London had their colonial administrators on the ground in India. The latter were trained to ensure that the will of those in London was carried out always and everywhere in India. Even when the colonial administrators were native Indians their mentality was colonial and British. Whenever there was unrest or crisis in India and news of the uprising reached headquarters in London, those in London did not panic. They knew how the colonial administrators

---

103. Cernera and Morgan, "The Catholic Intellectual Tradition," 201–2.

104. Andrew M. Greeley, "The Catholic 'Intellectual': An Empirical Investigation," in *Examining the Catholic Intellectual Tradition*, ed. Cernera and Morgan, 179–97, at 181.

105. Ibid.

106. Lonergan, "The Role of a Catholic University in the Modern World," 112–13.

would react because their mentality was colonial (British). Catholic education, Lonergan assured, does not aim to produce colonial administrators.[107] In a colonial administration, to expand the metaphor a little further, the dictates of the master are faithfully repeated and meanings of words are devalued and contracted to fit a narrow horizon.[108] CIT is not something foreign "to be dropped into [Catholic] schools by magisterial savants from a far-off headquarters."[109] It is a tradition from which all draw and to which all contribute. Catholic colleges and universities are "heirs and trustees of [this] great intellectual and cultural tradition founded on Christian faith and enhanced by grace and by many centuries of testing for fidelity and authenticity."[110] Because Catholic colleges and universities play a major role in preserving and disseminating this rich treasury, and because "the conditions for fidelity to our trust have changed a good deal in the twentieth century,"[111] it is up to each and every Catholic institution of higher learning to do an assessment—a self-study regarding the understanding of the institution's Catholic identity, and perhaps do it with some sympathetic imagination,[112] i.e., a compassionate spirit that attends to the needs of Catholics and non-Catholics alike.

Critical to the crisis of identity and mission that is plaguing Catholic colleges and universities today "is the uncertainty, even ignorance, of many regarding the tradition."[113] Catholicism is about more than Catholics.[114] Catholic tradition is not a closed system and does not exclude non-Catholics. The rich Catholic intellectual heritage is for the benefit of Catholics and non-Catholics alike. All who work in Catholic institutions of learning—faculty, staff, students,

---

107. Lonergan, *Topics in Education*, 103.

108. Ibid., 95–96.

109. John Haughey SJ, *Where Is Knowing Going? The Horizons of the Knowing Subject* (Washington, DC: Georgetown University Press, 2009), 153.

110. Hellwig, "The Catholic Intellectual Tradition in the Catholic University," 18.

111. Ibid.

112. M. C. Nussbaum, *Cultivating Humanity: A Classical Defense of Reform in Liberal Education* (Cambridge, MA: Harvard University Press, 1997), 85.

113. Cernera and Morgan, "The Catholic Intellectual Tradition," 199.

114. O'Brien, "The Renewal of American Catholicism," 85.

cooks, drivers, drivers, gatekeepers, et al.—all contribute to CIT in so far as they support the teaching, research, and service objectives of the college or university. Every department or unit of a Catholic college or university supports in a unique way that college or university's self-understanding of CIT.

A self-study of CIT by each Catholic institution of higher learning is both warranted and necessary because CIT is more meaningful when it is "local and embodied."[115] To draw an analogy from the immigrant American Catholicism that prevailed in the United States prior to Vatican II, the paradox of ethnic American Catholicism is this: although the French, German, Irish, Polish, and Italian parishes were always intentionally ethnic parishes, they were "also living embodiments of Roman Catholicism, with its universal claims, among them, the idea that 'the goal of history is the creation of a common humanity.'"[116] The point here is that a carefully worked out self-study of CIT on the part of Catholic colleges and universities would not only serve as a local and embodied expression of this vast body of heritage known as CIT but would also witness to these colleges' "vastly expanded understandings of human solidarity."[117] A self-study might be conceived as an instance of a Catholic college's or university's understanding of a Catholic "way of doing things," a "Catholic sensibility," a "Catholic imagination"[118] or an instance of a "Catholic mind."[119]

Further Reading

Banks, James A. "Diversity, Group Identity, and Citizenship Education in a Global Age." *Educational Reseacher* 37 (2008): 129–39.

---

115. Ibid., 85.

116. Ibid., quoting Timothy Smith, "Religion and Ethnicity in America," *American Historical Review* 83 (December, 1978): 1155–85.

117. O'Brien, "The Renewal of American Catholicism," 85.

118. See John B. Breslin, "'The Open-Ended Mystery of Matter': Readings of the Catholic Imagination," in *Examining the Catholic Intellectual Tradition*, ed. Cernera and Morgan, 157–78.

119. See Gerald McCool, "The Christian Wisdom Tradition and Enlightenment Reason," in *Examining the Catholic Intellectual Tradition*, ed. Cernera and Morgan, 75–101.

Bryk, Anthony S., Valerie E. Lee, and Peter B. Holland. *Catholic Schools and the Common Good*. Cambridge, MA: Harvard University Press, 1993.

Carley, Moira T. "Bernard Lonergan and the Catholic Teacher." In *The Philosophy of Catholic Education*, edited by Caroline F. DiGiovanni, 75–88. Collected Papers from the OSSTA Symposium on the Philosophy of Catholic Education, February 28 and March 1, 1991. Ottawa: Novalis, 1992.

DiGiovanni, Caroline M. "The Philosophy of Catholic Education." *Grail: An Ecumenical Journal* 13, no. 2 (June 1997): 35–46.

Happel, Stephen, and David Tracy. *A Catholic Vision*. Philadelphia: Fortress Press, 1983.

Heft, James. "Academic Freedom: American and Catholic." *Origins* 28, no. 35 (February 18, 1999): 614–23.

Hollenbach, David. *The Common Good and Christian Ethics*. Cambridge: Cambridge University Press, 2002.

Laplante, Richard L. "The Catholic School: A Community with a Changing Language." In Caroline F. DiGiovanni (ed.), *The Philosophy of Catholic Education*, edited by Caroline F. DiGiovanni, 31–55. Collected Papers from the OSSTA Symposium on the Philosophy of Catholic Education, February 28 and March 1, 1991. Ottawa: Novalis, 1992.

Marmion, Declan, ed. *Christian Identity in a Postmodern Age: Celebrating the Legacies of Karl Rahner and Bernard Lonergan*. Dublin: Veritas Publications, 2005.

Matustik, Martin J. "Democratic Multicultures and Cosmopolis: Beyond the Aporias of the Politics of Identity and Difference." *METHOD: Journal of Lonergan Studies* 12, no. 1 (Spring 1994): 63–89.

Ogilvie, Matthew C. "Is the Catechism Enough? A Theological Perspective on Using the Catechism in Education." *Compass: A Review of Topical Theology* 38, no. 1 (2004): 33–40.

Palmer, Parker J. *The Courage to Teach: Exploring the Inner Landscape of a Teacher's Life*. San Francisco: Jossey-Bass, 1998.

Roy, Louis. "Lonergan on Catholic Education: A Few Suggestions." In *Faith Seeking Understanding: Learning and the Catholic Tradition*, edited by George C. Berthold, 155–63. Selected Papers from the Symposium and Convocation Celebrating the Saint Anselm College Centennial. Manchester, NH: Saint Anselm College Press, 1991.

Trafford, Larry. "The Evolving Language of Catholic Schools: Its Relationship to the Catholic Community." In *The Philosophy of Catholic Education*, edited by Caroline F. DiGiovanni, 58–62. Collected Papers from the OSSTA Symposium on the Philosophy of Catholic Education, February 28 and March 1, 1991. Ottawa: Novalis, 1992.

INDEX

Illustrations, charts, and sidebars are referenced using i, c, or s after the page number. Footnotes are indicated with n followed by the footnote number.

United States Department of
Education, 152–53
unity, 25, 43, 165
universal humanism, 242
universality, 20–22
universities. *See also* Catholic colleges and universities, overview
definition, 239–40
development of modern, 54–61
function of, 60, 240, 243
history of, 28–29
University of Berlin, 54
University of Louvain, 61–62, 126
University of Notre Dame, 100

V

value, 216
values, as authenticity formulation
component, 122
Vatican, 58, 72, 214
Vatican I (First Vatican Council),
132, 133, 134
Vatican II (Second Vatican Council)
American Catholic subculture
collapse and, 76–77
Catholic identity impacted by, 87
catholicity and ecumenism, 21,
26
ecumenism and staffing patterns,
84
educational ministry, 94

history, acknowledgment of, 196
identity comparisons, before and
after, 30–31
manualist tradition, 121n22
tradition models, 32
verbal linguistic intelligence, 157
verum-factum principle, 179
vetera novis augere et perficere, 117,
222
Vietnam War, 76
Vincent of Lerins, 31, 50
virtually unconditioned (term), 126
virtues, theological, 232, 240, 241
vocations
communal life influences, 90
decline in, 72–73, 74, 77, 87, 88
Vœgelin, Eric, 194

W

war, 34
Weber, Max, 30, 130
we-mode (we-perspective), 228, 232
Wissenschaft als Beruf (Weber), 30
women
ordination controversies, 73
religious vowed, 73, 74, 77,
89–90

Y

Yale University, 102, 103